COLD WAR

COLD
WAR

How Organized Crime Works in Canada and

Why It's Just About to Get More Violent

JERRY LANGTON

HARPERCOLLINS PUBLISHERS LTD

HarperCollins books may be purchased for educational, business, or sales
promotional use through our Special Markets Department.

HarperCollins Publishers Ltd
2 Bloor Street East, 20th Floor
Toronto, Ontario, Canada
M4W 1A8

www.harpercollins.ca

Library and Archives Canada Cataloguing in Publication

ISBN 978-1-44343-255-9

Printed and bound in the United States
RRD 9 8 7 6 5 4 3 2 1

To my own gang, T, Dame and HooHoo

CONTENTS

INTRODUCTION

When the news broke that Toronto mayor Rob Ford had admitted to smoking crack, I received plenty of calls and e-mails from people all over the world who wanted to know exactly what was going on in Toronto.

Most of them came from the US. After having lived in New York City for a very long time, I still have plenty of friends in the United States. They're often quite surprised to find out that I write about organized crime in Canada because they didn't know there was any organized crime, or even regular crime, up here. Their media, as well as what they see of ours, generally portray Canada as a relative safe zone located north of a crime-infested neighbor to the south.

It's not actually true. While the US certainly has a much higher murder rate (which is often the only statistic used by media to compare national crime rates even though it's not a good indicator of actual violent crime), the overall violent crime and property crime rates for both countries are about the same, according to United Nations crime statistics, with Canada having higher assault, and especially sexual assault, rates. But the cultural differences and memories of more dangerous times, along with the American hope for a better place and Canada's habit of patting itself on the back, keep those beliefs intact.

So it was with much surprise that my American friends reacted to Rob Ford's November 2013 admission that he had smoked crack. My American friends were shocked to learn that we even *had* crack up here and that it was supplied by street gangs with links to international organized crime. My Canadian friends seemed irked that the world was finally learning that fact, as though it were a family secret they'd rather keep quiet.

In truth, the history of organized crime has linked the two countries (and others) for a century. When it was Canada that first instituted alcohol prohibition in 1918, gangsters brought liquor and beer in from the US. For a short period of time, both countries (except the province of Quebec, which gave up the idea after a few months), had Prohibition, leading to something of a gangster's paradise. Then, after Canada dropped Prohibition while it lingered in the US, illegal liquor started going south instead of north. That's the period that people in both countries still tend to talk about when they refer to Prohibition, and what gangster movies often portray.

When Prohibition ended in both countries, the bootleggers and smugglers made an informed business decision and turned to moving drugs. After brief introduction periods, drugs like heroin, cocaine, methamphetamine and others become immensely popular among users and lucrative for sellers. In fact, it was the French Connection—an operation that moved tons of heroin from Southeast Asia and Turkey through France, then through Canada to the US—that actually established the Italian Mafia families as the dominant crime organizations in North America. Despite the fact that Canadians like John Papalia and Vic Cotroni were key primary players and that the bulk of the drugs and money went through Canada, there was little mention of this country in the classic film about the operation.

As heroin's allure faded when the public began to realize what it did to addicts, it was largely replaced by cocaine, which enriched many Canadian crime organizations, some of which used Montreal as a distribution point for the northeastern US, helping to fuel the wildly violent crack wars of the late 1980s and early 1990s.

Later, Canadian organized crime groups diversified and regularly pushed billions of dollars worth of drugs, cash, weapons and other products over the border. In the late 1990s and early 2000s, things heated up as the value of British Columbia–grown marijuana began to increase rapidly. Suddenly, the Lower Mainland region of BC was overrun by growers, dealers, smugglers and would-be gangsters who started shooting it out on the streets.

Since I have been writing about organized crime in Canada, I have been asked the same question in almost every interview. People always want to know if legalizing marijuana would reduce the amount of organized crime in this country.

The answer, disappointingly, is yes at first, but ultimately no. Marijuana, of course, makes up a huge proportion of the illegally traded commodities and services in Canada. Naturally, making it legal would reduce the amount traded by organized crime groups within Canada. But it would not stop them from exporting it to other places, just like in the days of Prohibition. As it stands now, Canadian-grown marijuana is popular not just at home and in the US, but also in places like Japan and Australia. Making marijuana legal in Canada could easily result in organized crime groups exporting it to the rest of the world in greater amounts, just as happened with alcohol when the US had Prohibition and Canada did not. It should be noted that two US states—Colorado and

Washington, which borders BC—have made recreational marijuana legal, and the response from the public has been phenomenal. Retail stores have experienced long lineups, million-dollar sales days and empty storerooms. It's too early yet to see legalization's effect on organized crime in those states but it certainly hasn't made a significant difference.

Even if marijuana were magically made legal all around the world on the same day, organized crime groups would find other products to move, like heroin, cocaine, meth, steroids or, as is currently popular in many parts of Canada, prescription drugs. Keep in mind too that there are always non-drug products to move, like weapons, prostitutes and stolen goods (particularly cars and car parts to China). That wouldn't stop, just like it didn't when Prohibition was finally lifted.

And even if all of that were made legal, there would still be the old-fashioned organized crime activities, like extortion, kidnapping, illegal gambling, shady investments and other strong-arm moves. They never stop.

It's foolish to think that organized crime isn't around and mawkish to believe it can be legislated out of existence. Instead, it's a better idea to get to know who the players are.

That's why I wrote *Cold War*. Following the evolution of organized crime in Canada makes it much easier to understand which factors incubate organized crime, what helps it to mature and what prompts it to become more violent.

The title, *Cold War*, reflects the fact that as organized crime has evolved in this country, its players have always fallen into one of two sides, and those two sides have become interconnected. In every community where organized crime exists, its practitioners end up on one side and invariably hate the other side. Take, for example, 14-year-old Winnipeg crack dealer Sirak "Shaggy" Okbazion. He was a member of a street gang called the Mad Cowz, which was made up primarily of immigrants from the Horn of Africa, including Sudanese, Somalis and Eritreans like himself. They wore white, defended their territory against gangs like B-Side, which was also composed of East African immigrants, and received product and some modicum of support from a Native Canadian gang called the Native Syndicate. The senior partners, the Native Syndicate, wore black, fought turf wars with Native gangs like the Indian Posse and the Manitoba Warriors, and bought their drugs from a biker gang called the Zig Zag Crew. The Zig Zag Crew were a support club, essentially a minor-league affiliate, for the Hells Angels. They wore white-and-red patches to show their allegiance to the Hells Angels red and white, and along with the Hells Angels, faced off against biker gangs like the Spartans, the Outlaws, the Bandidos and the Rock Machine. Of course, the Canadian Hells Angels started in, and were originally mostly run from, Montreal. And the Hells Angels were established in Montreal and gained dominance there and throughout Canada because of their ties to the Italian Mafia. Depending on the time, the Canadian Hells Angels have been allied with either the Sicilian or Calabrian factions of the Mafia. So, Shaggy certainly didn't know it, but he was a foot soldier in a cold war between the Sicilians and Calabrians. Just like the proxy wars of the Cold War between the US and the USSR, the people selling drugs on Canadian streets might have their own motivations for doing so, but they are also representing one of the two superpowers. Shaggy, through the Mad Cowz, the Native Syndicate, the Zig Zag Crew and the Hells Angels, was representing, defending and strengthening the Sicilian families in Montreal. By default, his opponents in B-Side—who shot him three times in the chest and killed him outside a crack house he worked—were, through the Manitoba Warriors, the Bandidos and others, representing the interests of the Calabrians. The names and alliances sometimes change—the Mad Cowz are now the African Mafia, and the Bandidos basically morphed back into the Rock Machine—but the cold war continues, occasionally falling into violence. There are some deviations from the norm—some British Columbia–based gangs rely on Asian connections for drugs instead of on the Italian Mafia—but every guy selling heroin in Surrey, crack in Hamilton or prescription drugs in Corner Brook is on one side or the other, linked to one side or the other, and is putting his life on the line because the other side wants his territory.

I really believe that it's long past due that Canadians, not only those in law enforcement, recognize the fact that organized crime is very real in this country, and that it doesn't just cost us money, it compromises some of our elected officials and even puts the lives of innocent people in danger.

CHAPTER 1

GANGS INVADE THE ROCK

Everyone knows that motorcycle gangs originated in the middle of the twentieth century. Popular lore—which the clubs like to promote—is that they were started by World War II veterans unable to fit into mainstream society after seeing the horrors of war. There's scant evidence of that actually having occurred. Some motorcycle gangs—like the Outlaws—predate the war, and none had an especially high proportion of veterans in their ranks in the late 1940s.

Instead, motorcycle enthusiasts of all stripes found one another and met for races, customization and shows. As motorcycles became more popular, the numbers of motorcycle-enthusiast clubs began to grow. Few considered those clubs a problem until 1947, when a gathering of motorcycle clubs in Hollister, California, disintegrated into drunken violence and clashes with police.

The incident was reported—with wildly exaggerated levels of violence—internationally. The embattled American Motorcycle Association, eager to calm the public outrage directed at all motorcyclists, issued a statement that blamed the violence on "one per-cent" of the motorcycling community. That phrase found resonance with many—including clubs that were at Hollister, like the Booze-fighters and the Pissed-Off Bastards of Bloomington—who quickly adopted it as a badge of honor. To this day, motorcycle clubs that consider themselves outlaws call themselves (and are referred to by law enforcement as) "1% clubs," and their members, "1%ers."

In 1953, Hollywood released *The Wild One*, starring Marlon Brando. Based on a short story that was itself based on the Hollister incident, *The Wild One* was a massive critical and popular success. Soon, motorcycle-club members began to emulate the stars in the movie—particularly Lee Marvin's rough and ready character, Chino, rather than the more introspective Johnny that Brando played. In fact, 1%ers still dress in much the same way as the actors in the 60-year-old movie.

In fact, the outfit is essential. The uniform of a 1%er centers around a leather jacket or vest given to him by the club. Within the club, it is considered the member's most precious possession and can't be touched by nonmembers. On the back of the jacket is a three-part patch consisting of the club's name, logo and ter-ritory. Since these patches are given out in stages, full members of the club are often referred to as "full-patches." On the front of the jacket are sewn other patches. There's always a 1% patch, and others may be acquired for service to the club.

Membership is not easy to acquire. Clubs usually reach out to suitable recruits, preferring that to unsolicited requests to join. Recruits must be of legal drinking age, own and operate a motorcycle (most clubs stipulate a Harley-Davidson or at least an American-made bike), have never served as a sworn peace officer in any capacity and, in most cases, be white.

Recruits are usually known as "friends" or "supporters" until they have gained a basic level of trust, and they can then become "hangarounds." Hangarounds are allowed more privileges, like attending club events, but have no official standing with or protection from the club. If the hangaround gains the unanimous acceptance of every full-patch member of the club, he then graduates to "prospect" (or "striker") status.

Prospects are given their jacket or vest with a partial patch and are officially considered part of the club. While their privileges expand, so do their responsibilities. In fact, being a prospect means being at the beck and call of every member. No request from a full-patch—no matter how difficult, expensive, demeaning or illegal—may be refused. Depending on the personalities in the club, being a prospect can be hellish, and many recruits fail.

If a prospect serves his duties proficiently enough, his full-patch sponsor will then plead his case to the club. If every full-patch votes for him, he then becomes a member. If even one refuses or abstains, he does not.

Membership has its rewards, which vary from club to club. According to law enforcement, the primary purpose behind some motorcycle clubs is not to ride but to make money selling drugs and other vice. Every full-patch, they say, gets a cut of the action.

The biggest and most famous of all 1%er clubs is the Hells Angels. Founded in San Bernardino, California, in the late 1940s, the Hells Angels expanded rapidly and can now be found in 27 countries.

Their rather successful model has been emulated by other 1%er clubs throughout the world. By the 1960s, the Hells Angels drew a lot of attention for their lifestyle and for their involvement in crime and were the subjects of many books and movies. It was widely believed by both the public and law enforcement that they were deeply involved in organized crime—and there were many arrests to back that notion up.

But when the US federal government finally brought its case against the Hells Angels in 1979, it came up flat. Despite using the same Racketeer Influenced and Corrupt Organizations Act (RICO) that crippled the Mafia and other crime organizations, the government was unable to prove that the Hells Angels committed crimes as a unit. That proved to be of the utmost importance. While many members were found to be criminals—national president Sonny Barger himself admitted during the trial to selling heroin—the prosecution failed to disprove the bikers' claim that they associated because of their common interest in motorcycling, and that any crimes committed were incidental, the actions of individual members working independently of the organization.

That distinction—that some motorcycle clubs may have nothing but criminals for members but that their actions are not the legal responsibility of the club—has become of vital importance to bikers. That's why they always correct me when I call their clubs gangs.

The idea that biker gangs contain criminals but are not criminal organizations has been a successful concept, and it has been repeated, franchise-style, all over the world.

Biker gangs emerged in Canada in the late 1950s. They were made up mostly of guys who hung around together, rode their bikes and partied. There were exceptions. In cities where the Mafia was strong—primarily Montreal and Hamilton, Ontario—bikers picked up a few bucks here and there by helping the Italians as paid muscle.

In the early 1970s, much of Toronto's drug trade—particularly in the then run-down and now prohibitively expensive Yorkville district—was run by a biker gang called Satan's Choice. In fact, at the time, Satan's Choice (with chapters in Montreal as well as Hamilton, Oshawa and several other Ontario cities) was the second-biggest 1%er club in the world. In 1973, representatives of Satan's Choice actually turned down an offer to merge with the Hells Angels.

They might have wanted a do-over on that. Four years later—with Bernie Guindon, the club's founder and national president, in prison—the four most powerful chapters of Satan's Choice patched over to the Outlaws on July 1, 1977.

The Outlaws are another large, corporate-style American 1%er club, but they aren't the Hells Angels. Originally based in suburban Chicagoland, they later moved to Detroit, right across the mile-wide Detroit River from Windsor, Ontario. They expanded in much the same way the Hells Angels did, but their brand did not have the same impact. While the Outlaws would never rival the Hells Angels for the number-one biker spot in the US, they held their own, have traditionally controlled a great deal of the Midwest and are particularly dominant in Florida.

At the same time, the Hells Angels were also looking to expand to Canada. They were actively courting clubs in southern Ontario, but failed to make much headway there primarily because John "Johnny Pops" Papalia—who controlled the Ontario Mafia from Hamilton—refused to work with them.

Instead, the Hells Angels first came to Canada through Montreal. The Mafia there (more closely associated with New York City, while Papalia answered to the Buffalo family) had no problem with them. In fact, the gang the Hells Angels patched over—the notorious Popeyes—had a long history of working for the Italian Mafia. On December 5, 1977, the Hells Angels established themselves in Canada.

Over the years, the Hells Angels aggressively expanded throughout Canada. Careful not to arouse Papalia's ire, they flew under the radar in Ontario but auditioned and absorbed other clubs throughout the rest of the country.

Their choice for the Maritimes was not difficult. In the early 1980s, much of the drug trade and prostitution in Halifax and the region was controlled by a gang called the 13th Tribe. After a year-long probation period that included standing guard for badly injured future Hells Angels national president Walter "Nurget" Stadnick in a Hamilton hospital after a motorcycle accident, the 13th Tribe became the Halifax chapter of the Hells Angels.

From that strategic location, the Hells Angels Halifax chapter and their allies served all of the Maritimes with drugs and other forms of vice. The product made its way to Newfoundland primarily by ferry, but also by private planes and seacraft, courier and even Canada Post. For years, it was easy to get drugs to Newfoundland via commercial airlines, but increased security measures put an end to that.

Things did not go easily for the easternmost Hells Angels. Four Halifax members, including their president, David "Wolf" Carroll, were charged in 1985 in connection with the Lennoxville Massacre, in which the Montreal Hells Angels chapter in Sorel invited the Montreal chapter in Laval to a party in Lennoxville, Quebec, and then shot them dead for not following their rules.

The four from Halifax were acquitted, but in 1986, the chapter's hubris got them in trouble again. Sensing their increased profile as Hells Angels, they demanded a huge increase in what the prostitutes they controlled paid them for management and protection. That was too much for one of the women, who went to police and told them everything she knew about the chapter's operation. Carroll and two others were convicted of living off the avails of prostitution on May 30, 1986, and each spent a year in prison.

That put the club in a major bind. The Hells Angels charter requires that a chapter must have at least six full-patch members at any time—and the members in prison don't count. So to keep the valuable Halifax chapter alive, the Hells Angels rotated in other full-patch members, primarily from British Columbia, while Carroll and his pals were in prison.

After the members were released, the chapter enjoyed a period of relative wealth and ease until its leader found a better offer. Carroll, who had some very powerful friends in Montreal, left the Halifax chapter in 1995 to join the Nomads—an elite chapter of the Hells Angels—who made massive sums of money by distributing drugs, mainly cocaine, supplied chiefly by the Montreal Mafia. Carroll relocated to Montreal and did his business in the ski resorts of the Laurentians.

Without Carroll's charisma and support, the Halifax chapter withered. A massive police raid targeted the Hells Angels, and the Nomads in particular, in 2001. Operation Printemps resulted in the arrest of 122 people, including most of the club's management structure in Montreal. All of the Nomads were put behind bars except Carroll, who eluded arrest. These days, he is largely thought to be living under an assumed name, probably in the Caribbean, but several people I spoke with who knew him have told me that they firmly believe he is living under witness protection after cooperating with law enforcement.

Either way, he was in no position to support the Halifax chapter when it ran into trouble again. A series of arrests brought the number of members to below six again. In fact, after convictions sent members Clay McCrea, Art Harrie, Jeffrey Lynds and Neil Smith to prison in 2003, there were just three left on the streets.

Of what remained of the gang in Halifax, Clay McCrea's brother Mike, who had admitted to being a Hells Angel but long denied he was the chapter's president despite media and police allegations, handed in his patch and opened a legitimate IT support company. Member Daniel Fitzsimmons was visited by some Ontario members who demanded his patch. He complied. With Smith sentenced to life, Clay McCrea and Harrie retired from the club in prison— dashing the widespread belief they would revive it while freed. That left just one Hells Angel on the streets of Halifax.

Michael "Speedy" Christiansen, one of the founding members of the 13th Tribe and the last free Halifax Hells Angel, left the area at about the same time. He relocated to the West Coast, joining first the East Vancouver chapter of the Hells Angels, then later moving to the Kelowna chapter. With him gone, there were no more Hells Angels in the Maritimes.

When Lynds was released, he joined the Ontario Nomads before being convicted of the murder of two men outside a Montreal McDonald's. He died of an alleged suicide in prison.

But drugs still needed to be sold and prostitutes still needed to be handled on the East Coast. Besides, Halifax's port was far too valuable for the bikers to ignore. Their solution came from New Brunswick.

While big motorcycle clubs like the Hells Angels and Outlaws acquire new chapters by patching over existing gangs—as happened with the Popeyes in Montreal and the 13th Tribe in Halifax—they also actively reach out to and recruit other clubs they have no intention of patching over, instead using them almost as employees. These allied clubs are called "puppet clubs" by cops because they are so stringently controlled by the parent club. Although the parent club is firmly in charge, the relationship is usually symbiotic. According to many members of law enforcement I have spoken with, the puppet club supplies manpower, a recruiting pool and a buffer from prosecution, while the parent club supplies product, connections, guidance and the chance for advancement.

One such club was Bacchus. Centered in bucolic Albert County, New Brunswick, they were small-time players until the void in Halifax needed filling. According to public statements from authorities including the Royal Canadian Mounted Police (RCMP) and local forces, Bacchus had a long-standing relationship with a powerful Toronto club called the Para-Dice Riders.

After Papalia died in 1997, the Stadnick-led Hells Angels rode into Ontario and patched over several clubs, including the Para-Dice Riders. When the Montreal power structure collapsed in 2001, the former Para-Dice Riders—by then the Hells Angels' Downtown Toronto chapter—became the power center of the Hells Angels in Canada.

With their help—and that of the notorious East Vancouver chapter, which by then included Christiansen, according to an RCMP report—Bacchus became the Hells Angels' primary representatives on the East Coast. Their reputation in the area was not great. Many considered them lazy, disorganized and not all that bright. But there weren't a great number of options, and they did supply manpower.

In the tradition of Maritime bikers, they got into trouble early and often. Three members and an associate—all from the Halifax area—were arrested on November 29, 2006, on charges of trafficking cocaine, Ecstasy, marijuana and prescription drugs into Prince Edward Island. They were found guilty. A few months later, a raid against the Hells Angels and their associates in Edmonton implicated Bacchus in the methamphetamine trade into oil-rich Fort McMurray, according to an RCMP statement.

Nonetheless, they continued to expand. On the night of January 10, 2010, the RCMP watched as eight Harleys pulled up to the Bacchus headquarters out in the country near Hillsborough, New Brunswick. The men walked into the clubhouse wearing East Coast Riders patches. The following day, they walked out wearing Bacchus patches. And, perhaps more important, 1%er patches. Once outside, they burned their old patches.

When asked by CBC News if the first appearance of 1% patches on a Halifax club since the Hells Angels' evaporation in 2003 had any significance, RCMP Intelligence Unit inspector Greg Laturnus told them that it was "an open claim of outlaw status" and added, "We have a national strategy to combat outlaw motorcycle gangs, and certainly the Bacchus motorcycle club is considered an outlaw motorcycle gang."

At the same time, the newly minted members of Bacchus' Nova Scotia chapter brushed off claims of being involved with organized crime (as bikers always do). "We are far from organized, and we're not a crime group neither," Paul Fowler, who police and media alleged was the club's president, although he never confirmed or denied this, told a group of journalists. "In our mind, the true meaning of the one percent is that we are the one percent that doesn't fit in with the other ninety-nine percent of society, for whatever reason. You know, we like to do things our own way. We like to hang out together, ride motorcycles and party."

Things did not start smoothly. On February 26, 2010, just weeks after the patch-over, a friend dropped by the Barr Settlement, Nova Scotia, home of Bacchus member James "Rustie" Hall and his wife, Ellen. Finding the door open and receiving no answer when he called out to them, the friend knew something was wrong. When he spotted their bodies, he called 911. James and Ellen Hall, both 53, had been murdered.

At first, much of the speculation fell on Bacchus and the Hells Angels. Hall was known as a friendly and kind man—perhaps too gentle for the 1%er life—and could have been seen as a liability by the parent club if they intended to dominate the drug business in the area.

When the Halls' funeral was attended by members of Bacchus and the Hells Angels–leaning Red Devils of Chatham, Ontario (widely misreported in the media as being from Chatham, New Brunswick), few considered it an inside job anymore. Although speculation was rampant, the new members of Bacchus appeared to deflect the idea that the killing had been done by rival bikers. "It was a random psycho," one of them, who did not want to be identified, told assembled reporters. "The police don't know anything." Nobody has ever been charged in connection with the deaths.

While the police didn't "know" anything for sure, that did not stop them from considering that the historically lucrative Maritimes drug trade and its valuable ports could also be summoning other, rival, bikers who might be willing to kill for their right to share the wealth. "I don't think we're staring at any biker war," said RCMP biker cop Stephen MacQueen on a CTV news report. "However, I would say there is some concern among the [local] outlaw motorcycle gang members that rivals to the Hells Angels are looking at Atlantic Canada."

It is true that the Rock Machine—the Hells Angels' most bitter rivals in Canada, who were struggling to re-create themselves from a stronghold in Winnipeg—had attempted to establish a chapter in Nova Scotia but failed to make much headway and scrapped the plan about the time Bacchus patched over the East Coast Riders.

Still, without any official Hells Angels presence, rival bikers felt free to flaunt their colors on the streets of Atlantic Canada, particularly the much-desired Halifax region. "Over the last few months there have been sightings of Rock Machine, sightings of Outlaws in Atlantic Canada, which has probably spurred the East Coast Riders to make a decision of where they were going to stand on the issue," MacQueen continued. "Rival groups coming here wearing their colors in bars is a show of a lack of respect for the Hells Angels."

To further strengthen their position in Nova Scotia, the Hells Angels also reached out to a group called the Dartmouth Harley Club, which then changed its name to the Dark-Siders and occupied the old Halifax Hells Angels clubhouse. They also acquired the loyalty of the Antigonish, Nova Scotia–based Highlanders, who promptly opened a second chapter in Sydney on Cape Breton Island, a region with a depressed economy and a hunger for drugs.

Speculation that Bacchus was importing drugs to the Maritimes was strengthened when, acting on a tip, members of the Cumberland Integrated Street Crime Enforcement Unit and the Criminal Intelligence Service Nova Scotia stopped a full-patch member of the club on the Trans-Canada Highway in Amherst, Nova Scotia, on April 18, 2011. The 48-year-old man, who was not identified, was charged by the RCMP with trafficking and weapons offenses and breach of probation after police found eight ounces of marijuana, trace amounts of cocaine and a Taser in his car.

A few months later, in October 2011, police raided the Bacchus clubhouse on Pitt Street in Saint John, New Brunswick, on warrants received under the suspicion that the club was operating an illegal bar. While there were no important arrests, the raid did allow the cops inside the building and what they saw allowed them to order a fire safety inspection. The fire department ordered the club to make costly renovations or leave the premises.

On July 14, 2012, just a few days before they were to vacate the building, Bacchus hosted a party in front of the clubhouse. A closed-circuit security video taken from the clubhouse that day and made public by police shows a 31-year-old man named Michael Thomas Schimpf approach the guests. He has a brief conversation with chapter president Matthew Foley (who is wearing his full colors), then retreats. Foley—a 50-year-old who started his biker career with Satan's Choice in Ontario in the 1980s—then hands his drink to an associate, pulls a handgun from under his vest and follows Schimpf offscreen. The other members of Bacchus hold their positions, nervously looking up and down the street. Foley returns, reloads the handgun and leaves again in the same direction in which he followed Schimpf.

Schmipf's body—with a bullet hole in his chest—was found a few yards away later that day.

Foley later admitted to shooting at Schimpf, but said he felt his life was in danger when he saw Schimpf reach for something behind his back.

A police investigation failed to uncover any connections between Schimpf and organized crime, but he had been accused of throwing a brick through the window of Foley's tattoo shop a few days before the incident. "The investigation certainly doesn't tell us that the victim was associated to the motorcycle club, and he certainly didn't have any working relationship that we're aware of," Saint John police chief Bill Reid said to the CBC. "There is absolutely no evidence thus far to include organized crime, motorcycle gangs or an affiliation to motorcycle gangs at this time. It just happens to be where it took place and who's involved. At the end of the day, it's where two people have a problem and one person just happens to be the president of a motorcycle club and the other person is a citizen and then we have a confrontation." He failed to mention that Schimpf had spent time in prison for trafficking.

Facing overwhelming evidence, Foley admitted to shooting at Schimpf eight times, hitting him just once, while pleading guilty to the reduced charge of manslaughter. He received a sentence of 10 years in prison and a lifetime firearms ban. A Web site—freematt.ca—was launched in an effort to solicit donations for his legal team and "to help him get reestablished when he is free."

Law enforcement kept the pressure on. On September 20, 2012, the homes of several Halifax-area Bacchus members and prospects were raided. Police managed to find small quantities of marijuana, steroids and psilocybin (magic mushrooms), but could lay charges on only three members—Patrick James and David Pearce of Dartmouth and Duane Howe from nearby Grand Desert—for uttering threats and intimidation. Later, they would add to those charges as more evidence came to light.

Trouble showed up for hard-luck Bacchus again later that month. What happened at the 20/Twenty Club—a gray, low-slung strip-mall establishment that calls itself "Fredericton's #1 party spot"—at two in the morning of September 29, 2012, has no official timeline. But there was a person who claimed to witness the incident and told the media his version of events—anonymously. According to the witness, who spoke with several media sources, 54-year-old Walter "Buddy" Wheeler, a father of four, picked a fight with the wrong guy. "It all started out on the patio section of the bar," the witness said. "There was a Bacchus in his full colors with his vest on having a smoke. This guy walks up to him, pushes his drink away from him and starts mouthing to him. He's being real disrespectful to the guy, so things heated up."

According to the witness, the confrontation moved outside when the bar closed. He went on to say that when Wheeler—who did have a history of getting into fights—threatened the Bacchus member one last time, the biker snapped his fingers and pointed at Wheeler. On that command, the anonymous witness then told the collected media, another man, who had been at the biker's table, rushed up to Wheeler and sucker punched him in the face. Wheeler, he said, fell to the ground and hit his head on a curb, passing out.

Although that witness did not mention it, others on social media reported that the biker and his associate then kicked Wheeler while he was down. He fell into a coma. According to the same witness "the man didn't twitch or anything for the forty minutes it took to get him out of there."

On October 3, 2012, Wheeler died.

On October 8, Fredericton police arrested the biker's friend at his home. They charged him and released him pending an investigation. After a month-long investigation, they declined to press any charges and released the following statement: "As a result of this in-depth and thorough analysis of the evidence and factual information contained in this file, it has been determined that the events that lead to the death of Walter 'Buddy' Wheeler did not meet the elements required to successfully prosecute a charge of manslaughter or a charge of criminal negligence causing death."

While those sorts of charges—pursued or not—reflected a personal brush with the law, they were very much in keeping with how motorcycle clubs say their membership may behave. The police, however, made no secret of their desire to label the organization itself, not just its members, as criminal.

Canadian prosecutors have been trying for years to lay gangsterism charges against bikers—without much luck. A landmark Ontario case in 2005 determined that a pair of Hells Angels who were extorting a car dealer while wearing their colors were actually using the club's reputation as an intimidating weapon. It didn't exactly get rid of the Hells Angels in Ontario, but it did allow law enforcement more leeway to lay charges against its members and judges to put down much harsher sentences.

On January 2, 2013, police charged the three Bacchus members arrested in September 2012—James, Pearce and Howe—with extortion and, more important, committing crimes on behalf of the club. They have pleaded not guilty and their trial has been set over.

Not much later, a joint RCMP–Halifax Regional Police investigation into drug smuggling into Dartmouth's Central Nova Scotia Correctional Facility ended on March 25, 2013, when 14 people were arrested on charges related to a complex organization dedicated to smuggling drugs into the institution.

The ringleader, police alleged, was Bacchus full-patch David Bishop. They charged him with trafficking cocaine, trafficking steroids, possession of steroids for the purpose of trafficking, resisting arrest, unsafe ammunition storage, possession of cannabis resin, possession of prohibited weapons and breaching court conditions.

A search of his Chelmsford Place house in Halifax also uncovered a bulletproof vest.

Although only one member of the club was arrested, police made a point of stressing the idea that the entire club was behind the whole operation. "The Bacchus have a significant presence in Nova Scotia," RCMP inspector Joanne Crampton told the media. "It's important, though, to recognize that the club works as a large group rather than independently. They're interconnected with the other groups in the other Atlantic provinces." She then made a point of saying that Bacchus is "a criminal organization" with longtime links to the Hells Angels.

But while Bacchus was growing large—with about 80 full-patch members throughout the East Coast—it had acquired a reputation as being sloppy and prone to unnecessary arrests and bad press. While Bacchus had been stumbling around over the winter of 2012–2013, the Hells Angels—allegedly, the powerful London, Ontario, chapter—sponsored yet another small club in the Halifax area. In the sleepy little village of Musquodoboit Harbour, a new 1%er club, the Gate Keepers, began to wear colors. Significantly, their colors were red and white, a combination reserved in the 1%er world for the Hells Angels and their very closest allies.

The police reacted as though it was an aggressive encroachment into Atlantic Canada by the Hells Angels, which was Bacchus turf. It was already common knowledge to everybody else, however, that Bacchus was a Hells Angels ally. The establishment of the Gate Keepers was more likely an effort by the Hells Angels to have more boots on the ground or by the London chapter to have their own presence there. It's not unprecedented for two, or even several, Hells Angels–aligned clubs to share turf amicably if the market will support it.

Law enforcement in the Maritimes portrayed the establishment of the new club as a harbinger of fierce rivalry, perhaps even a war. "There's approximately eighty Bacchus here, and they feel that they have Atlantic Canada as their territory. The concern now is that the Hells Angels have made it clear that they want Atlantic Canada to be their territory and they are now doing it through the Gate Keepers," the RCMP's Crampton told CBC News. "It can bring a lot of violence to our community. It can bring tensions between the two groups as they look at how they are going to establish territory and how they are going to take over the Atlantic Canada area."

Not long after, both Bacchus and the Gate Keepers were seen partying together.

There would be no war in Nova Scotia. The days of rival bikers flying their colors in that province or New Brunswick or Prince Edward Island had come to a close. Through their series of puppets, the Hells Angels effectively controlled the drug trade in those provinces and the huge amount of drugs and other contraband that came through their ports.

That was hardly the case in Newfoundland, though. Newfoundland was more complicated, almost like two provinces. In and around St. John's, the economic boom brought about by the oil industry has caused a migration of young men (and some women) to the area. They are a natural market for recreational drugs because they have money. The rest of the island (which was seeing no such economic boom) is a natural market for recreational drugs because the locals have no money. Very quietly, Bacchus established a chapter in Grand Falls-Windsor to take advantage of both groups. In January 2011, Bacchus patched over a little-known 1%er club called Easton's Crew.

The location made perfect sense. While the big drug and vice markets are in burgeoning St. John's, dealers don't feel safe setting up shop there. Accurate or not, the belief among 1%er culture is that dedicated police forces drawn from the region are much more effective than national police forces, especially in communities that are not among the more desirable in which to live. St. John's, on the island's east coast, and Corner Brook, on the west, both house branches of the Royal Newfoundland Constabulary, a local police force composed of Newfoundlanders serving their home communities. Grand Falls-Windsor—right in the middle of the island, and its next biggest community—makes do with an RCMP detachment. Many 1%ers regard RCMP officers, who are drawn from the entire country and are often assigned less desirable locations based on a lack of seniority or rules violations, as careerists who try to ruffle as few feathers as they can while putting in enough time to be transferred to more plush assignments. Not to mention that the Hells Angels have had their run-ins with the Royal Newfoundland Constabulary before.

From Grand Falls-Windsor, Bacchus had quick highway access to St. John's and Corner Brook, but were out of effective range of the Royal Newfoundland Constabulary; they had unpatrolled ports nearby and even a small airstrip not far away in Botwood. They also had what amounted to a captive audience in central Newfoundland. Although the population was relatively small, its hunger for drugs was more than enough to support a biker chapter.

Of course, it's not as though the Hells Angels had ignored Newfoundland in the past. As the province—or at least St. John's—grew more prosperous, it became a higher priority.

As early as 2004, people in St. John's popular George Street nightlife district felt the presence of the club. A very large, imposing man who went by the name Patrick "Big Pat" Champoux started showing up at bars and nightclubs, bragging about carrying a handgun and being a member of the Hells Angels. He told those he felt he could trust that his intention was to start a Hells Angels chapter in the city and open a strip joint to serve as its headquarters. The would-be Tony Soprano also warned everyone who would listen that, henceforth, St. John's was a Hells Angels town and that anyone selling cocaine or marijuana there without his say-so was putting themselves in danger.

Big Pat kept his intimidating presence large. He'd enter bars and help himself to beer, daring the owners to stop him. Later, he and some friends ransacked a rival strip joint. According to the Royal Newfoundland Constabulary and a CBC documentary on the situation, he did everything short of renting a billboard to advertise the fact that he was the town's dominant drug dealer.

Police began to see more cocaine, and its effects, on the streets. Violent confrontations and petty crime in the area skyrocketed. Fights were frequent, and weapons, including knives and handguns, were increasingly becoming involved. When asked about the violence, Royal Newfoundland Constabulary sergeant Marlene Jesso acknowledged to a CBC documentary team that it was on the rise and added, "Another big thing in the city right now is home invasions, and that's drug dealers ripping off other drug dealers for money and drugs." The precipitous rise in violence prompted the Royal Newfoundland Constabulary to investigate its cause. It did not take long for many accusatory fingers to be pointed in Big Pat's direction.

True to his word, Champoux did actually open a strip joint on George Street—Bubbles Gentlemen's Club—which was managed by Champoux's girlfriend, Sonia Delisle. Quickly, it became well known in the area for pushing the limits of legality. One of its performers—Montrealer Marie-Andrée Lauriault, who performs as Tangerine Dream—was charged with an obscure part of the Criminal Code, "immoral theatrical performance," after a show in which she allowed 177 men to penetrate her with a dildo. Charges were dropped against Lauriault, but the club was fined $7,500, the maximum allowable penalty.

Bubbles was also known as a dangerous place. Fights there were frequent, and at least two people went over the balcony rail.

One, who was accused of being a police officer, was paralyzed and the other died. Another man, who was said to have angrily kicked down a sign on the sidewalk in front of Bubbles, was chased down George Street and stomped on by several men.

While its effects could be seen there, I've been repeatedly told that cocaine was never sold at Bubbles. Instead, it was distributed through nearby bars on George and New Gower Streets. At one of them, Backstage, a bartender with a half ounce of cocaine divided into individual servings was arrested. He pleaded down to lesser offenses.

According to the arrest report, Champoux eventually returned to Montreal, but he left behind a second-in-command. Patrick "Little Pat" Dickson—a longtime Hells Angels associate who had actually been convicted along with Walter Stadnick and others in 2001's Operation Printemps—stayed in St. John's to handle the business. When the police looked deeper into their files, they found a great deal of evidence, including scores of photos and videos that linked both Champoux and Dickson to the Hells Angels. The police then saw that several prominent Hells Angels members from Quebec came to visit both Champoux and Dickson, even staying over at their houses.

With Dickson and Delisle in Big Pat's fold, the Royal Newfoundland Constabulary alleged in court that Champoux also recruited some manpower and muscle. Locals John Stanley and Mark Kane operated out of a Waterford Bridge Road gym called Hard Tack Boxing & Fitness. Rumors of steroid use and availability at the facility were rampant when they were there.

Under surveillance used in the Crown's case against the group led by Big Pat, police saw that the group would stash and package drugs in Kane's west-end apartment. The main distribution and business center was at Stanley's house across town. Aware of that, police obtained a warrant that allowed them to enter Stanley's house more than a dozen times to take pictures—being extremely careful to leave everything as they had found it—and install surveillance equipment including a hidden microphone in the office area and bugs on the landline and a number of cell phones. Royal Newfoundland Constabulary constable Tim Hogan, who took part in searching the house, told the CBC he was surprised by the fact that he never found more than $10,000 to $20,000 in the house at any time. That led him to believe, he said, that the money was being stashed elsewhere.

He was right. As the business became more successful, the operation needed more stash houses. They established them in modest apartments and houses in Portugal Cove, Mount Pearl and central St. John's, being careful to avoid high-crime and otherwise run-down areas.

The police did find a kilo of cocaine—divided into dealer-ready two- and three-ounce packages—and two suitcases full of marijuana in Stanley's house and charged him with trafficking. Inside one of the suitcases was a receipt indicating that they had been purchased in suburban Montreal just days before. Armed with this information, the Royal Newfoundland Constabulary recruited the RCMP and police forces in Quebec, New Brunswick and Nova Scotia to help.

Police figured Dickson was the primary contact when they noticed that each time Champoux visited Newfoundland, he and Dickson would exchange packages that were sometimes wrapped as gifts. Their assumption was that Champoux was delivering cocaine and that Dickson was trading it for bundles of cash. The police put Dickson under surveillance. The project was named Operation Roadrunner.

In September 2007, they followed his minivan, assuming he was headed to a post office to mail a package but changed their guess once they noticed him heading for St. John's International

Airport. He didn't stop there but continued west to Portugal Cove. There, he boarded a ferry to Bell Island. Once on the island, he headed to its tiny airstrip. Bell Island Airport has no terminal, let alone security, and it issues the following cautions to pilots headed there: occasional radio-controlled aircraft activity, possibility of wildlife on the runway and occasional ground-vehicle racing on the runway.

As seen in a videotape that the court made public, Dickson then drove his minivan to the edge of the airstrip's tarmac. As soon as he stopped, a small, white, twin-engined Cessna appeared in the sky. It landed and police witnessed a number of cardboard boxes being thrown out of the plane. Dickson then packed them into the minivan. He also moved a suitcase from the minivan into the plane. Royal Newfoundland Constabulary inspector Jason Sheppard wrote down the plane's marker number and tracked it down. He determined that it had taken off from near Montreal, had flown at less than 1,000 feet for the entire journey and had its transponder turned off. The exchange at Bell Island took about 40 seconds, including a quick refuel. The Cessna's engines were never turned off and it was back in the sky as quickly as it came.

Police estimated that the group was importing about $1 million worth of cocaine, and a similar amount of marijuana, per month to Newfoundland by boat, cars and buses via ferry, plane and even the mail. Investigators also determined that the cocaine was being distributed all over the island and into Labrador as well.

When the police felt they had acquired enough evidence, and noticed through their surveillance that the operators were taking increased security precautions—Champoux, Dickson, Stanley and Kane went through more than 60 cell phones in just a few months, changing them frequently to keep them from being tapped—they struck.

On the quiet morning of October 11, 2007, police raided 11

homes in the St. John's area, arresting 12 people associated with the Champoux cocaine operation, including Dickson, Stanley and Kane. The police seized 9 kilograms of cocaine, 25 kilograms of marijuana and a number of handguns.

Champoux, the main prize, was still in Quebec. At the same time as the raids were going down in Newfoundland, a Sûreté du Québec SWAT team broke down the door of Champoux's house. He wasn't there, but inside, they found Sonia Delisle with Marc-André Hinse. A former president of the notorious Trois-Rivières chapter of the Hells Angels, Hinse had been on the run from police since an operation to break up his own cocaine smuggling ring in 2004. There was no evidence that Hinse was involved in the Newfoundland drug operation, but he had outstanding warrants for trafficking and gangsterism and was convicted of both.

That put Champoux on the run. He was successful at hiding—for a while—but he had the worst of luck. On the following May 24 weekend, Eric Vecchio, a veteran Montreal detective, took his girlfriend trout fishing in eastern Quebec. He stopped at a gas station in La Tuque (widely and hilariously reported in most English-speaking media as "La Toque"), a tiny and remote town far from just about anywhere, and just happened to recognize the guy in line in front of him. It was Champoux, buying groceries. Vecchio arrested him before he paid for his gas. He probably should have bought a lottery ticket.

In a short trial, Dickson received 10½ years, Champoux 8½ and Stanley 7½—not including time served. Kane and Mark Samson, who had been recorded taking cocaine orders from Dickson and was caught with cocaine and $81,000 in his car, both received two years of house arrest.

Getting rid of Big Pat and his loyal minions did not stop the flow of drugs into the province. Much as they had in Ontario during the pre-expansion days, the Hells Angels operated in the province by proxy. As the 2008 Criminal Intelligence Service Canada threat assessment put it, "In Newfoundland and Labrador, despite their lack of physical presence, the Hells Angels continue to exert their criminal influence in this region through associates and/or local criminals."

One set of their associates, Bacchus, showed up on July 18, 2010. Sixteen members from New Brunswick and Nova Scotia, along with a few local bikers, were stopped at Cape Spear, a popular tourist site. To nobody's surprise, they claimed merely to be taking in the sights. "We are just on vacation, like everybody else in the parking lot," said a Bacchus full-patch who gave his name as Kentucky. "But somehow, we just aren't allowed to do that. . . . It happens when we go on a trip like this. We aren't doing anything. We're just trying to have a vacation." The police, however, claimed in a media release that they had heard chatter as early as January 2010 indicating that Bacchus were looking for a Newfoundland club to patch over.

While there were a few established clubs on the island, including Easton's Crew in Grand Falls-Windsor and the Leonards and the Vikings in St. John's, law enforcement was more interested in a new 1%er club that opened just outside the small town of Cupids, not far from the capital. Named after the ax-like club used in the controversial harvesting of baby seals, the Hakapiks MC were secretive, refusing to identify themselves or speak with the media. They did, however, post a sign with their logo—red and white—on their clubhouse and have been known to associate with the Naiwa Rebels, a largely Mohawk club based in Beuace, Quebec, who are said to have ties with the Hells Angels.

Ultimately, it was the Grand Falls-Windsor–based Easton's Crew—named for Peter Easton, a seventeenth-century pirate who operated from Newfoundland—that received the official nod and were patched over to become Bacchus Newfoundland in January 2011.

At about the same time, Bacchus were thought to be setting up a new chapter in Fredericton, New Brunswick's capital. "If we rewind the clock a year ago to January 2010, when the Charlotte County Mariners were absorbed, they claimed stake to Nova Scotia, and there was a patch-over ceremony absorbing the East Coast Riders of Nova Scotia," said Constable Sebastien LeBlanc, a member of the RCMP's Southeast Integrated Intelligence Unit, at a press conference. "So they now claim stake to two provinces. In January 2011, they [Bacchus] absorbed the Easton's Crew to form Bacchus Newfoundland. Now they have Newfoundland, Nova Scotia and New Brunswick, so we're noticing a trend here. There's definitely an expansion going on here."

Indeed there was. Grand Falls-Windsor was such a desirable location for bikers that another chapter was established there in August 2011. But it wasn't Bacchus or some other Hells Angels puppet. In fact, it wasn't a puppet club at all. It was the Outlaws, the Hells Angels' oldest rivals.

While the Outlaws actually came to Canada before the Hells Angels, they were never quite as successful. The two clubs had a series of violent clashes in the US and later in Canada. After the Lennoxville Massacre established the Hells Angels' credentials in Montreal, they turned their attentions to the small Outlaws chapter in the island's largely English-speaking west end. The resulting war was bloody and one-sided. Any Outlaws who still existed in Montreal dared not wear their colors in public.

Ontario, on the other hand, was a different story. The Outlaws reached their greatest Canadian success with multiple chapters in Ontario in the 1980s under president Mario Parente, but massive arrests and the invasion of the Hells Angels after Papalia's death in 1997 crippled the Outlaws there. For years, imprisoned members, legal conditions on those still on the streets and the Hells Angels' near-hegemony in Ontario kept the club weak. But massive raids against the Hells Angels starting in 2001 and the implosion of the Bandidos after the Shedden Massacre in 2006 allowed the club to regain a little traction, at least in Ontario. Although it was far from the glory days of the '80s and '90s, the Outlaws operated in Ontario and flew their colors without fear.

Even so, it was a huge surprise when the Outlaws opened a chapter in Grand Falls-Windsor. Not only was it a long drive from Ottawa—the Outlaws' easternmost existing chapter—but it happened just a few months after the Hells Angels had declared the town theirs by establishing a Bacchus chapter there. The newly established chapter was, notably, an actual Outlaws chapter, not merely a puppet club. The use of their own men and name instead of proxies indicated the Outlaws meant business there.

While the police and the CBC had jumped the gun by predicting a gang war in Halifax when the Gate Keepers were established, they were both strangely quiet about the presence of both Bacchus and the Outlaws in a single, nondescript Newfoundland town. Historically, the Hells Angels have not tolerated other 1% clubs in the territory they claim, particularly the Outlaws. "The unique thing about Grand Falls-Windsor . . . is Newfoundland and Labrador is the only Atlantic Canadian province with two 'one percent' outlaw motorcycle gangs, and there are chapters of both in town," the RCMP's Mike Fewer told Grand Falls-Windsor *Advertiser* reporter Andrea Gunn. "We see them almost on a daily basis. But then we also see, through the year, increased presence periodically of members from other chapters of Bacchus and other chapters of the Outlaws . . . [and] we also see members of other clubs, other chapters, from all over Canada coming here."

While tempers may have been simmering in the middle of the island, it was actually in St. John's that they flared up next. In their long and exhaustive investigation of the Kitchener chapter of the Hells Angels, the Ontario Provincial Police (OPP) found enough evidence to charge two Newfoundlanders—Scott Hutchings of Bell Island and Jocelyn Dunn of St. John's—with trafficking cocaine and steroids, which the investigation determined were obtained from contacts in the Kitchener chapter, seven of whom were later arrested. Police also seized $50,000 in cash and an unspecified quantity of steroids from the pair. Charges are still pending and the trial has been set over. While Hutchings and Dunn have neither claimed nor denied gang membership, their connection to the Hells Angels is part of the Crown's case against them.

The Outlaws didn't stay quiet, either. As the location of their 2012 annual Canada Day national run—a party at which club matters are also addressed—they chose Grand Falls-Windsor. The local RCMP contingent (with reinforcements from around the country) kept a close eye on the proceedings, which passed without any arrests. "There were no incidents, and that's exactly what we anticipated," Fewer told Gunn. "They have a right to assemble and they have the right to socialize, but we just want to make sure that it's done safely and no laws are broken."

While the two gangs seemed to be able to coexist in relative peace in the middle of the island, there was trouble again in St. John's. It started with a suspicious fire. At 3:26 in the morning of May 25, 2013, emergency personnel responded to a 911 call directing them to a house on Hamilton Avenue. When they arrived they saw that the house and a car and motorcycle parked out front were all engulfed in flames. By the time the fire was extinguished, the car and the bike—a Harley-Davidson, of course—were write-offs. The house was severely damaged but salvageable, and the house next door suffered major damage as well. Spectators reported an overwhelming odor of gasoline at the site. A large unidentified man threatened to knock the camera out of the hands of a TV reporter while the fire was still raging. The incident was later widely reported as a firebombing, most likely the result of a gasoline-filled Molotov cocktail.

Just before midnight on the same day, automatic gunfire tore from inside a car at several houses on Dauntless Street in the Kenmount Terrace neighborhood. Nobody was hurt. Police, who recovered the weapon at the scene, said it was a case of mistaken identity, as none of the houses' residents were involved with the drug trade or organized crime. "We heard a couple of loud bangs and originally thought it was my dad coming back trying to scare us because they were in Florida," said Kenneth Neal, who was inside one of the houses when the shooting occurred. "But it was pretty loud so we came outside. My buddy ran out and he noticed the tires on the truck going flat. So I came out to look at it and noticed there were actually bullet holes in the window."

From interviews with witnesses and suspects, the Royal Newfoundland Constabulary believed that both incidents had to do with two men who were attempting to establish a Hells Angels chapter in the city.

In June, the two were arrested. Allan Winfield Potter and Bradley John Summers—the residents of the Hamilton Avenue house that had been set on fire—were both charged with four counts of assault, and Summers was also charged with four counts of uttering threats, one of which was also tied to Potter. The charges included George Street assaults dating back to March 2013—a stark reminder of the fights that had spawned Operation Roadrunner years before. At their initial arraignment, both men were wearing "Support 81" T-shirts, which are traditionally worn by friends and associates of the Hells Angels, as nonmembers are forbidden to wear the club's actual logo. Their trial is still pending, and they have pleaded not guilty.

"Outlaw motorcycle gangs may be involved in these events. Persons interviewed in the course of this investigation to date indicate an association to the Hells Angels," Royal Newfoundland Constabulary chief Robert Johnston told the CBC. "One person interviewed indicated that he is in the process of establishing a Hells Angels chapter in St. John's." It was later claimed by the Crown that that person was Summers. He and Potter have since been released on bail under the condition they do not associate with known gang members.

As the Hells Angels once again failed to find any traction in St. John's, the Outlaws apparently found great success in Newfoundland. So great that on September 27, 2013, they opened a second chapter an hour down the Trans-Canada Highway from Grand Falls-Windsor in Gander. Unlike most 1%er clubhouses, which are usually freestanding structures that can be easily armored, defended and monitored, the Gander Outlaws set up shop in a former check-cashing outlet between the Corner Pocket pool hall and a bar called Sidetrax in a strip mall on Airport Road.

As if to stake their territory, they rode loud-piped Harleys and wore their colors everywhere. That was new to Gander, which had not really seen bikers before, other than those passing through. Unlike most new 1%er chapters, the Outlaws did not patch over an existing club in Gander, but instead imported veterans from Ontario, who then recruited a few local tough guys.

A somewhat more affluent community that grew around a giant airport built as a transatlantic refueling stop during World War II, Gander is now also the home of a large Canadian military base. As such, it has a far higher number of bars and motels than a town its size normally would. It's an attractive place to sell drugs.

Unlike their "brothers" in Grand Falls-Windsor, the Gander Outlaws found trouble right away. There were persistent reports of loud parties and illegal beer sales, but nobody had the guts to make an official complaint. Then there was the fighting. While bar brawls are hardly uncommon in places like Gander, it was something of an open secret that the membership of the Outlaws had been recruited from the guys most likely to mess you up. That's a good asset to have when it comes to selling drugs or participating in any number of businesses that could be lucrative on the streets of Gander.

For the most part, they got away with it. Not only is there a macho code of not snitching after a bar fight, but fear of reprisal is a big part of why 1%ers let people know they're bikers.

Just two days after they christened their clubhouse, the Outlaws got into a huge bar brawl. What they did not realize was that two of the guys they got into it with were off-duty RCMP officers and a third was an auxiliary (he was knocked unconscious by a beer bottle to the head).

After the brawl, the RCMP issued a warrant for a local kid who was also an Outlaws full-patch. Patrick Bemister—on parole stemming from an earlier assault conviction—was on the run, and the RCMP issued a warning that he should not be approached. But just before 5:00 p.m. on October 7, Bemister walked into the RCMP detachment in Grand Falls-Windsor and turned himself in. He was released with several conditions about what items he was allowed to carry and whom he could speak with, and is still awaiting trial.

As the news of firebombings, drive-by shootings, automatic weapons and wannabe Hells Angels in St. John's—not to mention full-patch Outlaws allegedly breaking beer bottles over cops' heads—was still gripping the island, a man named Jason Skinner was murdered in a dispute over drugs in his room in a small house on 18th Avenue in Grand Falls-Windsor. There were no bikers directly involved, according to law enforcement, just a pair of drug-starved petty thieves.

What happened in Grand Falls-Windsor was actually closer to the organized crime game plan than all the goings-on in St. John's. The people who supplied the murdered Skinner with drugs—bikers or not—have no desire to be shot at by rivals or arrested by law enforcement. All they want to do is sell product, make money and not get caught. What happens after the sale is not their concern. What the clients do afterward is their own business (unless they turn rat).

But that's how organized crime works in Newfoundland. And, with a few regional variations, how it works all over Canada.

CHAPTER 2

HOW WE MAKE CRIME
ORGANIZATIONS IN CANADA

Organized crime doesn't just happen; it's created.

Before I explain that, let's set some terms straight. "Organized crime" is defined as collaboration between a group of people (it can be as few as two) for the purpose of committing crimes habitually. A "mafia" is a crime organization based on ethnic, cultural or clan relationships. In Canada, we have seen Italian, Irish, Jewish, Russian, Albanian, Indian, aboriginal and countless other mafias. It is only recently that truly multiethnic crime organizations—in that their leadership has been made up of two or more ethnicities—have emerged in Canada.

But when we say "the Mafia," we generally mean either of the two branches of the Italian Mafia—the Cosa Nostra and the lesser-known 'Ndrangheta. These are the guys you're familiar with from movies: the guys with the sharp suits, fedoras and machine guns in violin cases.

For the most part, mafias develop not from greed, but from need. Take, for example, the Cosa Nostra, or Sicilian Mafia. Over the centuries, the Mediterranean island of Sicily has been success-fully invaded and controlled by the Greeks, Carthaginians, Romans, Vandals, Byzantines, Arabs, Normans, French, Spanish and, finally, Italians. At the time of Italian unification in 1860, Sicilians were a poor, agricultural people who had a different language and culture than the rest of the country. The central government in Rome had little to do with them in any real terms—the only time most Sicil-ians had any contact with it was when paying taxes or having their sons taken off to war.

The lack of an effective government presence left a power vac-uum on the island. The people of Sicily instead went to prominent members of their own community—people who spoke their lan-guage and knew their ways—for conflict resolution. As years and generations passed, those families who distinguished themselves as community leaders became increasingly rich and powerful. Answering only to themselves, the big families used the threat of violence to take whatever they wanted. In fact, they acquired their status and lifestyle in much the same way as the crowned heads of Europe had centuries before, and they felt every bit as entitled to them.

As the system evolved, those involved called it the *Cosa Nos-tra* ("Our Thing") and others referred to them as the *mafia*, which comes from an old Arabic term meaning "braggart." An individual family group—called *cosca*, a reference to a tough-skinned plant that does not give up its fruit without a fight—would claim ownership of a territory, operate in it and defend it from encroachment. One cosca might work with another when it was advantageous, and the groups generally did their best to avoid conflict with one another.

Most members of a cosca were born into it, and after a few generations, when their names had become synonymous with their lifestyle, the Cosa Nostra became a de facto class—an easily identified and defined subset of the population. Joseph "Joey Bananas" Bonanno, a lifelong member of the Cosa Nostra in New York and the man responsible for much of Canada's organized crime, describes life in the Mafia in his memoir by saying: "Mafia is a process, not a thing. Mafia is a form of clan cooperation to which its individual members pledge lifelong loyalty. Friendship connections, family ties, trust, loyalty, obedience—this was the 'glue' that held us together."

A similar situation existed in Calabria—the toe of Italy's boot—which gave birth to the 'Ndrangheta. In fact, the 'Ndrangheta is so entwined in the government and businesses of Calabria that a cable made public by WikiLeaks from the US embassy in Rome to the US State Department claimed that organized crime has infiltrated government and business so profoundly in Calabria that it would be considered a "failed state" along the lines of Somalia if it were an independent nation.

There are few differences between the 'Ndrangheta and the Cosa Nostra, and even they are mostly subtle or outdated. Their terminology is not the same, as it comes from different dialects. For example, a family or clan unit is referred to by the Calabrians as an 'ndrina—from the old Greek word for "unbending"—rather than a cosca.

In North America, the Cosa Nostra and 'Ndrangheta have often worked together, especially in communities with few Italians, with one usually more dominant than the other.

Other situations also bred these de facto shadow governments that pulled the strings in their communities and evolved into mafias themselves—as in the case of the Irish, who were dominated by the British until 1922, and many European Jewish communities, which often found themselves ruled by antagonistic governments.

More recently, the fall of the Soviet Union and its client states in Eastern Europe and Central Asia between 1989 and 1992 jump-started a massive new organized crime movement in that region. Suddenly, nations that had been under totalitarian but stable rule for generations were turned upside down. The dreary predictability of the Communists was replaced by a vile burlesque of Western democracy. With all the rules suspended, the tough, the strong, the ruthless and the well-connected took over. It was a gold rush mentality in which those who could took everything they could put their hands on. The only way for many to get ahead was to steal or help someone else steal. And the police—inhumanely unpaid and tragically underequipped—could be easily bought off or threatened on the rare occasions they tried to stop anyone. Many governments were seen as little more than farces or criminal organizations in their own right.

After the crash, it seemed like every ethnicity had its own mafia, many of which posed as independence movements in attempts at legitimacy and as a way to obtain weapons. Particularly hard hit were the Albanians. From 1944 until 1985, Albania was under the atavistic rule of dictator Enver Hoxha, and then until 1992 by the kleptomaniacal Ramiz Alia. During that period, Albania was always the poorest and most backward European country, with technology and culture befitting an earlier century. There was a great deal of hope after the Communists fell, but the next regime, led by Sali Berisha, fell apart when the economy collapsed after billions were lost in government-sponsored Ponzi schemes. Millions of Albanians then took their personal economies into their own hands, in varying degrees of legality.

So, the first step in creating crime organizations is to build massive distrust or lack of cooperation between a cultural group or ethnicity and its government.

The second step is to keep that group together, self-sufficient and distant from the government, even if its members move to another country. Poverty helps too.

When Italians came to Canada in the early twentieth century, they were treated as outsiders, forbidden to take on certain occupations and often considered suspicious. According to historian Franca Iacovetta as well as current and retired law enforcement personnel I have spoken with, in some communities—like Hamilton, which later became one of the epicenters of Italian Mafia in Canada—gatherings of three or more Italian men were illegal and frequently broken up by police.

Other ethnicities received similar treatment. Often segregated into monocultural near-ghettos, Italians, Chinese and others rarely had any contact with the mainstream society, and their experience of the government was limited to the odd visit by police and the tax collector. These groups needed internal leadership, and—as in the cases with the Cosa Nostra and 'Ndrangheta—some was already in place.

Of course, the process of transforming neighborhood leaders into organized crime dons can be accelerated by moves that change their relationship with authority from distant to antagonistic. When the federal government outlawed opium in 1908, it was a huge blow to the Chinese community, who not only considered it a near-essential part of life, but also relied on it for much of their commerce. Later, alcohol prohibition affected Canada's Italian community—for whom wine was almost as important as opium was to the Chinese—in much the same way, especially after Ontario, where virtually all of Canada's Italian immigrants had settled, passed its own prohibition laws in 1916, a few years after several other provinces.

By the time the government started rounding up prominent Italian men and throwing them into distant internment camps in 1940, the relationship between much of the Italian community and the government was wildly embittered. The government's theory was that ethnic Italians in Canada might be more loyal to their former country than to their new one, and that locking them up would prevent them from becoming spies or saboteurs. Add to that soured relationship a healthy dose of institutionalized and cultural racism along with frequent police brutality and you can understand why shadow governments and powerful secret organizations among these groups and others, like aboriginals and people of African descent, developed and matured.

In early twentieth-century Canada, organized crime often stemmed from segregated ethnic communities in large cities. For the most part, these communities kept to themselves, and mainstream Canadians were little concerned with their goings-on unless they wanted to partake in a little vice themselves.

The only significant exceptions to the live-and-let-live equilibrium were those Canadians with a political agenda who needed a scapegoat to stoke the fires of moral indignation. In 1907, then-Deputy Minister of Labor Mackenzie King went on a fact-finding mission to Vancouver's Chinatown. Upon declaring that the opium trade in the city was "corrupting . . . white youth" in his report "The Need for the Suppression of Opium Traffic in Canada," he sponsored the Opium Act, which became law in 1908. Later, temperance societies and the politicians they supported vilified ethnic organizations for allegedly affecting other people's children in similar ways. The process probably hit its apex when Gerry McGeer conducted an investigation into crime in Vancouver, concluded it was primarily the fault of the large Chinese and tiny black communities (the latter of which numbered no more than a couple dozen people at the time), and won the mayor's seat in 1934 with the biggest landslide in the city's history.

Such demagoguery was thankfully rare. When organized crime did catch the attention of the Canadian public, it was actually because of the wealth, ego and conspicuous consumption of one particular Calabrian immigrant and his equally ostentatious wife.

Rocco Perri was born in Platì, the epicenter of 'Ndrangheta activity in Calabria. He came to Canada in 1913 to work on the fourth attempt at a shipping canal from Lake Ontario to Lake Erie through Welland to bypass Niagara Falls. When World War I put an end to government funds for the project, Perri, like many Italians who had been hired as laborers, was out of a job. To his credit, he tried working both in a local bakery and then as a door-to-door pasta salesman but didn't succeed at either. When Ontario passed its alcohol prohibition law in 1916, he knew what his future was.

Alcohol may have been illegal, but it was still very popular. Perri began to brew his own wine, then beer, then spirits and distribute them, first to Hamilton's Calabrian community, and then—with the protection of some beefy young men—to anyone who could afford them. Much of Perri's success could be attributed to his common-law wife, Besha "Bessie" Starkman, known as Bessie Tobin during her first (failed) marriage. Loaded with business acumen—and Jewish, a combination the stereotype-hungry media at the time adored and exploited—Bessie helped Rocco with payoffs to local law enforcement and politicians and arranged deals with shipping and storage companies.

The Perris were already quite wealthy when the US government passed its own prohibition act in 1920, instantly expanding the market from modest to enormous. While other would-be entrepreneurs scrambled to break into the American market, Perri—already known as the "King of the Bootleggers"—was more than ready. Instead of moving product over water or trying to sneak it across remote parts of the border, Perri, with his contacts and payoffs, had no problem shipping booze, disguised as turnips, into the US by train.

By the mid-1920s, Perri had expanded his product line to include narcotic drugs. It was a smart business plan. Not only had the alcohol market become crowded with increasingly ruthless competitors, but any smuggler worth his salt could see that Prohibition was coming to an end, first in Canada and then the US.

Rocco, with his dapper suits, big cars and constant boasts, became something of a media sensation. While he made little secret of his profession, his untouchable status with law enforcement earned him some perhaps grudging respect from the public at large. But his star paled beside that of Bessie, who was a media and society darling because of her inability to keep from saying the most ostentatious things. At a time when society was much less tolerant of such things, Bessie told the *Toronto Telegram* that she had left her first husband, children and religion back in 1916 because she found them boring compared to Rocco. In 1917, she was convicted of keeping a house of ill-repute, although she always maintained that she had no idea that her boarders were prostitutes.

After a tell-all newspaper article about Rocco featuring a one-on-one interview with Bessie, the two were called to testify at the federal government's inquest into liquor smuggling. Both claimed to have no knowledge of the liquor industry or smuggling, but Bessie failed to explain why there had been several dozen phone calls between her own line and that of the Gooderham and Worts Distillery. The pair was charged with perjury; while Rocco served six months, Bessie was allowed to walk.

In 1929, she just happened to show up at a warehouse full of whiskey with hundreds of dollars in her purse when an RCMP raid went down. Although she couldn't explain why she was there, there was no evidence she was making a deal. The suspicion her presence there drew allowed federal police, who hadn't been paid off, to watch her. Undercover officer Frank Zaneth (whose real name was Francesco Zanetti) began to follow her. Posing as an American drug smuggler, Zaneth met with Bessie, but—perhaps she was tipped off—no deal took place.

As would be the case with many other Canadian mafiosi, the Perris had far less to fear from law enforcement than from their competitors and colleagues.

Bessie was not well liked. Sharp-tongued and bossy, her attitude was not appreciated by the men, largely Italian, who worked for her husband. She was also notoriously cheap, which stood in stark contrast to her great fondness for showing off her expensive possessions like cars and jewelry. Stories about her legendary harshness were rampant. According to one particularly popular one, Rocco promised to pay a settlement to the family of one of his men who was killed on a smuggling run. When the poor man's uncle arrived to accept the money, as Mafia expert Antonio Nicaso writes in his biography of Perri, Bessie was enraged and told the grieving man to "go to hell."

At 11:15 on the evening of August 13, 1930, Rocco and Bessie returned home after a night on the town. While Rocco was still shutting down the car and Bessie was headed to the stairs that led from the garage to the kitchen, shotgun blasts tore through the air—and Bessie. She died immediately; Rocco was unharmed.

Although Rocco always claimed the incident was a robbery, none of the estimated $10,000 in jewelry Bessie was wearing was touched.

After Bessie's murder, Perri's star lost its shine. Many believed he was lost without Bessie's business acumen. He did take up with another woman, Annie Newman (as with Bessie, the media made a big deal out of the fact that she too was Jewish), but he was no longer considered a boss or leader or force to be reckoned with. On April 23, 1943, Perri went for a walk and was never seen again. The Hamilton police received several tips from reliable sources that his body, encased in cement, was at the bottom of Hamilton Harbor. Because no body was ever recovered, he is still listed as missing.

I think it's safe now to say that Bessie wasn't essentially cut in half by opportunistic thieves. And Rocco didn't start sleeping with Hamilton Harbor's legions of carp because he slipped and fell.

Most of the people who have made it their business to become familiar with the Perris or remember them are sure that the reason they both met untimely ends was because of their professional activities.

• • •

As well known and powerful as the Perris were, they—like generations of Canadian mafiosi after them—answered to American bosses.

You have to keep in mind that it was a very different time. Back then, Buffalo was not the hollowed-out rust-belt outpost it is now. When the Perris were in charge, Buffalo was at least the size of Toronto and, in most respects, more important. And it had a mafia to back it up. It was well known among local contemporaries that the Perris, especially Bessie, had several outstanding debts to the Buffalo Mafia. It is also important to note that, while the Perris were Calabrian, the real power in the region was Sicilian.

Italians came to Buffalo for the same reasons they came to Hamilton—to work. By the start of the twentieth century, Buffalo had its own Little Italy, in which much of the authority was held by the local Mafia. The first recognized godfather was Angelo "Buffalo Bill" Palmeri. He was from Castellammare del Golfo, Sicily, and had strong ties to other Cosa Nostra coscas from the same town, including the influential Bonannos and Magaddinos, who settled in Brooklyn.

A war between Brooklyn coscas—which stemmed from a rivalry between the Bonanno and Buccellato families in Castellammare del Golfo—led to widespread violence. In 1921, when a failed ambush by a Bonanno loyalist against the insurrection's two young leaders, Gaspar Milazzo and Stefano "the Undertaker" Magaddino, left two innocent bystanders dead, it was clear that the Williamsburg neighborhood was too crowded and full of gangsters. Thirty-four-year-old Milazzo moved to Detroit and thirty-year-old Magaddino to Buffalo.

At the time, Buffalo was controlled by Giuseppe "the Chief" DiCarlo, a close ally of the Brooklyn Sicilian families. He welcomed Magaddino and set him up as the local underboss because Buffalo did not have a family of its own. Magaddino opened a funeral parlor, which would remain a successful and legitimate business for decades.

DiCarlo, who had been in poor health, died less than a year after Magaddino arrived, but there was no question who would replace him at the top. Buffalo, with its lucrative border crossings and proximity to the freewheeling tourist trap of Niagara Falls, was Magaddino's. Still just 30, he quickly became one of the most wealthy and important mafioso in America, smuggling in Canadian booze from Perri and others and distributing it all over the region between Detroit and New York City.

In fact, business was almost too good. Lacking enough manpower to handle all of the product that needed to be moved, Magaddino allowed other gangsters to operate in Buffalo as long as they kicked a hefty amount of revenue back to him. It's indicative of Magaddino's status that the first of these was Detroit's Morris "Moe" Dalitz. A veteran of the notorious Purple Gang, Dalitz operated a smuggling ring known as the "Big Jewish Navy" and often dealt with Al Capone, Meyer Lansky and even Capone's archenemy, Bugs Moran. He was later instrumental in Lansky's re-creation of Las Vegas as a gambling mecca.

In 1930, when war broke out between the Bonannos and other Williamsburg families from Castellammare del Golfo and families from Corleone (another Sicilian town) who had established themselves in Manhattan, Magaddino was there to help. He sent cash to the Castellammarese every month and took in and hid members who were in danger.

The war ended when Salvatore (later Charles) "Lucky" Luciano, a high-ranking member of the Corleone faction, switched sides to the Castellammarese and invited Giuseppe "the Boss" Masseria, leader of the Corleones, to a sit-down at Nuova Villa Tammaro, a popular Coney Island restaurant. When Luciano excused himself to go to the men's room, four gunmen burst into the establishment and filled Masseria full of holes. One of the triggermen was Bugsy Siegel.

The victorious Castellammarese, under the leadership of Salvatore Maranzano, established themselves as the exclusive Cosa Nostra families of New York City. While he was still celebrating, Maranzano decided he could not trust Luciano and hired notorious Irish assassin Vincent "Mad Dog" Coll to kill him. But Luciano was tipped off and sent his own men, including Lansky, to a meeting Maranzano had set up as a pretext for a hit. Dressed as police, they disarmed Maranzano's guards and attacked the boss. After an intense struggle, Maranzano was finally taken down by blades and bullets. Coll arrived at the meeting late and, since Luciano's men did not recognize him, he was allowed to leave.

With Maranzano gone, the leadership fell to Magaddino's cousin, Giuseppe (later Joseph) "Joey Bananas" Bonanno. He established what he called the National Commission, a group that oversaw Cosa Nostra activity in the US, established rules and punishments and met once a year to give out its "Man of the Year" award. The original members were the five Castellammarese families of New York. He put himself in charge of the Brooklyn Bonanno family and the greater organization; Luciano received the Masseria organization in Manhattan's Little Italy; Gaetano

"Tommy" Gagliano led the Reina family of the Bronx; Giuseppe "Joe" Profaci remained head of Long Island's Profaci family and Francesco "Don Cheech" Scalise took over the D'Aquila-Mineo family of Bensonhurst in Brooklyn—and the Five Families allied themselves with Al Capone of Chicago and Magaddino, who now controlled Buffalo.

As powerful as he was, Magaddino was not without enemies. A rival gambling ring had established itself in nearby Batavia. Frank A. LoTempio and his brother Russell ran a gambling den from the Savoy Athletic and Social Club and a nightclub called The Cocoanut Grove, where illegal bets could be placed. Almost immediately, the Magaddino organization put some pressure on the LoTempios to pay up or pack up. Feeling bullied, Frank actually went to the police and asked for protection. They refused. So the upstarts decided to get rid of the boss.

On the evening of May 19, 1936, a blast ripped through 1651 Whitney Place in Buffalo, igniting a huge blaze. Hundreds watched as the house burned to the ground. A woman died from the blast and her three daughters were badly injured by smoke and flames. One of the people watching, with great concern and anger, was Magaddino. The firebomb was clearly meant for him, but had been delivered to the wrong address. He lived next door at 1653. The dead woman was his younger sister, Arcangela Longo, and the girls were his nieces. Her husband, Nick Longo, was in New York City at the time.

Not long after, on June 27, Frank LoTempio was leaving a wedding reception with his family. After he had, in a rather gentlemanly manner, seated his wife and sister in the car, he was walking around to the driver's side when a large black car pulled up and its passengers unloaded a hail of gunfire. Frank stumbled to the sidewalk, his bright white suit stained dark red from the eight bullet holes (four in the chest, three in the neck and one in the face) he had sustained. He died at the scene.

He had been driving Russell's car, a fact that must have made Russell feel like a moving target. Indeed he was. On October 29, 1936, Russell was in the backseat of his limo on the way home to Batavia after checking in on one of his bookies in Medina. The limo was about halfway back when a bomb that had been attached to the bottom of the car exploded. Russell's left foot was obliterated; the chauffeur, William Yates, was mostly unhurt.

Russell survived, minus his foot, but was soon out of the gambling business. On August 14, 1937, a group of gunmen shot up his last remaining pool room, killing one client, Alfred Panepinto, with a shotgun blast while he was playing poker, and badly injuring another, Sam See. With that, any conflict between the two groups was over.

With Prohibition now a bad memory in both countries (it was repealed in the US in 1933), the Mafia was desperate for other money-making enterprises. They still had the old standbys of loan-sharking, illegal gambling, extortion, carjacking, prostitution and labor racketeering, but all of that combined could not replace the revenue bootlegging had generated.

Slowly, and against the wishes of much of the old guard, the Mafia turned to trafficking illegal drugs. At the time, the real money was in heroin. Marijuana was trafficked into the US largely by Mexicans and was a low-profit, niche product. Cocaine was not yet popular and amphetamines were still mostly legal.

Heroin, an opiate with intense effects and an ability to be profoundly addictive, quickly found a market. Derived from poppies grown in Southeast Asia and later the Middle East, heroin became popular with soldiers in World War II.

Its massive popularity in the West can be linked to one man, Paul Bonaventure Carbone, a Corsican. As a young man in the 1920s, he and his friend François Spirito ran a scam in which they promised young women high-paying jobs in Egyptian tourist resorts. But when the women arrived, they were robbed of their cash, possessions and identification and forced into prostitution. He later relocated to Marseille, a rough and bustling port on France's Mediterranean coast, where he operated a series of brothels, ran rackets on tourists and even smuggled expensive cheeses in from Italy.

He was part of the Corsican Mafia, known in France as L'Unione Corse and in English as the Corsican Gang, an even more tight-knit and secretive society than the Cosa Nostra or 'Ndrangheta. Although just as powerful and violent as the Italian Mafias, the Corsican Gang is little known in North America; they operate here only by proxy because very few Corsicans ever migrated to Canada or the US.

It was in the 1930s that Carbone learned that there was a huge demand, particularly among sailors and soldiers, for opium. It had been used in Southeast Asia—much of which was a French colony at the time, with an administration that was composed of a disproportionate number of Corsicans—for generations and had developed an enthusiastic market among those stationed there. Carbone and Spirito traveled to Indochina, as it was then known, and returned with opium, from which they manufactured heroin. Although the profits made the trips worthwhile, Carbone was delighted to learn that farmers in much-closer Turkey were growing opium poppies legally for pharmaceutical companies and were willing to sell their excess directly to him. Before long, Carbone was the biggest heroin trafficker in the world. At the time, his reach extended only to Western Europe and the remaining French colonies, which were overwhelmingly poor. To make real money, he had to get his product across the Atlantic.

That would have to wait. Carbone had to consolidate his empire first. To keep things running smoothly, he put Marseille mayor Simon Sabiani on the payroll and allowed him the use of his thugs as strike breakers. Carbone also made another powerful friend—fellow Corsican gangster Auguste Ricord. When the Nazis invaded France in 1940, the as-yet unoccupied southern half of the country agreed to act as a client state for Germany. Named after its capital, Vichy France served as a semi-autonomous puppet state for the Nazi regime, rounding up Jews and others in exchange for a promise that the two million French held in Germany would not be sent to forced labor camps.

Many of the citizens of Vichy France supported the Nazis, and no group was more likely to collaborate with the Vichy government than the Corsicans, whose relationship with France was not unlike that between Sicily and Italy. In fact, Corsicans and Sicilians share much, and each of them spoke a native language that had more in common with the other than with French or Italian.

Among the high-level collaborators were Carbone, Spirito and Ricord. In fact, Ricord was so dedicated to the Nazi cause that he became a high-ranking officer in the Carlingue—the French auxiliaries of the Gestapo—and his influence kept the authorities, either in Germany or Vichy, from interfering in Carbone's business.

In 1943, Carbone was headed to Turkey on a train carrying Wehrmacht troops back to Germany for rest and relaxation. A bomb planted on the tracks by French Resistance derailed the train, killing several and injuring dozens. According to contemporary reports, Carbone—both legs severed and a cigarette hanging from his lower lip—shooed away medical personnel, telling them to concentrate on those who could still be saved.

His businesses were taken over by other members of the Corsican Gang. As the war started to turn in the Allies' favor, the Corsican Gang changed sides and regularly assassinated high-placed collaborators in Marseille. After the war, the Corsican Gang was allegedly funded and trained by the CIA to help put down the Communist movement in France. At any rate, it was well documented that members of the Corsican Gang were hired as goons to help break Communist-inspired strikes in Marseille in 1948 and even assassinated some pro-Communist union leaders.

The Corsicans realized that in order to make really big money, they had to get the heroin to America. Without a Corsican presence on the western side of the Atlantic, they would have to rely on their friends from Sicily. To pull off what would later become known as the French Connection, the Cosa Nostra would rely on two Canadians—Vic "the Egg" Cotroni in Montreal and John "Johnny Pops" Papalia in Hamilton.

CHAPTER 3

THE MAFIA INVASION

After laying out the National Commission with himself at the top of the heap, Joseph Bonanno was clearly the most powerful mafioso in America. In the 1950s, he was about to become unbelievably wealthy. While the other families in New York were reluctant to move heroin, the Bonannos were anything but. Still, it was a challenge for Bonanno to establish an infrastructure for its movement and a network of willing partners for its distribution.

Bonanno directed his underboss, his cousin Frank "Carroll" Garafola, to move back to Sicily and coordinate the European side of the operation. With him gone, Bonanno needed a new underboss—and knew exactly who he wanted.

Carmine "Lilo" Galante was one of the toughest of all the New York Mafia enforcers during their bootlegging heyday. In 1930, an NYPD cop named Joseph Meenahan caught him hijacking a truck in Williamsburg. When Meenahan shouted for him to stop, Galante replied with all the bullets in his gun. He didn't hit Meenahan, but he did manage to shoot a six-year-old girl who just happened to be at the scene. She survived, but Galante, finally apprehended miles away, received a 12½-year sentence for aggravated assault.

Almost immediately upon his release, Garafola had a job for him. At the time, Garafola distributed an Italian-language newspaper in New York called *Il Progresso* (*The Progressive*). It was staunchly in support of Benito Mussolini's Fascist government and ideology. At the same time, a rival paper, *Il Martello* (*The Hammer*), was being published in New York by a self-described anarchist named Carlo Tresca. It was full of antifascist, anti-Mussolini rhetoric and frequently made mention of Garafola and his best friend, construction mogul Generoso Pope, who was a big financial supporter of the Mussolini government.

Garafola tolerated Tresca as a minor annoyance for a while, but he crossed a line in September 1942. Garafola, Pope and Tresca had all been invited to a formal event specifically for New York's Italian-American community to raise funds for war bonds. When Tresca arrived and saw the other two, smiling in their tuxedos, he shouted, as quoted by *The New York Times*, "Not only is there a Fascist here, but also his gangster. This is too much, I'm leaving!" He could just as easily have politely asked Garafola to kill him, because it would have had the same effect.

In truth, Tresca had a lot of enemies inside and outside the Italian-American community. Accordingly, the police watched him constantly. On January 9, 1943, officers on foot saw an unidentified driver deliberately try to run him down as he was walking in Manhattan's Little Italy. Two days after that, Tresca managed to ditch the officers following him but showed up again two hours later at the corner of 13th Street and Fifth Avenue. As the police in a squad car watched from a discreet distance, a Ford sedan stopped directly in front of Tresca, blocking his path. A short and thickly built man hopped out of the car and shot him twice—once in the chest and once in the face. The man then jumped back into the Ford, which sped off. Due to wartime gas rationing restrictions, the police were unable to give chase. The car was later found abandoned.

Speculation as to who killed Tresca was everywhere. Many believed it was Stalin's NKVD (the forerunner of the KGB) because Tresca had turned his back on the Communists and tore into them in his paper just as deeply as he had the Fascists.

The killer turned out to be Galante, who was actually seen near the scene of the crime but not followed (again, because of rationing—at least, officially).

After proving himself with the Tresca murder, Galante was groomed for years to take over for Garafola. With the old underboss sent off to Sicily, Galante was promoted and sent to Canada in 1953. Importing heroin to Canada made sense to Bonanno because its points of entry (like seaports and airports) were much less strictly patrolled than those in the US and because the Cosa Nostra had well-established smuggling routes from Canada dating back as much as 30 years.

The first place Galante went was Montreal, which was then Canada's biggest and most important city. After thoroughly investigating and interviewing potential candidates, he settled on one enterprising Calabrian immigrant named Vincenzo Cotroni. There were Sicilian mobsters in Montreal at the time—most notably, Luigi Greco and the Cuntrera brothers, Pasquale and Liborio—but Galante settled on Cotroni. Greco and his partner, Frank Petrula, had strong ties to Lucky Luciano, so that may have swayed Galante's opinion. The Montreal Sicilians remained part of the operation but under Cotroni's authority.

Cotroni's family came to Canada when he was 13. Rather than attend school—he never learned to read or write—Cotroni worked as an assistant in the carpentry business run by his father,

Nicodemo. Between them, they declared an income of $35 a week. They supplemented that with petty crime.

By the time Vic was 16, he knew carpentry was not his future. He'd already established a name for himself as a street brawler when he drew the attention of Armand Courville. A professional wrestler of some esteem, Courville taught the local boys the finer points of the sport and was impressed by Cotroni. Soon Courville had the lad fighting under the name Vic Vincent. The money wasn't great, so Courville introduced Vic to his side business: muscle for hire. Courville's primary client for muscle was the local Liberal party, who greatly appreciated his operation's ability to clear rivals from a polling station with a baseball bat and his lack of hesitation when it came to stuffing ballot boxes. He once proudly told a reporter that he was "the Liberal party's chief of police."

He taught Vic all of it—from buying off cops, prosecutors and judges to intimidating witnesses and debtors. His young protégé jumped headlong into the business. He was a natural.

Vic's first arrest, in 1928, came after he allegedly raped a girl when she refused to marry him. While he was out on bail, the alleged victim, Maria Bresciano, withdrew her complaint and married him anyway. After that, he had a series of brushes with the law, including selling liquor without a license, passing bad checks and possession of counterfeit money. In 1936, he was charged with assaulting an elections officer. It was the last time he was ever convicted and marked the beginning of his maturity as a mobster.

Vic and Courville, along with two (French, but not Corsican) brothers from Marseille, Edmond and Marius Martin, opened a nightclub at the corner of Saint-Laurent and Sainte-Catherine in 1942. The 600-seat Cabaret au Faisan Doré (Golden Pheasant Cabaret) featured the best in French and Québécois music and entertainment, and it was extremely popular.

But that wasn't how Vic the Egg made his real money. Instead, he relied on gambling, loan-sharking, prostitution and illegal bars, which were then called "blind pigs." Recent crackdowns on gambling in the US led a steady stream of Americans to Montreal. Gambling wasn't exactly legal there, but it was largely tolerated. Before Atlantic City legalized casinos, Montreal wasn't just a great place to go, it was the only place to go.

Under Vic's direction, a Jewish mobster named Harry Ship (who had once been referred to as the "King of the Gamblers") rented a building close to the Faisan Doré and converted it into a sort of mission control for gambling. It was equipped with ticker-tape machines reporting results from horse races and other sports from all over Canada and the US. It was manned round the clock by bookies who each received bets over five phone lines. It was raided no fewer than 34 times over six years. According to contemporary reports, Ship would pay the fine out of petty cash while the bookies still took calls. It may have been chump change for Ship and Vic, but it was an important source of revenue for the cops. "The fines we paid took care of the police department's salaries, or a large part of them," he later told historian William Weintraub for his book *City Unique*. "And the city's coffers were getting fat."

By the time Galante arrived in 1953, Vic was a very important man in Montreal's underworld, insulating himself from prosecution by having dozens of rackets run by other people, like Ship, who would kick money from their operations up to him. Once New York was part of the picture, however, he was always a subordinate to Galante and would frequently have to get his hands dirty. On one occasion, a well-known club owner, Solomon "Solly Silver" Schnapp, refused to allow Galante's prostitutes to ply their trade in his flagship club, Chez Paris. In return, Vic and some of his friends walked into the club with sledgehammers and baseball bats and wrecked the place. Although the damage was estimated at

$30,000, Schnapp dropped his complaint after Vic agreed to pay him $200.

Vic was quickly rising, but was still well below Galante in the big picture and was required to kick up a "tax" on all operations and rackets he ran in Montreal. Galante, in turn, kicked a portion of that up to the boss, Bonanno.

With Montreal secure, Galante turned his eyes toward Ontario. He needed a man like Vic Cotroni there. He found one in John Papalia.

Born in Hamilton to Calabrian parents, Papalia was a career criminal, involved in burglary, fencing, prostitution, intimidation and gambling rackets in the city since his teens. He briefly relocated to Toronto, where he was arrested for a break and enter. It may have seemed like bad luck at the time, but it was actually the spark that launched his career. Papalia made lots of friends in prison and when he was released in 1947, he started moving heroin on the streets of Toronto for drug kingpin Harvey Chernick (the Jewish mob did not share the Cosa Nostra's reluctance to get involved in the drug trade even then).

When he was arrested in front of Toronto's Union Station in 1949, according to Mafia expert Antonio Nicaso, he received only two years because he convinced the judge that the white powder he was carrying was actually syphilis medicine, not heroin. That story was backed up by contemporary newspaper reports, including one in the *Toronto Star*.

Upon his release in 1951, Papalia headed to Montreal to work as an enforcer for Greco. While there, he caught the eye of Galante. The New Yorker took him under his wing, teaching him the finer points of extorting gamblers, intimidating witnesses and setting up phony stock-market scams.

His Cosa Nostra apprenticeship over, Papalia returned to Hamilton in 1954 and put together a crew. In defiance of how things had been done in Hamilton (and the old country) for generations, Papalia collected a multiethnic group, including Calabrians, Sicilians, Anglos, Irish and French-Canadians, but, as the rules dictated, all the men in charge were Calabrians. They ran gambling, extortion, loan-sharking and stock scams from behind the front of a taxi company. He too kicked money upstairs to Bonanno via Galante, who was considered the Cosa Nostra's top man in Canada.

Huge changes were in store in 1957. The Canadian government got tired of Galante's frequent arrests and deported him. That left Cotroni in charge in Montreal, reporting directly to Bonanno. With Galante out of the picture, Buffalo's Stefano Magaddino appealed to Bonanno about Papalia. He pointed out that Papalia's father had worked for him and that Hamilton was only an hour from Buffalo. Bonanno agreed that Papalia had the necessary qualities to lead a crew and gave his blessing. From that point forward, Papalia was in charge in Hamilton, reporting directly to Magaddino.

Both men were given the title *caporegime*, meaning they were the boss of their territory but answered to an underboss in the US (Cotroni to New York, and Papalia to Buffalo).

In October 1957, Bonanno, Galante, Magaddino's cousins Antonio and Gaspare (who represented Buffalo), Detroit's Santo Volpe and Lucky Luciano traveled to Sicily to meet with the local Mafia and the Corsicans to set up what would become the French Connection. It was a huge deal. In fact, Italy's minister of foreign trade, Bernardo Mattarella, actually met the US delegation when it changed planes in Rome.

Later in 1957, a meeting of Mafia representatives in bucolic Apalachin, New York, was raided by cops. Most of the mafiosi who fled into the woods were caught and questioned, but those who remained inside the house—like Galante—weren't bothered because the police did not have a warrant to search or even enter the building. Many blamed the disaster on Magaddino, who had recommended the spot. But business went on as planned, and the French Connection was established by those smart enough to not get arrested.

Soon heroin was flooding into North America, much of it through Montreal and Hamilton. In order to coordinate getting the heroin from Papalia then over the border to Buffalo, Magaddino recruited a pair of Sicilians who owned a bakery in Toronto. The Agueci brothers, Albert and Vito, devised a plan in which they loaned trunks and suitcases to tourists and immigrants flying into Toronto's Pearson airport from France. The bags all had false bottoms in which heroin was hidden. They moved it to Papalia, who doled it out to the distributors (including the Aguecis), with most of what went over the border headed to New York City.

It worked without fail for a few years, but disaster struck twice in 1961. The first to go down was Papalia. On March 21, 1961, he showed up at the Town Tavern, a popular jazz joint in downtown Toronto. Everyone knew why he was there. He wanted a piece of the action. But owner Max Bluestein stood firm. When Bluestein refused a drink bought by Papalia, it was clear. No deal. The second Bluestein waved off the unfortunate waitress, Papalia and his men stood up. Johnny walked over to Max and smacked him in the jaw with a right augmented by brass knuckles. That was just the start. What followed was a brutal beating that left Bluestein inches from death. Papalia finished the job by shoving a broken beer bottle into his mouth while he was on the floor unconscious.

Although there were more than 100 people in the bar at the time, to use a timeworn phrase, nobody saw nothing. Even Bluestein, when he was well enough to speak again, told the police he had no idea who attacked him.

Of course everyone and his brother knew it was Johnny. Especially the police. They kept such a close eye on Papalia that he had no choice but to lie low. He was essentially useless to the French Connection. Under intense pressure, he eventually gave in and admitted to the beating. The charges were dropped when Papalia was later caught by US authorities for trafficking. He was extradited and in 1964 was given a 10-year sentence. He was housed at the Lewisburg federal penitentiary, better known in those days as the Mafia country club. He was reunited in there with Galante, who was serving his own 12-year sentence, also for trafficking.

At about the same time Johnny was pounding poor Max, Albert Agueci was arrested in Rochester with two capsules of heroin in his pocket. He was charged with conspiracy to traffic. Albert wasn't too upset, though; he knew Magaddino would take care of it. That was the deal.

But Magaddino didn't. He didn't even return Agueci's calls. Instead, Albert's wife would have to mortgage their family home in Scarborough to raise the necessary funds for his bail. Freed, he drove to Buffalo and met with Magaddino, by this time an old man. The cops captured the conversation via wiretap, but the recording was declared inadmissible in court, so it was never made public. It's the most open secret in Buffalo crime history that Albert, enraged, reminded Magaddino about their original deal. Unsatisfied with Magaddino's response, he then threatened the Undertaker. For his part, Magaddino is said to have told the upstart baker that threatening him was not a really well-thought-out idea. They agreed to meet again when both were less emotional.

On October 8, 1961, Albert told his wife he was going to talk with Magaddino and left their Scarborough home. He was never seen again. Alive, at least.

A couple of deer hunters tramping around the woods near a cornfield just south of Penfield, New York, came across what was left of his body on November 23, 1961. His hands had been tied behind his back with barbed wire. His teeth had been knocked out one by one. His ribs had been broken, his hands and face had been burned off and his skull had been fractured over the eight or nine days he was tortured before someone was kind enough to strangle him. He was missing more than 30 pounds of flesh from his legs. Contemporary reports in papers, including *The Buffalo News*, said the torturers took it off piece by piece.

There were no such problems in Montreal. In the mid-1950s, though, two men who would ultimately change the face of the Italian Mafia in Canada emigrated from Italy.

One was Paolo Violi. Born in Sinopoli, Calabria, Violi was a short, heavy man with a quick temper and a fondness for unnecessary violence and double crosses. Before he ever appeared in Montreal, he settled down in Hamilton. In his early 20s, he ran with a few smaller gangs. On May 24, 1955, he was arrested after shooting another Calabrian immigrant, Natale Brigante, to death in a parking lot in the nearby Niagara Peninsula town of Welland. He told the cops that they had been arguing over a woman and that Brigante had slashed him with a knife. Unable to escape because Brigante had him pinned, Violi admitted he shot and killed him, but in self-defense. To back up his claim, he showed police a fresh knife wound on his chest. Unable to produce any contrary evidence, they let him go. Still, many believed that the conflict was not about a woman at all, but the result of a long-running feud or vendetta from the old country.

Whether the killing was set up or just noticed by him, it certainly gained Violi an audience with Giacomo Luppino. The last of the truly old-school Canadian godfathers, when he came to Canada from Calabria, Luppino brought an ear he had severed from an old rival. It was more than just a memento; it was a reminder to all that he was not to be crossed. He ruled Hamilton's 'Ndrangheta for years before Papalia's star began to rise, but he too answered to Magaddino, the real power in the region. When Papalia was powerful enough to take over Hamilton, Luppino gracefully backed into a subordinate role.

Luppino put Violi to work right away. Even though liquor was legal in all of Canada after 1948, federal and provincial sin taxes made it far more expensive in some areas than others. The Ontario Mafia, of course, still had plenty of bootlegging stills and was industriously churning out 165-proof spirits at a time when the most powerful liquors legally available topped out at 80. Violi's job was to get them from rural Ontario to bars and nightclubs in Montreal. He did it well.

By the early '60s, Luppino had a decision to make. He knew Hamilton was too small for Papalia and Violi to coexist. One had to go. Although he had a great deal of personal fondness for Violi (who was dating his daughter, Grazia), Luppino chose the gruff Papalia, whose heroin connections were beginning to make ridiculous amounts of money and whose credentials as an enforcer were unparalleled. Violi was sent to Montreal.

While it has been reported that Magaddino disapproved of the decision and may even have wanted to kill Violi rather than lose him, the more widely accepted theory among law enforcement and Mafia experts these days is that he was happy to have an ally in the lucrative Montreal market.

Paolo opened Violi Pizzeria in the north-end neighborhood of Saint-Léonard and soon became involved in extortion and counterfeiting, as well as receiving bootleg liquor from Ontario to sell in Montreal. Of course, it was impossible to operate in Montreal without paying tribute to Cotroni, so a relationship was set up right away.

Vic and his brother Frank, who was also active in the organization, took a strong liking to Violi and began to include him in their activities. It was an advantageous position but one fraught with danger. Violi was still close to Luppino (he married Grazia on July 10, 1965), who answered to Magaddino, and he was now also a member of the Cotroni family, answering to the Bonannos. Those widespread relationships allowed Violi to act as an ambassador between the two families, as well as with the Americans and Italians, but they also gave him divided loyalties, something his mouth was not suited for. Violi could be opinionated and loud. He would occasionally complain about the Bonannos, and he advised Cotroni to cut the family free of them and become more than just the Bonannos' northern franchise. That particularly irked Greco, a Sicilian who was still very loyal to the Bonannos, even though they had bypassed him for boss of Montreal.

But it kind of didn't matter what Greco thought. The Cosa Nostra is all about loyalty. If you don't like what the boss says, too bad.

By 1970, the Mafia landscape began to change. Always a scammer, Papalia had been released from prison early because he had convinced US authorities that he was terminally ill. In reality, he was as healthy as an ox, and he quickly reassumed his position in Hamilton. In fact, with the aging Luppino fading, Papalia was the undeniably the top dog in Ontario—although he was working with the Cosa Nostra instead of the 'Ndrangheta despite his Calabrian roots. Other than Johnny and his men, the biggest operation in Hamilton was the 'Ndrangheta, led by a foul-mouthed and quick-tempered fat man named Domenic Musitano. His small army of street hoods generally ran operations too small to arouse Papalia's interest, or they could be recruited to the big man's cause when needed. They were best known for bombing the businesses, often bakeries, of rivals and debtors, briefly earning Hamilton the nickname "Bomb City."

Violi stayed in contact and on friendly terms with the legendarily hard-to-get-along-with Papalia. In fact, Papalia was the actual, not metaphoric, godfather of Violi's son.

More important, though, is the fact that Violi had risen so quickly in the ranks of the Cotronis. He quickly bypassed Greco and others—including Vic's own brother Frank—to become second-in-command and he was named successor to Vic the Egg himself. That was not just an honor, but a job. By the mid-1970s, Vic was old and had fallen very ill. He became less and less involved with the family business and had fallen into a figurehead role, rarely leaving his house. In fact, Violi was so hands-on and powerful that when police spoke about the organization to the media, they started calling it the "Cotroni-Violi family."

Although it was a lucrative relationship, things weren't always smooth between Violi, Cotroni and Papalia. A crisis loomed in 1971 when the DuBois crime family began encroaching on their turf. Originating with a biological family of French-Canadian thugs whose first successful scam was to act so obnoxious in restaurants and bars that the owners would pay them to stay away, the DuBois boys had created their own low-level empire and had plenty of unemployed and angry French-Canadian youth at their disposal. Violi's plan, captured on wiretap, was simple: Kill them all. Cotroni's cooler head prevailed, and the DuBoises were allowed to operate in their part of Montreal with impunity with the understanding that they would kick upstairs like everyone else.

Things did not go smoothly for Vic the Egg soon after that. The separatist Quebec Liberation Front, in its manifesto for a free Quebec, named him personally as one of the primary obstacles to democracy in the province due to his long history of voter intimidation, ballot-box stuffing and bribing politicians. That spurred investigative reporter Jean-Pierre Charbonneau to write a series of articles that outlined the connections between Montreal's major Mafia figures and politicians. Eager to clear his party's name, Quebec premier Robert "Boo Boo" Bourassa convened a province-wide organized crime probe. Montreal mayor Jean Drapeau, no stranger to controversy himself, called the investigation "useless and very costly . . . serving only to tarnish reputations."

Vic, the probe's primary target, was not helpful. He was sentenced to a year in prison after delivering testimony that was widely reported in the national media as "deliberately incomprehensible; rambling, vague, and nebulous" to Bourassa's organized crime inquisition in November 1973. His lawyer managed to get the sentence overturned, but not before the boss had spent a few weeks behind bars.

Later that year, a wiretap emerged in which Cotroni and Violi threatened to kill, of all people, Papalia. They had caught wind of Papalia using their names without their permission in a scam that netted him $300,000. Despite the fact that Cotroni did indeed say that he had considered killing Papalia, the meeting seemed genuinely friendly and the Montrealers were assuaged when Papalia told them the operation hadn't worked and he had made only a paltry $40,000 on it. They parted as friends, but Cotroni and Violi were arrested for the threat. They were both acquitted.

Later that year, Vic was implicated along with close friend William "Obie" Obront in a scheme to supply tainted meat to fast-food restaurants in Montreal including the concessions at Expo 67. A big wheel in Jewish organized crime, who has been referred to as Canada's Meyer Lansky, Obront became a close ally of Cotroni's once he saw that the young Calabrian immigrant was going to make millions through the French Connection. He quickly became Cotroni's primary money launderer, sending his heroin profits through 38 different companies he owned. The tainted-meat investigation was halted when it failed to acquire sufficient evidence.

Things got even worse for Vic when he lost his brother Frank. Known as "the Big Guy," Frank was unlucky and was frequently arrested. Once he was even picked up by the Federales in Acapulco,

Mexico, for using a stolen credit card. It all turned out to be an honest mistake because the police had been given the wrong credit card number. Normally, Frank had a handle on the operation, like when a Greek restaurant owner named Dionysos Chionsis told the cops that Frank demanded $250 a week as part of a protection racket. As became custom in the region, when the court date rolled around, Chionsis had changed his mind completely and denied he even knew who Frank was.

But things got bigger and slipped out of his hands when Sicilian-American gangster Giuseppe "Pino" Catania turned rat and implicated Frank as one of his major contacts in a small cross-border trafficking operation. After extradition to the US, Frank was given a 15-year sentence and a $20,000 fine.

A much bigger threat to Vic Cotroni than law enforcement would ever be came from the second man who arrived in Canada from Italy in the 1950s and who, along with Violi, would have a major impact on the Mafia in Canada. Nicolo "Nick" Rizzuto came to Montreal with his family from Sicily in 1955. A player back in the old country, he immediately hooked up with the Cotroni outfit through Greco.

Although Rizzuto quickly became a big earner, he caused a great deal of friction with his constant complaints over the fact that he, a Sicilian, had to take orders in the Cosa Nostra from a Calabrian. His anger turned to outrage in the early 1970s when Cotroni chose Violi—another Calabrian, and an ill-mannered and disrespectful one at that—as his successor and put him directly in charge of Rizzuto's family. Rizzuto was convinced that he himself deserved the position. He earned more, he had a much bigger network and more manpower, and—unlike Violi—he was not involved in two-bit operations like roughing up restaurant owners until they paid protection.

The Sicilian Greco, who many believed would succeed Cotroni and who had always handled the other Sicilians in Montreal, had died in a horrifying incident on December 7, 1972. Workers repairing the floor of his restaurant, Gina's Pizzeria, decided for some reason to clean the tile with kerosene. A flick of a lighter ignited the fumes, which then engulfed Greco's petroleum-based suit and incinerated him inside it.

In open defiance of his new Calabrian boss, Rizzuto refused to pay tribute to Violi and would not even speak with him, turning down several face-to-face meetings.

Major-league mafiosi from America and Italy were brought in to mediate. They cared a lot less about who came from where than how much money they were making running drugs through Montreal. But Rizzuto wouldn't budge. Cotroni had little choice. He put out a contract on Rizzuto's head.

CHAPTER 4

TWO TRIBES EMERGE

Upon hearing that Cotroni was finished with him, and unable to convince the Bonannos to back his plan of a heroin-cash-fueled Sicilian takeover of Montreal, Nick fled to Venezuela in 1974 because it was the nearest country that did not have an extradition agreement with Canada. He opened a pizza restaurant called Godfathers just outside Caracas. The blockbuster Mafia movie of the same name had been released in 1972 and was still very popular.

Nick used the pizza joint as a front for both money laundering and local trafficking. It was there that the Rizzutos were first exposed to the money-making miracle that is cocaine. For organized crime, it was a wonder drug—addictive like heroin, but easier to conceal, and instead of nodding off to sleep, its users get an energy boost, a feeling of confidence and an increased sex drive.

Nick's absence left his oldest son, 28-year-old Vito, in charge of the Sicilian faction in Montreal—known derisively among the Calabrians as the "Zips."

Before long, Vito would get the impetus to start a revolution among Montreal's Mafia. The war between the Calabrians and the Sicilians first took root back in 1973, when a tall stranger walked into Violi's bar, Reggio, and asked about the APARTMENT FOR RENT sign in the front window. He introduced himself as Bob Wilson, a journeyman electrician from Ontario. Judging him to be something of a big, dumb mook, Violi rented him the apartment right above Reggio.

It was a ruse. Wilson was, in fact, undercover cop Robert "Shotgun Bob" Menard. Unbeknownst to Violi and his colleagues, Menard was one of the primary movers in the Montreal police's notorious Night Squad, which was well known to have put most of the DuBois gang out of business through violent means. Menard has admitted in interviews that the squad's methods would not necessarily be approved of by outsider observers.

Shortly after Shotgun Bob moved in, he managed to plant listening devices not only in Reggio but also on its phone. The cops could hear everything said in the bar and from the bar.

The intel was a treasure trove, and it provided much of the evidence for Bourassa's crime commission, which had so disrupted business in the mid-1970s.

By the time the Mafia figured out what had happened and how it had been accomplished, Violi's reputation was in tatters. Allowing law enforcement so much information so easily made him, in many eyes, the equivalent of a rat by incompetence.

These circumstances allowed Vito Rizzuto to appeal to New York. He asked them: If Violi was stupid enough to risk his and everybody else's operation by allowing an undercover cop to live above his own bar, what else was he capable of? New York agreed; Violi should be punished. They were correcting Vic the Egg's mistake in his choice of successor a few years earlier.

With official approval, Rizzuto acted quickly. But he didn't want to get rid of just Violi. Rizzuto's plan was to remove the

Calabrian power structure in Montreal so that his own small but increasingly powerful family could take over.

His first target was Pietro Sciara. A Sicilian who worked directly for Violi, Sciara had attracted the Rizzutos' ire when he was one of the loudest supporters of the Calabrians during the negotiations that resulted in the order to kill Nick, which led to his self-imposed exile to Venezuela. It was particularly bothersome to Rizzuto that Violi called Sciara "Zio Petrino" (Uncle Pete). They weren't family; Violi was a Calabrian. To Nick's hard-core Sicilian pride, it was a huge offense.

If nothing else, Sciara was an old-schooler and loyalist. When the same commission that charged Cotroni with being too vague asked him about his own role in the Mafia, Sciara answered, "The Mafia? I don't know. What is that, 'the Mafia'?"

On Valentine's Day 1976, Sciara took his wife out to see an Italian-dubbed version of *The Godfather, Part II.* On the way out, the couple were approached by three men. One of them held a sawed-off shotgun to Sciara's head and pulled the trigger. He was killed immediately, and his wife was injured by the blast. The three men ran into the open side door of a white Chevy van and peeled away. The van was later recovered, but the men were never identified.

It was the opening shot in what would become a Mafia war in Montreal. It also set what would become a precedent for the brutality that would be seen there. The Sciara hit broke many long-held rules of Mafia etiquette. Not only was Pietro shot in the face, preventing an open-casket funeral, but his body was left in the street. Even worse, his innocent wife was hurt by flying bits of his skull.

At the time, Violi was in Montreal's notorious Bordeaux Prison for his own testimony before Bourassa's commission. He had left his big, ugly brother Francesco in charge in the family stronghold, the Reggio. Whichever one of them was actually making the decisions reacted quickly. On March 9, 1976, Sebastiano Messina, a well-known Rizzuto lieutenant, was hanging around outside a pool hall on Rue Tillemont when an ordinary-looking man walked by and shot him dead before making his getaway in a nearby Camaro.

Paolo Violi was still in jail on February 8, 1977, when he was informed that three masked gunmen had broken into Violi Importing and Distributing in the east end and pushed Francesco up against a wall before killing him with a shotgun blast to the back of the head. Judiciously, Corrections Canada did not let Paolo out to go to his brother's funeral.

But they did release him in December 1977 when his sentence was over. Desperate for money, Paolo sold Reggio to the Randisi brothers, Vincenzo and Giuseppe, Sicilians who, I have been told by sources who'd rather not be named, were aligned with the Cotronis. Violi tried to carry on with business as usual at the establishment, renamed Bar Jean-Talon by the Randisis, even though everyone knew his life was likely to end at any minute.

Police say that Vito Rizzuto had one last sit-down with Violi shortly before Christmas. They claim that the Sicilian usurper gave the old Calabrian boss a chance to save his own life by stepping aside, but that Violi refused the offer. His fate, many thought, was sealed.

They were right. But not immediately. Acting on a tip, Montreal police broke into a white Chevy van that had been parked in the lot of Carrefour Langelier, a shopping mall near Bar Jean-Talon. Inside, they found weapons and disguises, including balaclavas. Careful to return everything precisely as they found it, the cops waited to see who picked up the van.

It turned out to be two Sicilians well known to them, Domenic Manno (Nick Rizzuto's brother-in-law) and Agostino Cuntrera

(Liborio and Pasquale's cousin). The cops followed them as they went to Bar Jean-Talon when it was closed and watched as the two Sicilians took a good look around the place.

Early in January, in one of their many investigations into Violi's dealings, police overheard a phone call in which Vincenzo Randisi invited Violi to an important conversation at the bar. When the police arrived, they saw that Manno and Cuntrera were also there. In fact, they had parked their white Cadillac in the alley out back and entered through a secret door that led to the basement. Violi wasn't there. He didn't show. Later, phone taps determined that he had begged off due to an electrical problem at home.

Sure they were going to catch the men in the act of assassinating Violi, the police rented a second-floor apartment across the street, from which they could keep an eye on Bar Jean-Talon's entrance. On January 18, 1978, they saw two men, wearing white coveralls and balaclavas, drive a white Cadillac up to about half a block away from the bar and then approach it on foot. Suddenly, one motioned to the other and they both got in the Cadillac and took off. The cops guessed that they judged the snow too deep for them to make an effective getaway. The notorious Montreal winter may have saved, or at least extended, Violi's life.

It was proving expensive to follow Manno and Cuntrera, so the Montreal police decided to cut back on the surveillance, limiting it just to weekdays so they wouldn't have to pay higher weekend labor rates. On the very next Sunday—January 22, 1978—Vincenzo Randisi called Violi at home while he was eating dinner with his family and invited him to a card game. Violi left home and showed up at the bar. Walking through to the exclusive back room, he sat down with three old friends and accepted the hand he was dealt. One of the men is said to have kissed him on the cheek. A white Camaro pulled up in the alley beside the bar. Two masked men burst from it, made their way into the back room and one of them pressed a *lupara*, an Italian shotgun, into the back of Violi's head. Nobody else did anything. The guy with the lupara pulled the trigger and the extra-large buckshot tore through Violi's head and out his face. The other masked man shot him again with a handgun before they left.

Manno, Cuntrera and Giovanni DiMora were arrested and charged with his murder, but a shortage of evidence allowed them to plea bargain down to conspiracy charges. They got 10 years apiece.

With Violi out of the way, the war was essentially over. Giuseppi "Pep" Cotroni, Vic the Egg's younger brother, who had basically lain low after his release from prison in 1971, died of natural causes in September 1979. When Frank Cotroni was paroled from his American prison days later, he returned to a very different Montreal. But he wasn't going to make any waves. He went to work for the Rizzutos, swearing his allegiance to the man who had taken down his family's empire.

Not all the old-school Calabrians were welcome in the new family. Violi's brother Rocco, who was never much of a gangster, was killed while reading a newspaper at the kitchen table of his home on October 19, 1980. That was three months after two guys on a motorcycle shot at him with a shotgun, inflicting major head injuries.

Nick Rizzuto returned from Italy and reassumed his position as head of the family, which was reinforced by Sicilians, including the Cuntrera-Caruana group, who had been loyal to the cause while the Cotronis were still in charge. Nick's first priority was to make peace with the ailing Vic Cotroni. Then he had to establish a working relationship with the Bonannos in New York. It wasn't a problem. Sicilians themselves, the Bonannos had intended all along to give the Rizzutos essentially the same deal they had with the Cotronis.

The Rizzutos had a new pipeline of cocaine coming in from South America. It was almost more business than they could handle. The incredible amount of wealth that could be made through drugs was far too important to risk with petty crimes. An order came down from Rizzuto to his men. Henceforth, the Italians in Montreal would not engage in small-time crime. No more extortion, bookmaking, loan-sharking or any of that. Those jobs were no longer befitting their status as drug barons.

Things had changed in New York as well. Joseph Bonanno had become the last surviving family head of the Cosa Nostra's National Commission after Joe Profaci died of cancer in 1962. Even he faced many challenges, both from Magaddino and from within his own family. In 1968, he suffered a heart attack and retired to Arizona. A new set of gangsters rose to the fore—new families with new capos and bosses and, usually, new names. And they had their own way of doing things.

The only one of the original five families to survive into the '70s with the same name was the Bonannos, but they were by then headed by Philip "Rusty" Rastelli. At least officially. The family had actually fallen into two factions, one behind Rastelli and the other behind Galante, who was still handling tons of heroin. The split was so bad that the Bonannos were actually suspended from the Commission until they got their act together.

The rift was resolved from within. After some members of the Gambino family (formerly the D'Aquila family) of Little Italy started to move in on Galante's territory in Brooklyn, he had eight of them killed in very rapid succession. It was too much for the Commission. Galante had to go.

The end came on July 12, 1979. Galante had just finished a meal on the open-air back patio of his favorite place, Joe and Mary's Italian-American Restaurant, when he lit up one of his signature cigars. Three masked gunmen made their way from a car illegally parked on Knickerbocker Avenue, through the restaurant, out onto the patio and up to the table. The first shot went right though Galante's right eye, sending his dead body slumping to the floor, cigar still clenched between his teeth. Also killed were his cousin Giuseppe "Joe" Turano, owner of the restaurant, and bodyguard Leonardo Coppola.

That one gang hit in the Bushwick neighborhood of Brooklyn marked the end of an era in Canadian organized crime. Only a few years earlier, Galante had come to Canada to upgrade a bunch of strong-arm guys from Montreal and Hamilton into real drug-running wiseguys. Under the direction of the most powerful mafioso in America, Joey Bananas, he had brought them untold riches through the French Connection.

But things changed. A stint in a US prison scared Hamilton's Papalia off heroin trafficking, and that particular region had been long ago annexed by the Magaddinos anyway. In Montreal, Galante's original partners were usurped by a new gang that found heroin to be less attractive than cocaine and had started taking steps toward autonomy even before Galante went down.

Although the Bonannos would always have a presence there, the Rizzuto-led Montreal organization would gain more and more autonomy as the years went along and both cities' dependence on heroin waned. As both the Canadians and Americans turned away from Europe's heroin toward Latin America's cocaine, making their own deals, the link between the two became weaker. Eventually the Rizzutos would be less a northern franchise of the Bonannos than an actual family in their own right. Though never invited to break bread with the top families, they were no longer seated at the kiddies' table.

CHAPTER 5

HOMEGROWN ORGANIZED CRIME

Organized crime in Canada has hardly been limited to recent immigrant groups. While it is true that much of Canada's early organized crime stemmed from tightly knit ethnic enclaves, many of which suffered isolating and embittering relationships with government and mainstream culture at large, there was a group considered by many to be the majority that also turned to organized crime.

Canada had changed—particularly in the almost uninterrupted period of Liberal control of the federal government under Lester B. Pearson and Pierre Trudeau, from 1963 until 1983. Ties with the UK—both literally and culturally—were loosened, Quebec nationalism and French-language rights bloomed, immigration restrictions were revised—leading to huge influxes of non-English-speaking, often non-white, newcomers—and multiculturalism became official policy. Other sweeping changes, like gun control, the adoption of the metric system and the massive reduction of the military, made Canadian life almost unrecognizable to many, after just a generation.

There were other changes, as well, that were not directly attributable to the Canadian government. The first petroleum crisis in 1973 and the rise of the Middle Eastern states was followed by the gutting of the Canadian manufacturing industry through technology and the opening of low-wage labor markets like Mexico and China. All of these had profound effects on the Canadian economy.

What essentially happened in that period was that almost all of the advantages that English-speaking, native-born white Canadians had enjoyed for decades disappeared. None were hit harder than the less educated. All of their lives they had been promised a lifetime of factory employment—and thus the ability to buy a house, a car, maybe even a cottage—but when they got out of high school, the factories were gone. A similar process occurred with native-born French speakers. Though they were emboldened by the rise in Quebec culture, they faced the same economic challenges.

Suddenly, uneducated whites were on equal footing with recent immigrants. Their own perception was that they had fallen behind the newcomers due to what they called "government handouts" like welfare, housing subsidies, job-creation schemes and other programs they felt favored immigrants and people of color over themselves.

The entire process led to the creation of yet another isolated group in Canada—uneducated whites—that was wildly disillusioned with government and what they perceived as mainstream culture. Many of them had views we'd now consider sexist, racist, xenophobic, homophobic and militaristic that not only ran contrary to the trend in mainstream culture, but also were considered almost dangerous to express in public. Eventually, like other groups, they started to keep to themselves and develop their own communities.

Not surprisingly, those cultural and economic realities led to crime and, eventually, organized crime. Unlike most other groups who looked to community leaders, however, these people—who felt betrayed by their leaders—looked to their dropouts and outsiders.

Motorcycle gangs have a long and storied history well known by the public. Much of it is imaginary, but it is true that young men bonded over their combined love of motorcycles and that some of them, the 1%ers, lived an "outlaw" lifestyle in which they regularly flouted laws they thought unnecessary, or that stood in the way of their own personal fulfillment.

By the 1970s, there were literally hundreds of motorcycle clubs in Canada. Some, like Satan's Choice in Ontario, were as big and influential as any in the world.

But it was two other, smaller motorcycle clubs that would change the organized crime landscape in Canada and later come to dominate it. Or, at least, these two clubs—the Popeyes of Montreal and the Wild Ones of Hamilton—had members who would later become the biggest players in Canadian crime.

In the late 1960s, bikers were everywhere in Canada. Most were better at making mayhem with petty vandalism, public urination and bar fights than they were at making money. Many of their members did engage in criminal schemes, often related to stolen cars and motorcycles, and one enterprising club in suburban Quebec City actually charged motorists and pedestrians a two-dollar fee to use any street or sidewalk they happened to be hanging out on.

Montreal was different. Canada's Sin City has always been a very criminal place, and there were plenty of street gangs doing plenty of work. Every neighborhood had its gang, and when territories overlapped, violence was usually the result.

Downtown, especially—with its transient population of partiers and tourists—was different. Nobody really came from there, so the turf belonged to whoever was tough enough to take it. Two of those contenders were motorcycle clubs who shared little affection for one another—the Popeyes and the Devil's Disciples. Both clubs were entirely French-Canadian; the English names were just part of the biker tradition.

Years of competition and animosity turned to all-out war in 1968. Many believe the spark that started it was five Devil's Disciples gang-raping a South Shore woman. I've been told that she was related to at least one Popeye.

On the night of May 18, 1968, seven Popeyes were attempting to cross the Jacques Cartier Bridge from the South Shore into the city when they, and all other inbound traffic, were stopped by about 50 Devil's Disciples. The Popeyes backed off and retreated back to the South Shore, but some of the Devil's Disciples followed them. According to one of the Popeyes, Yves "Apache" Trudeau, the Devil's Disciples president—a man Trudeau identified only as Fidel—was surrounded by a circle of young toughs. They were all mouthing off, but when one of them—18-year-old Montrealer Jean-Yves Picquet—threatened his life, Fidel had had enough. He pulled a knife and plunged it into the kid's chest. Bikers on both sides scattered for the safety of home as Picquet died on the pavement.

No charges were laid, but the police couldn't ignore the next incident. About two weeks later, more than 100 members of both gangs showed up at a pre-determined east-end location and just started going at it with chains, ax handles and any other weapons they could lay their hands on. When the first cops arrived, they fired warning shots in the air, but the bikers kept bashing one another. It took 60 cops to finally bring it all down. Four bikers were seriously injured.

The cops ordered the two sides to have a sit-down to clear up their differences. It backfired. Pissed off at what their rivals said, both sides declared all-out war. Over the next year or so, two Popeyes were shot and killed, and the sergeant at arms for the Devil's Disciples, Jacques "Coco" Mercier, went to prison for life for shooting and wounding two others. A sort-of tacit, police-enforced peace followed, but not for long.

Although it was not a big war when it came to body counts and headlines, the fight between the Popeyes and the Devil's Disciples set the stage for a rivalry that would cost hundreds of lives in later gang wars, still exists today and has spread throughout the entire country. It all came down to who the gangs' respective friends were and which drugs they sold.

In those days, long before *Breaking Bad*, few people knew exactly what methamphetamine was. In fact, amphetamines—also known as speed—had been legal in Canada until the early 1970s. It's hard to believe now, but they had been quite popular, and doctor-recommended, as pep pills, weight-loss aids and stimulants for years. Most people considered amphetamines little more dangerous than the energy drinks people consume now.

Methamphetamine is a lot different from amphetamine. Profoundly addictive with deep, lasting psychological effects, meth is now widely considered one of the most dangerous drugs on the market.

It originally became popular in the late 1960s with bikers from southern California. It was the only stimulant drug that could be produced domestically—important to the xenophobic bikers—and be easily concealed. It was very popular with bored suburbanites. Although generally limited to bikers and their friends, meth was largely available throughout the western and Midwestern states by 1971.

It got to Canada through Satan's Choice. Although it was the Hells Angels who began dealing meth in the US, the Outlaws quickly followed suit and made it available to their Canadian friends in Satan's Choice. Meth didn't take off in Ontario (at least not then), but it did find a willing market in Montreal, mainly in the Gay Village and the Latin Quarter.

The Montreal chapter of Satan's Choice needed a set of middlemen to sell their meth. They found them in the Devil's Disciples. After a brief skirmish to rid Saint-Louis Square of a few DuBois family loyalists that was detailed in the *Toronto Telegram* and *Allo Police!*, the Devil's Disciples made the small park into an open-air meth market. But the profits were too easy and a rivalry emerged in the gang's leadership. Their president, Claude Ellefsen, was a huge fan of French singer Johnny Hallyday and styled his hair, mustache and clothes to look just like Hallyday's. At first, everything was cool as all the Devil's Disciples were getting rich off meth, until a few of them noticed that Ellefsen and his buddies were getting richer than the rest of them.

True to its nature, meth caused aggressive, suspicious and even psychotic behavior among the gang, all of whom used as well as sold the drug. Quickly a rebel faction coalesced within the Devil's Disciples behind burly Gil Forget. Words became blows, fists turned to knives, then guns. In the period between May 20 and September 29, 1974, no fewer than 23 people—all associated with the Devil's Disciples—were murdered over the meth trade.

The Devil's Disciples effectively ceased to exist after that. Satan's Choice continued to survive in the west end, however, until they patched over to the Outlaws in the summer of 1977.

Although never celebrated for their intellect, the Popeyes made an astute strategic move in avoiding Satan's Choice and meth. At about the same time, they made richer and more powerful friends, who had a better product.

Even before the Rizzutos ousted the Cotronis in Montreal, they were in charge of most of the country's cocaine supply and needed manpower—and the need became almost a crisis after Nick Rizzuto returned from Venezuela and banned his men from getting their hands dirty. They had to have more soldiers. There was no shortage of tough guys in Montreal, but most of them were already allied with groups—like the West End Gang, the DuBois family or the McSweens—that the Rizzutos would rather not deal with. But the Popeyes were not. They were tough, strong and independent. The Mafia put them to work right away doing all the jobs their men weren't supposed to any longer. When it came to extortion, loan-sharking, prostitution and many other rackets, the Popeyes were now in charge of downtown. And, although it started small, they also broke into cocaine trafficking.

What made the Popeyes so desirable as an organization was their boss, Yves "le Boss" Buteau. Tall, blond and handsome, he had a ready smile, an indelible charisma and an ability to speak and lead. He wasn't afraid to get his hands dirty, though, whether punching out a debtor, selling coke in a bar or planting a bomb on an enemy's motorcycle.

It wasn't just the Rizzutos who had taken a liking to the Popeyes. The Hells Angels had been looking to expand into Canada for years—at least since 1973. They had been rebuffed in their attempts in Ontario because the most powerful existing clubs had formed an alliance to keep them out and because Papalia didn't trust them and would not allow his men to work with them.

Montreal was a different story. The Parti Québécois—with a mandate to strengthen the French language and identity in the province—took over the provincial government in 1976, but even afterward, Montreal was still a welcoming city for the Hells Angels. English speakers were everywhere; the city even had a major league baseball team. And, of course, it also just happened to be the drug and prostitution capital of North America.

New Hells Angels chapters need to be sponsored by an existing chapter, and the Popeyes found a willing benefactor in the Hells

Angels' near-legendary Manhattan chapter. Their own close relationship with the Bonannos would hardly be an obstacle.

The Popeyes aced their prospect period and set up their headquarters not in Montreal but in the decaying industrial city of Sorel, about an hour's drive down the St. Lawrence River. In fact, it was actually closer to Trois-Rivières than it was to the big city. As though predicting the violence that they would see over the next few years, the club armored and barricaded the building, turning it into a veritable bunker with 24/7 video surveillance.

On December 5, 1977, they held a party to celebrate their patch-over. It was huge and loud. There were dozens of American Hells Angels there, mostly from New York. And there was one other notable guest, Sonny Barger, the widely reported Hells Angels international president and one of the club's founding members, who has been convicted of several felonies. He was there to bestow something special on the guest of honor. At the party, he presented Buteau with a Hells Angels International patch. He was, and still is, the only Canadian ever to wear that title.

At the same time that the Popeyes were establishing themselves as the dominant biker gang in Montreal, a young man was moving up the ranks in Hamilton. In the late 1960s, Walter "Nurget" Stadnick was a high school hash dealer who was quiet and polite but also known for his skill with vehicles and engines and for his wild, almost ridiculous, taste in clothes. After he finished school, he ran with a street gang for a while before starting his own motorcycle club, the Cossacks. They failed to coalesce into anything stable. He approached the Hamilton chapters of both Satan's Choice (Canada's biggest 1%er club) and the Red Devils (Canada's oldest 1%er club), but they wouldn't have him. Though tough, smart, capable and easy to get along with, Stadnick had one major handicap to success in their world—his height. At five foot four, Stadnick found it hard to be taken seriously in a culture that put a premium on physical size and strength.

He did manage to get into one of Hamilton's lesser motor-cycle clubs, though—the Wild Ones. While the Wild Ones were neither a big nor impressive group, they did have friends. It was well known that Papalia would not allow his men to work with bikers, especially Hells Angels. But there were other Mafia families in Hamilton—more closely connected to the 'Ndrangheta back in Calabria than to the Cosa Nostra in New York—who were more than happy to employ them for a variety of jobs. In the mid-1970s, the Wild Ones found themselves making money from the Italians by intimidating witnesses, committing extortion, selling stolen goods and even setting fire to or firebombing the businesses of debtors and rivals.

They weren't exactly the most competent of gangs. They had a habit of getting arrested, and two of them accidentally blew themselves up while putting together a bomb. Even so, their status of being unaffiliated with other biker gangs but closely aligned with the 'Ndrangheta drew the attention of the Hells Angels.

Still, the Sorel-based Hells Angels had something they had to take care of before they considered expanding to Ontario and potentially facing Papalia's men. It's Hells Angels policy not to allow direct competition in their territory, and Montreal had lots of 1%er and wannabe clubs (and even more drug dealers and muscle-for-hire guys who had nothing to do with motorcycles). More importantly, a few months before the Popeyes became Hells Angels, some of the chapters of Satan's Choice—including both Montreal and Hamilton—had patched over to the Outlaws, bitter rivals of the Hells Angels.

Over the winter of 1977 and into the spring of 1978, both the Hells Angels and Outlaws campaigned hard for the hearts and minds of the local bikers. Not surprisingly, the Hells Angels—with their cocaine, ties to the Mafia and their fame from Hollywood movies— came out ahead of the Outlaws, with their meth and little else.

That meant it was open season on Outlaws in Montreal. It began on February 15, 1978, when Outlaw Robert Côté and a friend walked into a bar full of Hells Angels allies. After a few angry words were exchanged, a phone call was made and Apache Trudeau showed up. Shots were fired and Côté was fatally injured.

A little more than a month later, May 21, 1978, Outlaws president Gilles Cadorette was showing off his customized Camaro to sergeant at arms Donald McLean when it exploded. Cadorette was killed immediately, and McLean was badly injured, losing sight in one eye.

After several other assassinations, and an incident in which a Hells Angel actually knocked on the door of the Outlaws' clubhouse, was let in and started shooting up the place (no one was hurt, because his gun jammed), the war was particularly one-sided. The few Outlaws who hadn't been killed moved to Ontario or quit, lay low and never wore their colors in public. But they were still there.

Confident that he had won the war, Buteau ordered a meeting with the Wild Ones. Stadnick, Gary "Gator" Davies and French-speaking George "Chico" Mousseau rode up to Montreal on October 12, 1978, for a meeting with Hells Angels Louis "Ti-Oui" Lapierre, Bruno Coulombe and Jean Brochu.

Two other guests also showed up at the Le Tourbillon bar that night. Wearing geeky-looking Windbreakers and slacks, Lapierre quickly made them as undercover cops and basically told them to get lost.

Lapierre was wrong. The two men were professional assassins hired by the Outlaws. One pulled out a sawed-off shotgun and the other a semiautomatic handgun. In a flash, they started pumping the booth full of lead. Mousseau and Brochu died on the scene, Davies a few days later. Lapierre and Coulombe were badly hurt. Stadnick, essentially unharmed, rode back to Hamilton alone.

The Wild Ones ceased to exist. The other surviving members told Stadnick that the life was too dangerous for them.

While his gang was gone, Stadnick was not without friends. He stayed in contact with the Montreal Hells Angels and quickly became a favorite of Buteau's.

Le Boss had other priorities before he could even think about Ontario. First he had to consolidate his own hold on Montreal. His method was to pit clubs that were aligned with his against those that weren't. At any time on the streets of Montreal in the late 1970s and early 1980s, you could find fistfights and shootings between members of clubs like the SS against the Hondix. The territory the Hells Angels' allies controlled was being taken block by block, black eye by black eye.

The Outlaws, on the other hand, with their meth money and friends in Ontario and the US, were another story. The Hells Angels took care of them themselves. In fact, Buteau was part of a three-man team that planted a bomb on McLean's Harley-Davidson that killed him and his girlfriend, Carmen Piché, on May 9, 1979.

Buteau's second priority was to extend his reach (and product) throughout the province. He sent emissaries who quickly won over established clubs like the Missiles in Quebec City and the Gitans in Sherbrooke, bringing them into the fold.

He was very successful at both of those tasks, building himself an impressive empire. In fact, it was getting so big and popular that it was growing beyond his control. It was becoming clear that there were two factions in the Sorel clubhouse. One followed Buteau and emulated his ways. They'd rather sell drugs than take them, rarely rode their bikes or wore their colors, preferring to look more presentable, and never got involved in petty crime or fights. They were business-like and serious, almost straitlaced, by biker standards. They were all about getting rich.

But there were others, mostly older, who sought to retain the partying and brawling ways of the old Popeyes. They sold drugs, sure, but took plenty too. They rumbled around town on straight-pipe Harleys and wore their colors constantly, taking immense pride in showing off their membership in the biggest, most dangerous club on the island.

Facing a great deal of tension within the gang, Buteau came up with a diplomatic solution. Solomon-like, he split the club in two. Those who were more like Buteau stayed in Sorel, and those who were more old-school—under the leadership, at first, of Apache Trudeau—were free to form their own chapter in Laval, which opened on Boulevard Arthur-Sauvé on September 14, 1979. In a quirk of local geography, the Sorel chapter was named "Montreal South" because it was on the south shore of the St. Lawrence and the Laval Chapter was named "Montreal North" because Laval is on an island north of Montreal. Neither clubhouse was in Montreal proper, and Laval is actually several miles farther south than Sorel.

Quickly, both clubs established their identities. Sorel sold drugs and had others do their dirty work for them. Laval sold drugs, took drugs and relished the opportunity to take on the strong-arm work both from the Mafia and, increasingly, from Sorel members who found such work beneath them. Laval also had a thriving practice in which their resident chemist, Jean-Guy "Brutus" Geoffrion, would cook meth, which the chapter would trade to Sorel, the West End Gang or representatives of the Rizzutos for cocaine, their drug of choice.

Before long, Trudeau became the go-to guy for assassinations for both organizations. Although most of his victims were shot, he also used his experience working at the C-I-L dynamite plant in McMasterville to make several bombs.

His first target was an interesting one. On the otherwise quiet Saturday afternoon of October 27, 1981, two luminaries, such as they were, from Montreal's Irish Mafia—the West End Gang, which controlled much of the shipborne traffic in the city and worked closely with the Italians—were driving through Westmount. At the wheel of the garish yellow Mercedes-Benz was Patrick "Hughie" McGurnaghan, who'd been associated with organized crime and trafficking since 1956. Beside him was Joseph Frankel, close friends with several well-known Mafia figures, who once described himself to Bourassa's organized crime inquest as a "reformed bookie."

Just after noon, the car exploded. The blast shattered windows in a nearby apartment building and the shredded Mercedes continued to roll, flames and smoke trailing, until it came to a rest in a park across the street from a primary school. A young doctor happened to be in a nearby antique shop, and he heard the blast. "I knew it was a bomb right away because I heard a lot of them go off when I was traveling in East Africa," he told the *Montreal Gazette*, although he asked the paper not to use his name.

He rushed to the car, opened the driver's side door and used his belt to furnish a tourniquet to stop the bleeding from McGurnaghan's left leg, which had been severed above the knee. Upon noticing that McGurnaghan's left arm was in similar shape, he sent an onlooker to call an ambulance and find another belt. Frankel had suffered cuts and bruises, and both his eardrums were shattered, but he was otherwise okay. The guy looking for another belt flagged down a nearby private ambulance, but it refused to take McGurnaghan because the vehicle's lights and siren weren't working. When a police ambulance arrived, paramedics loaded up the two men and sped to a hospital. Things were not looking good. McGurnaghan was losing blood at too quick a rate for the paramedics to handle. "He died in my arms when we were fifty feet away from the hospital doors," one of them reported to *The Montreal Star*.

Not long after, Frank "Dunie" Ryan—boss of the West End Gang and the most likely person to have ordered the McGurnaghan hit—visited Trudeau in Laval. He complained to the chapter president about some of his men. Ryan singled out Charles "Charlie" Hachez, who drove around town in a Corvette despite owing Ryan in excess of $150,000, and Dennis "le Curé" Kennedy, who also had fallen into significant arrears for cocaine. Trudeau assured Ryan he'd take care of it.

Trudeau told the pair that they had to pay Ryan or face the consequences. Their reaction may go down as the stupidest decision in Canadian organized crime history. They, along with Laval prospect Robert "Steve" Grenier and Hachez's girlfriend, Marjolaine Poirer, decided to kidnap one of Ryan's kids and use the ransom money to pay their debts. Even worse, Kennedy shot his mouth off and told his friends about the plan. Word got back to Trudeau, and within days, Hachez, Poirer, Kennedy and Grenier were all at the bottom of the St. Lawrence.

While Laval was partying and paying the price, Sorel was getting richer and attracting more talent that fit Buteau's mold. One of those prospects was Stadnick. Not long after the Le Tourbillon massacre, Stadnick—a personal favorite of Buteau's—became a Sorel prospect. In an unprecedented turn of events, he was allowed to serve his period as a Sorel prospect in Hamilton, which prevented him from having to perform the menial and sometimes humiliating tasks most prospects face.

Stadnick's French was very poor, so he often traveled with his friend Noel "Frenchy" Mailloux, who spoke French fluently. While Sorel had no interest in extending Mailloux membership—he would have fit in better with Laval—Stadnick was made a full-patch member of the Hells Angels Montreal South chapter on May 26, 1982.

Stadnick still lived in Hamilton, which was a dangerous proposition. The former Satan's Choice chapter there had since become Outlaws, and they felt the city was theirs to defend. But they, and

Papalia's men, tolerated his existence in their realm. In fact, his biggest problem was Mailloux.

On February 17, 1983—at the tail end of a cocaine binge that had started the previous Christmas—Mailloux lost his grip on reality and shot his girlfriend, her best friend and her four-year-old son. His girlfriend, stripper Connie Augustin, survived. The other two did not. While police were chasing down Mailloux in a wooded park, finally finding him babbling and drooling in the bushes, someone—described as a short man on a Harley-Davidson—came to his house and removed a box full of items. Mailloux was convicted, but a search of his home uncovered no trafficking- or gang-related paraphernalia.

Back in Montreal, Trudeau continued to work as a freelance assassin. He'd already made kills for his own club and the West End Gang (including blowing up Paul April, who was in hiding after having killed Ryan), but he soon stepped up into Montreal's big leagues.

Michel Desormiers was Frank Cotroni's brother-in-law. His name was well known to Montrealers since a 1967 plan in which a team he was leading was caught trying to tunnel under a city street and into a bank vault from a house Cotroni rented across the street. Desormiers's older brother, Richard, had been killed in 1973 for selling in the DuBois brothers' territory. Throughout the '70s, Michel had been quietly but efficiently moving drugs from the Cotroni family to Montreal's far west end.

At 3:00 a.m. on July 15, there was a loud knock on the door of his beautiful home in the genteel Senneville section of the island's far west end, overlooking lac des Deux Montagnes. Unwisely, Desormiers went to see what the racket was. Seeing nobody at the door, like a doomed teenager in a 1980s horror movie, he walked out onto his large veranda and called out to whoever was there. Predictably, Trudeau—who later described the story to the Sûreté du Québec (Quebec's provincial police, also known as the SQ) and, later, the RCMP as part of his confession—emerged from the shadows and sent two bullets zipping through Desormiers's head.

An imperfect rat, he never did say who paid him to kill Desormiers, attributing the hit just to "the Mafia."

In fact, while the Rizzutos had stabilized things among the Italians, there was still a great deal of housecleaning to do. The Cotronis, though defeated and now secondary to the Rizzutos, were far from gone. Not to mention they had their own version of Apache Trudeau.

In the 1970s, Réal Simard graduated from being a petty crook to a professional bank robber. On one job, in which he was the getaway driver, he managed to escape, but one of the guys who didn't—Jean-Paul Saint-Amand—fingered Simard and his partner, Raymond Martel. With no defense, Simard received a six-year sentence.

In the Parthenais Detention Centre & Laboratoire de Sciences Judiciaires et de Médecine Légale (a jail better known as the Parthenais Hotel), he was spotted by Frank Cotroni, who was being held there while the Americans were getting their papers in order for his extradition. As Armand Courville's nephew, Simard was almost family to the Cotronis. Frank told him he'd protect him and connect him.

Later, when they were both free men (Frank was paroled on April 25, 1979), Simard happened to see Cotroni in a bar and they reconnected. Before long, Simard found himself working for Cotroni, doing everything from handling his dry cleaning to giving his friends rides to the airport. The two, in fact, became so very close that Simard started calling his boss "Uncle Frank"—something many other Italians had a hard time stomaching.

Spending so much time at Frank's house gave Simard an inside look at how the Mafia really works, which he describes in detail in his book, *The Nephew*. True to their roots in Sicily and Calabria, the members of the Mafia not only operated to enrich themselves but also served as adjudicators and as an enforcement organization within the Italian community. In his book, Simard describes how Italians would come to Frank—who was, for better or worse, the ranking Cotroni at the time—for help. One woman needed help leaving her abusive French-Canadian husband, so Frank sent Simard over to protect her while she moved out and to let the man know any retaliation on his part would not be tolerated.

As a reward, Frank set Simard up as the manager of Prestige Entertainment, a stripper agency. It was a dream job; he interviewed new talent and the money just rolled in. Even more than you might expect. The girls of Prestige were more than just dancers; many were also street-level cocaine dealers (and, many of them, users). It was a very effective system that was later, I've been told, incorporated as part of Stadnick's master plan.

Simard recounts in his book that after a month, he handed his boss an envelope with $5,000 in cash in it. Cotroni was pleased and told Simard that he had a job for him. While Frank wasn't deluded enough to think he could wrest control of Montreal back from the Sicilians, he did have some scores to settle. Michel "Fatso" Marion was a French-Canadian nightclub owner and hashish distributor who Frank had heard was influential in helping the Rizzutos kill some of his allies. Simard's next job was to kill Marion.

It didn't take long. On January 18, 1980, Simard followed Fatso into a restaurant and, after Marion sat down, shot him twice in the chest. After Marion slumped onto his table, Simard put another shot into the back of his head. Later Simard would say that he remembered Frank's advice to always leave a bullet in the head to make sure the target was dead. He then went back to Frank's house and kissed him on both cheeks. Frank knew what that meant.

Simard's second victim was small-time heroin dealer Nicholas Morello, younger brother of big-time heroin dealer Giuseppe "Joe" Morello. As Nicholas staggered toward his car after several drinks at a Saint-Léonard bar on the night of December 13, 1980, Simard emerged from the shadows and shot him several times, once in the head.

Simard was so good at killing that Frank gave him another job right away. Frank's son, Francesco Jr., had long been selling cocaine (and been convicted of it) to north-end dealer Giuseppe Montegano. In April 1981, the two had a meeting at Francesco Jr.'s headquarters, the Agrigento Social Club, like they often had before. This time, the two argued. Montegano was enraged because he believed that the coke he was getting was of far lower quality than what he had paid for.

When Frank heard about the disagreement—he had never liked the 26-year-old Montegano because he suspected him of being in league with the Rizzutos—he told Simard that it was his job to make sure Montegano's days would be numbered—in single digits. In an effort to do his due diligence, despite his near-slavish obedience to Frank, Simard met with both sides. After interviewing them both, Simard reported back to Frank. The boss's judgment, not surprisingly, was that Montegano had to die.

Francesco, pretending to reconcile, invited the doomed man to Agrigento on June 14, 1981. Simard recruited his friends Francesco Rao and Daniel Arena in a plot to abduct Montegano, stuff him in a car and kill him at a second location. But Montegano wouldn't cooperate. Sensing the double cross, he fought for his life and nearly escaped before Simard shot him dead. Charges were dropped against Rao and Arena after they agreed to cooperate with the investigation.

Montegano was hardly the last victim. For years, Michel Pozza was an important part of the Montreal Mafia, but he was a little different. He had no real stake in the Sicilian-Calabrian feud because he was from Trento, in the far north of Italy. He also had two degrees and was considered something of a financial whiz among a group whose literacy level was questionable at best. In the 1970s, Pozza worked very closely with Luigi Greco, a Sicilian working under Cotroni, a Calabrian. As the Cotroni family's power structure began to unravel, Pozza was seen more and more frequently with the rebellious Sicilian faction. In his book, Simard writes that Frank told him, "Something has to be done about [Pozza]."

Something was. On September 17, 1982—while Pozza was awaiting his appearance before the organized crime commission—Simard asked him out for a few drinks. They must have had several, because Simard stayed the night at Pozza's posh Mont-Rolland home. The following morning, as the two were having a quiet conversation on Pozza's front porch, as Simard admits in his book, he pulled out a .22-caliber handgun and put six bullets into Pozza, including two in the head. According to Simard's account, police found on his body, among other incriminating things, a $2.6 million deposit slip from a Swiss bank.

Pleased with Simard, Frank had bigger plans for him. When the Parti Québécois took over in Quebec in 1976, their new laws and policies irked English-speaking Quebecers so much that no fewer than 250,000 of them moved west, mainly to Toronto. By 1981, Toronto—derided by Montrealers for decades as provincial "Hogtown" or prosaic "Second City"—had taken the crown as Canada's biggest and richest metropolis away from Montreal. There was money to be made there, and Frank, who knew that the Rizzutos now owned Montreal, wanted a part of it.

Before he could do any actual work in Toronto, however, Simard had to meet with Papalia, because Toronto was part of his territory. Johnny Pops gave his blessing. So Simard—who went by the name David in Toronto—flooded Toronto's strip joints with dancers from Quebec, many of whom also sold coke for him. He claimed he stocked those same bars with street-level dealers posing as clientele who also sold for him. It was a pretty big operation, so Simard elevated his old friend Richard Clément to second-in-command.

While the Cotronis had established a beachhead in Toronto, disaster struck their operations in Florida. In the 1960s, Vic the Egg had had a son, Nick, with his girlfriend Ghyslaine Turgeon. In order to keep them from ruffling any feathers in Montreal, Vic set them up in Miami, and when Nick was old enough, he became part of the business. In fact, he was a huge earner, part of a $50-million-a-year scheme that sent Quaaludes (often deeply cut and sometimes altogether fake) to Miami and sent cash, or sometimes cocaine, back to Montreal.

The operation was taken down by the US Drug Enforcement Administration (DEA) in July 21, 1983. Altogether, 20 Canadians—including Obront, who was caught with a kilo of cocaine on his front porch, but not Cotroni—27 Americans and 2 Colombians were arrested. Obront was convicted of trafficking. The DEA told the CBC that they estimated the gang controlled about 70 percent of the Quaalude market in the US. Whatever your opinions of the DEA or the War on Drugs, you kind of have to hand it to them when it comes to Quaaludes—they went from commonplace to extinct in the US after this and several other mass arrests.

Meanwhile, the Toronto franchise was booming. In November 1983, Frank sent a couple of Montreal tough guys named Mario Héroux and Robert Hétu to Toronto with a big bag of cocaine for Simard's girls to distribute. After a few days, Simard and Clément—both of whom were pretty coked up at the time—started to believe that Héroux and Hétu were skimming from them. Without any more evidence than his word, Simard asked Frank if it would be okay to kill them. Frank agreed.

On November 19, 1983, Simard and Clément met and had breakfast at the sumptuous Sutton Place Hotel, at the time perhaps Toronto's finest, where Simard had been staying. Then they headed out to the seedy Seaway Motel (not Toronto's worst at the time, but close) on the western lakeshore, where Héroux and Hétu were staying. They each brought a handgun, and Simard took along a false beard, which he later ditched because he found it uncomfortable.

When they arrived, the first thing they did was block the fire escape of the room Héroux and Hétu were staying in. Then they went into the motel proper and knocked on the room's door. Hétu answered. Simard shot him twice in the mouth and once more in the temple. Hétu went down immediately. The two invaders stepped over Hétu, and Clément shot Héroux in the head five times, killing him immediately. As they ran from the room, Clément fired one more time at the prone Hétu, aiming, as he had been taught, for the head.

But Hétu was not dead. Perhaps it was his military training, but when the bullets hit his mouth, he made a conscious decision to play dead rather than try to defend himself. Somehow, both of the bullets that entered his mouth had missed his brain and spinal cord, instead exiting through his cheeks. The third bullet just grazed his skin. The fourth slug, from Clément, missed him entirely.

After the gunmen left, Hétu fell unconscious from blood loss. By the time police arrived, Hétu was sort of awake and sitting up in a blood-soaked armchair mumbling to himself. Despite his poor English and a shattered jaw hanging by a bloody sinew, Hétu was able to tell them that Simard and another man had murdered Héroux and tried to kill him.

Simard learned that Hétu was still alive and immediately fled up Highway 401 for Montreal. The cops picked him up the moment he arrived at his office in Montreal. Sure that Hétu had ratted on him, Simard started trying to cut a deal the second he got into the cop car. Hétu never named Clément, so Simard gave him up and then he ratted out his beloved "uncle."

Caught, even Frank made a deal, but only for himself. In exchange for trafficking and conspiracy charges being dropped, he copped to a manslaughter charge and was given three years.

Hétu was relocated to Penetanguishene, Ontario, under witness protection, but was convicted in 1989 of a series of sexual assaults on four girls between seven and twelve years old. He spent a few months in prison and was relocated again, this time to a part of Ontario with a greater proportion of French speakers.

Simard was housed in a relatively luxurious suite in Archambault prison until 1993, when he too was relocated under witness protection. His looks had been surgically changed to help hide his identity. He settled originally in Vermont, then later, France.

Clément fled to Lebanon after the killing but was caught almost immediately after he returned to Montreal in 1988 and ended up in prison, convicted of the killings with Simard.

Vic the Egg, who had been battling cancer since the mid-1970s, finally expired on September 19, 1984, at age 74. His funeral was as lavish an affair as Rocco Perri's had been. It featured 23 slow-moving cars bedecked with floral arrangements and a 17-piece brass band.

Frank couldn't come; he was in jail. So was Miami Nick, Vic's semi-secret son with Turgeon. But Vito Rizzuto was there, paying his "respects." The Cotroni empire was in tatters. Not completely extinguished, but not too far from it either.

CHAPTER 6

WITH THE MAFIA REELING,
THE BIKERS TAKE ADVANTAGE

As Frank and the Cotronis were going through tough times, things were looking up for the Hells Angels. About a week after he had killed Desormiers, Trudeau was partying with all of the other Canadian Hells Angels. In much the same way that the Manhattan chapter had taken an interest in Montreal, some California chapters decided to expand their reach into Vancouver and the Lower Mainland of BC. They settled on two candidates, the Satan's Angels and the Gypsy Wheelers.

The Satan's Angels, who had two chapters, were already famous for a 1968 incident in which they had kidnapped a 20-year-old man and held him for a weekend, torturing and sexually assaulting him the whole time. Simma Holt, later a member of Parliament, wrote a book on the case, called *The Devil's Butler*. In it, she lays out not just the gory details of the incident but the gang's fascination with Nazi memorabilia—a theme that shows up time and again with Canadian 1%er clubs.

Their prospect period began in 1981, and both gangs were tasked with eliminating or absorbing all of the other 1%er gangs in the area. By the summer of 1983, they had done so and were given their Hells Angels patches.

While the three new chapters were all in Canada, they had little to do with their "brothers" in Montreal, all of whom were French-speakers aside from Stadnick. In fact, the most well-known aspect of the Satan's Angels other than *The Devil's Butler* case was their habit of brutally beating up migrant French-Canadian agricultural workers in the Okanagan Valley every summer.

Now they were all brothers under the same winged skull flag. Since they were also all Canadian, their bosses south of the border expected them to play nice. In fact, officially, at least, they answered not just to California but also to Buteau, a favorite among the American management structure. They trusted that his leadership skills would more than make up for any language differences or bad blood.

It was widely reported that every single Hells Angel was expected to be at the patching-over party set for July 23, 1983 in Vancouver. Although they were expected to ride their Harleys the 3,100-mile distance, some flew, some drove and, according to the Ontario Provincial Police, two lesser lights from Laval—Michel "Jinx" Genest and Jean-Marc Nadeau—took the bus.

The OPP's evidence against them at the Sudbury Outlaws' subsequent trial said that witnesses told them the Sudbury Outlaws saw Genest's Hells Angels T-shirt pressed up against the window as he slept on the bus. When the bus stopped in Wawa, they shot it up. Eyewitnesses said that the car the shots came from, a Ford Taurus, had a "Support Your Local Outlaws" bumper sticker on the back.

Whatever happened, it did not come at a good time for Outlaws national president Mario "Mike the Wop" Parente, who was out on bail after the shooting death of a man in Hamilton.

Although he has personally told me he was not involved in the Wawa shooting, at his manslaughter trial for it, he pleaded guilty in hopes of putting the incident behind him and receiving a light sentence because he also intended to plead guilty to the killing in Hamilton. He didn't get it.

His absence changed things in Ontario. While Stadnick was not crazy enough to wear his colors in Hamilton, he did open up a bar there called Rebel's Roadhouse. Naturally, this did not sit well with the Outlaws. One of them, admittedly nervous over the prospect, turned informant and told the Hamilton police about a plan to use stolen antitank rocket launchers to assassinate Stadnick in his bar. The cop, Sergeant John Harris, who spoke with the informant and recovered the rocket launchers in a nearby park, told me that he believed that if Parente had not been behind bars at the time, Stadnick would have been blown to bits.

While things appeared to be looking up for Buteau and the Hells Angels—he was also negotiating with a few other clubs to potentially become prospective Hells Angels chapters—that good feeling left with the hot weather. On the night of September 8, 1983, Buteau and translator René Lamoureux were meeting with Guy "Frenchy" Gilbert at a Sorel bar called Le Petit Bourg. It was an important strategic meeting in that Gilbert represented one of the few Satan's Choice chapters that had not patched over to the Outlaws in 1977. His Kitchener chapter was, and would be for years, a very wealthy and powerful club. As they were leaving, an Outlaws hangaround named Gino Goudreau shot them all. Buteau and Gilbert died; Lamoureux, a former US Marine, survived. Goudreau was convicted of murder.

Things changed for the Hells Angels rapidly. Without Buteau, the new national president and president of the Sorel chapter was Michel "Sky" Langlois. It was an obvious choice. Businesslike and eminently presentable, Langlois owned several legitimate businesses, including a Harley repair shop, and was also the owner and pilot of a small private plane.

While he was no Buteau as a leader, he did share le Boss's concern about cocaine use. A little more than a year before his death, Buteau banned the use of cocaine among the Hells Angels. The members of Sorel either complied or at least covered it up well enough to get by. Laval, though, was a different story. Many of them used more coke than they sold and that resulted in huge debts, much of it to the members of Sorel but also to the West End Gang or even the Italians.

Langlois took it upon himself to warn the members of Laval that their irresponsible ways were leading them into grave danger. His words did not fall entirely upon deaf ears. Three members of the Laval chapter—Réjean "Zig-Zag" Lessard, Luc "Sam" Michaud and Robert "Ti-Maigre" Richard—saw the writing on the wall, gave up their coke habits and switched allegiances from North, which wasn't really north, to South, which wasn't really south.

With tensions between the two chapters running high, disaster struck. A year after Buteau's death, the South chapter planned an elaborate memorial ceremony to remember le Boss. They did not realize that they would be competing with a visit by the incredibly popular Pope John Paul II. Traffic was miserable, and the Hells Angels did their best to avoid it by using back roads. It worked for the most part, but they did not factor in the late-to-the-party priest who ran a stop sign and slammed into the procession of bikers.

He killed Daniel Matthieu outright, the impact of the speeding car throwing the biker clear of his Harley. Next in line happened to be Stadnick. His Harley collided into the priest's car, and its customized gas tank exploded. Emergency personnel found him literally fused to his bike in the spots where leather, rubber, plastic and flesh met.

At first, he was treated in Montreal, but Hamilton police told me his common-law wife, Kathi Anderson, was upset and worried by how little English the staff spoke and how flippant they seemed with his treatment. She demanded they move him to Hamilton General. But while he would be treated in English in the Hammer, he would also, defenseless, be exposed to its people. That could mean Outlaws, Cosa Nostra or 'Ndrangheta—any of which would have been more than happy to hasten his demise.

When she finally realized how dangerous the situation was, the Hamilton police told me, she called Langlois. He had an idea. The 13th Tribe, the Halifax-based club that so badly wanted to become a Hells Angels chapter, could earn their stripes by standing guard in his room. That could happen only during visiting hours, though. Desperate and out of options, Anderson called Harris, Hamilton's top biker cop, to ask for police protection. Harris told me he was flabbergasted by the call. It's not like there was any love lost between the tiny biker and the giant cop. A former professional football player and a strong believer in old-school police tactics, the towering six foot seven cop told me he made it a habit to annoy and taunt Stadnick every chance he got. In the interest of preventing a murder, he agreed.

With the ever-tactful Stadnick out of commission, things got worse in Montreal. Stretched thin, Langlois stepped down as Sorel president (retaining the title of national president). His replacement was a surprise. Réjean "Zig-Zag" Lessard, who had only a little while earlier been a member of Laval, was much more a man of action than the laconic Langlois.

Everyone at Sorel agreed that Laval had been given enough warnings about getting off the blow and paying their debts. There was also a great deal of resentment over the fact that Laval had two meth cooks working full-time and that they would not let Sorel in on the business. Lessard came up with a plan to fix the problem with Laval once and for all—eliminate the chapter. But he needed Manhattan's permission first. It didn't take long.

Robert "Ti-Maigre" Richard, himself a former Laval member and the closest confidant of Lessard, called Laval and told them there would be a party in Lennoxville to celebrate the patch-over of the Gitans, who would become the Hells Angels Sherbrooke chapter. The club, which had formerly been known as the Dirty Reich, had long been connected to the original Popeyes and had earned their patch by eliminating their primary competition in the area, the Atomes, murdering members Michel "Ballon" Fortier, Jean-Noël Roy, Ronald "Big" Sigouin and president Réjean "Farmer" Gilbert in quick succession. Attendance at the Lennoxville party, Richard said, was mandatory.

Only a few showed up from Laval, according to the transcripts from a later trial. Richard got back on the phone and ordered the remainder to come the following day, Sunday, March 24, 1985. They all showed up except for Trudeau, who was in rehab after snorting $60,000 worth of cocaine over a short period; his friend and fellow paid assassin, Régis "Lucky" Asselin, who could not be reached; and Jinx Genest. With members of the Gitans and 13th Tribe joining Sorel's own prospects outside, the members of Laval were herded inside. Prospects Normand "Biff" Hamel and Claude "Coco" Roy were held at gunpoint outside.

Seconds later, the air erupted with the sounds of shouting, gunfire and screaming. Laval president Laurent "l'Anglais" Viau and members Jean-Guy "Brutus" Geoffrion, Jean-Pierre "Matt le Crosseur" Mathieu, Michel "Willie" Mayrand and Guy-Louis "Chop" Adam were dead. Of the surviving members in Lennoxville (those the Sorel guys thought they could assimiliate), the Crown said, one—Gilles "le Nez" Lachance—was offered Sorel membership. He quickly accepted. The other two—Yvon "le Père"

Bilodeau and Richard "Bert" Mayrand (Michel's older brother)—were told to get lost.

While the prospects were eliminating evidence from the scene, two Sorel members, Jacques "la Pelle" Pelletier and Robert "Snake" Tremblay, drove Lachance to the Laval clubhouse to take possession of whatever they could find. One of those things was Jinx Genest, who was sitting at the clubhouse bar drinking beer alone. They explained to him what had happened and offered him prospective membership with Sorel. He, too, quickly agreed.

That left some other loose ends. Trudeau had done too much over the years just to be gotten rid of like the other Laval members. Besides, he had recruited many of the original Popeyes, was still well liked and could be of value. Biff Hamel earned his standing as a Sorel prospect by visiting Trudeau at rehab, explaining what had happened and telling him that he was being spared, though discharged from the Hells Angels, and that his possessions were now Sorel property. Trudeau later earned his bike back by murdering Jean-Marc "la Grande Gueule" Deniger, an old friend from the Popeyes who had been selling drugs for Laval, but when he asked if that would also allow him back into the club, he was once again told his membership was gone forever.

According to several media sources at the time, including Allo Police!, a $50,000 open contract was issued for Lucky Asselin's death, but he lived up to his nickname, surviving two assassination attempts before hightailing it out of town. He was eventually tracked down, not by bikers, but by Sûreté du Québec officers, in the northern mill town of Dolbeau (now known as Dolbeau-Mistassini) on March 10, 1986.

Lessard then allegedly decided to kill two birds with one stone by promising Jinx Genest a full patch if he'd kill Coco Roy, whom Lessard suspected of being less than loyal. Genest would have gotten away with it if he hadn't had eyes for Roy's coke-addicted stripper girlfriend, Linda Lord. After arranging to meet Roy in room 103 in the Motel Idéal in Laval for a coke deal, Genest beat him to death and stole the drugs. Instead of leaving, he called Lord and invited her to spend the night with him (and the coke) at the very same hotel. She refused, pointing out that she was his friend's girlfriend. Genest laughed at that. When he came to her home and knocked on her door later that night, Lord refused to answer and called the police, sealing Genest's fate. He was later convicted of Roy's killing. Lessard was not charged, but his alleged contributions to the Roy killing were used in a later trial.

Lessard was not suspicious of just Roy. There was another prospect, former Missile Gerry "le Chat" Coulombe, he was also worried about. A couple of other prospects noticed that Coulombe seemed to panic when the bullets started flying in Lennoxville, and that did not sit well with Lessard. On June 26, 1985, Lessard called the prospect and told him to come by the clubhouse to get his full patch. Excited and nervous, Coulombe called his friends, Hells Angels prospects Gaétan "Gaet" Proulx and Jean-Paul "Donat" Ramsay, but when they told him they had not been told of such a party, he began to worry. Luckily for him, the following day, a SWAT team broke into Coulombe's apartment. Facing certain death from his "brothers," he decided to turn informant.

He was the first Canadian biker to do so but would hardly be the last. In fact, he wasn't even the last one who had been involved in the Lennoxville Massacre.

The bodies, which had been put into sleeping bags weighed down by rocks and thrown into the St. Lawrence, began floating to the surface in June. At first, police thought the Outlaws were behind it, but they quickly realized it was a housecleaning. They told me that after Coulombe turned, they asked him if there was anyone else they could work with. Coulombe named Lachance, who was still horrified by what he had witnessed at Lennoxville and wasn't sure he wasn't next in line. The evidence he provided allowed them to approach Trudeau. When police told him what Lachance had said, he smiled and told them, "I killed for them and now they want to kill me—that's gratitude, eh?"

With Coulombe, Lachance and Trudeau—who admitted to 43 murders, 30 of which were bikers—providing evidence, the arrests came quickly. Of the 100 or so men arrested, including some members of the Gitans and the 13th Tribe, only Lessard, Tremblay, Pelletier and Michaud were convicted. Each received a life term. Chapter president Robert Richard was later acquitted on appeal and the other four were paroled between 2005 and 2008.

Langlois escaped police "by a hair" (as they told the *Montreal Gazette*) when, tipped off, he fled a motorcycle show they had arrived at. He absconded to Morocco, where he lived for a while. His conscience overcame him, and in 1988, he showed up at a Sûreté du Québec station and turned himself in. He received a two-year sentence for conspiracy.

The importance of the Lennoxville Massacre to Canadian crime history and its part in the cold war can hardly be overstated. The seeds of the cold war were sown by the bootleggers and smugglers. That connection to the big-time, big-money mafias of the US led Joey Bananas to send Carmine Galante to Canada to establish Montreal as the primary distribution center for the French Connection. That, in turn, precipitated the war between the Calabrian Cotronis and their Corsican heroin, and the Sicilian Rizzutos and their Venezuelan cocaine. When the Rizzutos won, they needed someone to do their dirty work and move their coke. That attracted the Hells Angels, who quickly became established. And, after the Lennoxville Massacre, they became even more powerful than ever.

CHAPTER 7

THE HELLS ANGELS RE-EMERGE, STRONGER THAN BEFORE

If you don't understand how a club can kill many of its members and prospects, have three more turn informant, lose a chapter president and three other members to arrest and have their national president flee to North Africa and come out stronger, it's because you aren't thinking like a strategic-minded 1%er.

As soon as the bloated bodies started floating to the surface of the St. Lawrence and fingers were pointed at the Hells Angels themselves, the few remaining Outlaws in Montreal did their level best to cash in. They stapled up posters with the slogan HELLS ANGELS BROTHERHOOD, depicting dead bikers at the bottom of the St. Lawrence, around the rougher areas of the city. This probably did them more harm than good in that it pointed out their lowly status in Montreal. The Hells Angels were in a moment of profound crisis, and all the Outlaws could do was hang up some childish, hand-drawn posters in the middle of the night and then crawl back into hiding when the sun came up—hardly good marketing for a tough-guy image.

The Hells Angels were the talk of the town. When it came to the element most likely to wind up in jail, opinions were divided. Take, for example, the SS. Drearily and predictably named after the much-feared Nazi guard of World War II, the SS were the primary source of manpower and recruits for the Hells Angels at the time—Biff Hamel, the Laval prospect who crossed over to Sorel, had been in the SS just weeks before.

Their leader, Salvatore Cazzetta, was aghast at what had happened. Like the other members of the SS, he had hoped to become a Hells Angel, but the Lennoxville Massacre changed his mind. To Cazzetta, brothers who would kill their own brothers weren't brothers.

He called a meeting at the clubhouse in Pointe-aux-Trembles on the far eastern tip of the island. Quickly, two factions formed. One, behind Cazzetta, his younger brother, Giovanni, and guys like Frédéric "Fred" Faucher and the gigantic Paul "Sasquatch" Porter, condemned the killings and argued in favor of severing ties with Sorel. The other faction, behind an equally if not more charismatic leader, argued that the killings were not only justified, but necessary. He argued that the guys who were killed were putting everyone else in danger, with their unnecessary arrests exposing the whole organization to law enforcement and their huge coke debts angering the West End Gang and the Italians. He quickly found support, especially with the SS's younger members.

The man was Maurice "Mom" Boucher. Born in tiny Causapscal on the Gaspé Peninsula, he moved with his family to Montreal's blue-collar Hochelaga-Maisonneuve neighborhood, where his father worked as a longshoreman. Boucher dropped out of school in the ninth grade and supported himself with petty thefts and stick-ups. Years later, the Crown would claim that he'd spent time behind bars for the knifepoint robbery of an elderly man and the knifepoint rape of a 16-year-old girl. He'd recently been released for the rape conviction when the Lennoxville Massacre went down.

The meeting ended in a way that is almost unprecedented in the 1%er world—they agreed to disagree. Cazzetta and Boucher decided to disband the SS and go their separate ways, remaining friends. Although amicable, the parting was the start of the two opposing sets of Canadian bikers, a rivalry that has cost hundreds of lives since. That day, the cold war expanded from two Italian factions to two forces throughout organized crime as the two gangs became each other's rivals and would be employed, and used against each other, by the two competing Mafia families.

With the SS behind him, Boucher joined his other old pal, Biff Hamel, in Sorel, quickly becoming a prospect.

He was exactly what they wanted. The Lennoxville Massacre had transformed the Montreal Hells Angels. The deaths, forced retirements, arrests and flights from law enforcement had not only cleaned out the cokeheads and stumblebums, it had also eliminated the old Popeyes—guys like Trudeau, Lessard and Langlois—from positions of power. Like a hammer that has had its head and handle replaced at different times, it was the same club, but entirely different. Gone were the old-timers who had joined the club to drink, get high, brawl and ride their Harleys—the reasons all bikers still coyly say they belong to such clubs. They were replaced by career criminals like Boucher, who joined the club to make money. Motorcycles were, if anything, an afterthought. They all owned at least one, and they rode them when they had to, but the Hells Angels in Montreal were a motorcycle club in much the same way that the Queen of England is Canada's head of state.

One of the other things that had bothered Sorel about Laval was that they allowed other motorcycle gangs not only to exist but to sell drugs within their territory. Since 1966, the Death Riders had been operating out of a motorcycle repair shop in Saint-Eustache on the North Shore just west of Laval. While they had done some work for Laval and Sorel in the past, and many of their members were friends with the Hells Angels, they were hardly what we'd now call a puppet gang.

Their independent streak came from their leader, 23-year-old Martin Huneault. Foolishly under the impression his gang could coexist with the Hells Angels as equals, Huneault took his girlfriend to watch the Habs game at a Laval bar on May 4, 1987. Just into the first period, a stranger walked into the bar, headed straight for Huneault and shot him three times (once each in the face, right arm and chest). Huneault fell forward onto the floor and bled out before help could arrive.

When questioned, none of the five other patrons, including his girlfriend, or the waitress, said that they saw the killer well enough to give an accurate description. No charges were laid. However, the following night, several newspapers reported that Boucher and Hamel were seen in a Laval bar drinking and meeting with Death Riders full-patches Mario Martin and André Richard. Soon thereafter, the Death Riders had a new boss, Sorel full-patch Michael "l'Animal" Lajoie-Smith (who connected them with Paolo "Paul" Cotroni as a connection for product, according to a trafficking conviction against Cotroni). Perhaps not entirely coincidentally, Boucher and Hamel received their patches.

The addition of the Death Riders as a puppet club marked another important step in the Hells Angels' development and pushed the country's crime organizations closer to war. It was the first part of a very successful formula. In territories the Hells Angels claimed, they made sure that everyone else who wanted to sell drugs sold them for the prices they set and kicked a portion of the profits back to them. The penalty for not complying, as Huneault learned, was death.

Two years earlier, the Hells Angels had two chapters in Montreal—one that followed the Buteau money-making formula and one that did not—and three very distant, isolated and not entirely friendly chapters in the Vancouver area. By the summer of 1987, there were three efficient chapters in Montreal, Sherbrooke and Halifax, a puppet club in Laval and a better relationship with the chapters in Vancouver.

Part of the reason the Quebec chapters had grown closer to Vancouver was that, once he recovered from his burns, Stadnick returned to the fold, along with another English speaker from Hamilton, Donald "Pup" Stockford. Badly scarred and missing parts of several fingers, Stadnick wore a patch on his jacket that read HELL, to commemorate the hell he went through after the accident. Later, when he was more powerful, a mutual acquaintance who would rather not be named told me, Stadnick ran into another Hells Angel in Germany with a HELL patch. Stadnick ordered him to take off the patch, believing he himself was the only one who deserved to wear it. Upon his return, he was well received in Montreal and his charisma and ambition led many of the Hells Angels to believe that their expansion plans would not be limited to Quebec and points east.

While the Hells Angels were thinking big, the Cotronis and their allies were struggling to stay alive, out of prison, valid and financially solvent. Simard was talking to anyone who would listen, and his close relationship with Uncle Frank meant that he knew everything.

The cops then launched Operation Si-Co (Simard-Cotroni), in which they arrested several men alleged to have connections to the Cotroni family. Frank Cotroni, his son Francesco, Claude Faber, Daniel Arena, and Francesco Raso were charged with the murder of Giuseppe Montegano. Faber, Frank's brother-in-law, who was caught on a wiretap recommending that the Cotronis should kill Papalia if he objected to them moving into Toronto, was just days away from moving from Montreal to Acapulco where he was planning to establish a headquarters at which he could buy cocaine cheaply in Mexico and send it directly to the Cotronis in Montreal, reaping huge profits. After Faber pleaded guilty to manslaughter, charges against the others were dropped.

Simard knew about Faber's plan to move to Acapulco and told the cops. Simard also told them that Faber had shot dealer Claude Ménard in the back of the head in 1982 for shorting him (although he was not charged), and that he traveled and dined on the Montreal Hotel and Restaurant Employees Union tab, even though he had never held a legitimate job, let alone a union position.

Frank was granted bail on the condition that he maintain employment at a company named Ital Video-Poker. Of course, what the Crown didn't know, or at least couldn't prove, was that Ital Video-Poker was a business owned by Frank that centered around illegal gambling, loan-sharking and, naturally, drug trafficking. Despite his best efforts, Frank was found guilty of manslaughter in the death of Montegano and was sentenced to eight years. He told the media, including the CBC, that the severity of the sentence made him want to change his ways. He promised to go straight after his release.

He may have been secretly pleased to know that things were not entirely smooth for his rivals, either. The RCMP had raided a boat, the *Charlotte Louise*, carrying 17 tons of hashish, off Newfoundland. Evidence came out that Vito Rizzuto and his friends were paying otherwise unemployed fishermen to move hash from Turkey though Newfoundland to Montreal for $17,000 to $25,000 a shipment. Rizzuto, his old pal Raynald Desjardins, Michel Routhier and Gerald Hiscock, the point man in Newfoundland, were all arrested. During their trial, however, the judge disallowed much of the wiretap evidence because it had been acquired illegally. The accused walked free.

While Vito was out on $150,000 bail, another ship full of drugs was found. On July 18, 1988, police and customs searched the *Jeanne D'Arc*, which was headed for port in Sept-Îles, Quebec, on the North Shore, about a 10-hour drive from Sorel. On board, they found 35 tons of hashish from Lebanon. The vessel's captain, Normand Dupuis, started cooperating with police before his feet were on dry land. He fingered Vito Rizzuto.

While Vito was out on a second bail agreement, Dupuis— the Crown's only witness—called Jean Salois, Vito's lawyer, and asked for a "lifelong pension" in exchange for forgetting everything about the hash. Salois had the presence of mind to tape the conversation, which, when presented at trial, destroyed Dupuis's credibility. Vito was free to go. But Dupuis wasn't. His limp extortion attempt netted him a 32-month obstruction of justice conviction to go along with the convictions related to his being in possession of 35 tons of hash.

Then, in December 1990, Vito was off the hook again. Part of the evidence against him consisted of an RCMP recording of conversations he had with his legal team in a hotel restaurant. Because of client privilege, it was inadmissible. The RCMP tried to explain that the conversation was merely overheard by the bug when they were listening to another suspect in the restaurant, but the judge wouldn't have it. Vito was freed again. The other four on trial were, however, found guilty.

Caught twice and acquitted both times, Rizzuto looked invincible. His standing was further enhanced by his juxtaposition to the Cotronis. Just a few months after Frank Cotroni sheepishly told reporters he was giving up his life of crime, Vito beamingly told the media: "One word can mean so much— especially when that word is *acquittal*."

While the Rizzutos in Montreal were breathing easy, tragedy befell Nick in Venezuela. In a February 12, 1988, raid, the Cuerpo de Investigaciones Científicas (Venezuelan national police) found 800 grams of cocaine hidden in a belt worn by a Montrealer who was in Nick's party. Four men, including Nick, were arrested. Although the drugs were found on another man, the prosecution in Caracas concluded that Nick was the ringleader and he was sentenced to eight years in prison—a harsh term by the current standards of the offense.

The Cotronis were far from finished. With Frank behind bars, the ranking family member was Paolo, also known as Paul. In fact, his relationship with the Death Riders—now channeled through Sorel, but still immensely profitable—had made him very wealthy. Unlike many in the Rizzuto clan, he could not resist getting his hands dirty with a little extra action. On August 30, 1990, acting on a tip, police found a boat in the backyard of his Repentigny home. Media reports often incorrectly said that the 26-foot, $125,000 craft was named *Fountain Fever*, but that was actually its model name. Either way, it was quickly and easily identified as one of two identical boats that had gone missing from the headquarters of Can-Am, Bombardier's motorcycle and all-terrain vehicle division. After a night in jail, Paul pleaded guilty to possession of stolen property, asked what the fine was and immediately forked over $15,000 in cash.

It was chump change for him, in large part because of the success of his connections with the Death Riders and Hells Angels. In fact, the Death Riders were so successful selling drugs and performing other tasks for the Hells Angels in Laval and the Laurentians that the Montreal Hells Angels decided to replicate the process in the city itself.

By 1992, the Montreal Hells Angels bore little resemblance to the hairy, bedraggled group of stoners and brawlers who had earned the patch in 1977. The new leadership was composed of men like Buteau's protégé, Stadnick, and his right-hand man, Pup Stockford, alongside local talents Mom Boucher and Biff Hamel, who earned their full patches back in 1987. Aside from Hamel's thick but tidy beard and Stadnick's scars and fondness for flamboyant affectations like his floor-length wolf-fur coat, the new breed of Hells Angels appeared to be presentable businessmen, hardly distinguishable from other successful Montrealers except when they wore their colors for ceremonial purposes.

The new guard had adapted to their new responsibilities. Tactful, amiable and English-speaking, the strategic-minded Stadnick was elected national president, a position with a job description that included fostering communication between existing chapters and, more important, recruiting new clubs all over the country to the Hells Angels cause. Bold, charismatic and bellicose, Boucher was elected chapter president. His job was to protect and further develop the Hells Angels' interests in Montreal. As the cold war devolved into an all-out conflict, both men would prove exceedingly adept at their jobs.

Another part of this new bikers-as-professional-criminals ethos was centered on protecting the full-patches from prosecution. While it had long been tradition for full-patches to hand off dangerous responsibilities to prospects, the Montreal Hells Angels realized that by handing their dirty work to another gang, they were one more layer away from prison in the event something went wrong.

On March 26, 1992, the Montreal Hells Angels created a new club, also in Montreal, called the Rockers MC. Their task was to run the street-level drug operations in Montreal and to enforce the Hells Angels' rules by any means necessary. Each of the Rockers had a Hells Angel to report to. For example, Hells Angel Paul "Fon Fon" Fontaine supplied Rocker Serge Boutin with cocaine, which Boutin then distributed through as many as 100 individual street-level dealers in his territory—Montreal's Gay Village.

As an added degree of safety, the Rockers employed three different street gangs—the Syndicate, Les Scorpions and No Man's

Land—to do jobs they found too small or risky. And, despite the white supremacist past of many Hells Angels and their associates, the Rockers also dealt directly with Montreal's most powerful black gang, Master B.

Even with all the gangs and subgangs and friends and associates, the Hells Angels were hardly the only people selling cocaine on the streets of Montreal or the rest of the country, for that matter.

In time, ordinary Canadians would watch as expansionist Stadnick and protectionist Boucher used their varied and complementary talents to establish the Hells Angels as the dominant crime organization in the country. Of course, that could not be done without a great deal of blood flowing in the streets.

CHAPTER 8

HOW MONTREAL BECAME A BATTLEGROUND

It's unlikely that in 1984, when Mom Boucher and Salvatore Cazzetta disbanded the SS and agreed to go their separate ways, they knew they would be precipitating a conflict that would kill more Canadians than the war in Afghanistan. In fact, they parted friends, even if they were no longer brothers.

A number of SS members, as well as other allied organizations, agreed with Cazzetta that Zig-Zag Lessard and his Sorel chapter had gone too far when they enforced a death penalty on their "brother" members in Laval. Cazzetta recruited his actual brother, Giovanni (who had been running with the ill-fated Montreal Outlaws for a while), and friends Paul "Sasquatch" Porter, Renaud Jomphe, André Sauvageau, Gilles Lambert, Martin Bourget, Richard Lagacé, Serge Pinel and Johnny Plescio to form a new organization.

Cazzetta made the bold decision not to call his new entity a motorcycle club. Despite the inherent legal protection motorcycle clubs enjoy by posing as mutual-interest organizations, he felt that their bikes and their clubhouses attracted too much attention from media and law enforcement. He came up with an it-could-only-happen-in-Quebec name—the Rock Machine.

For years they ran under the radar, but the growing influence of the Hells Angels forced changes. Under the reign of Boucher, a decree was passed that anybody who wanted to sell drugs in Montreal would have to follow their rules as far as pricing and product quality were concerned. Undercutting—which would erode the Hells Angels' market share and profit margin—would be punishable by death. Later, that imperial order would evolve into a demand that anyone selling cocaine on the streets of Montreal would have to buy their supply from the Hells Angels, regardless of price or quality.

Not everybody was happy with those decrees. Many Montreal drug traffickers—including members of the West End Gang, the still-powerful-in-the-east-end Pelletier Clan, what remained of the Dubois gang and a shadowy group of bar owners called the Dark Circle—refused to kowtow to Boucher and formed their own loose-knit group called the Alliance. There was no headquarters or official leader, but members could identify one another, according to police and prosecutors, by their pinkie rings. The Rock Machine were brought into the fold to act mainly as enforcers.

There are different schools of thought as to why the Rock Machine was allowed to survive relatively unmolested as long as they did. They even had a habit of giving out T-shirts and baseball caps with their logo—originally an eagle's leg then later an eagle's head—to cooperative dealers.

Some people think that it took Boucher years to gain enough power and support to declare war. It is true that the Montreal Hells Angels were in transition in the early 1990s. After long being supplied by and employed by the Cotronis, Boucher met with Raynald Desjardins—the highest-ranking non-Italian in the Rizzuto family and Vito's trusted confidant—on May 25, 1993. Police learned about the meeting through prison interviews and later had it confirmed when Desjardins spoke about the success of the meeting in a taped phone conversation.

Some weeks later, the connection between the Rizzutos and the Hells Angels became abundantly clear. On August 25, 1993, the RCMP announced via press release that they had arrested 20 people—including Desjardins, Richard "Bob" Hudon and André Imbeault of the Quebec City Hells Angels and Rocker Luc "Bordel" Bordeleau—for their part in a plan to ship 700 kilos of cocaine from Venezuela into Halifax. When the coke (hidden in metal drainpipes) went overboard, the military had to recover it with a manned submersible.

Desjardins was sentenced to 15 years in prison. On his first day inside, he shook hands with the warden and assured him all would go well. He wasn't being entirely honest. Although he did hire a construction crew to renovate the penitentiary's recreational facilities and cater a seafood feast for the inmates (police stopped the delivery before it reached the gate), I have been told by two people close to the situation, who would rather not be identified, that he is rumored to have ordered the deaths of two other inmates. He was not charged.

Others believe that Boucher tolerated the Rock Machine's existence because of his long friendship with Salvatore Cazzetta. Indeed, the Quebec Biker War, which pitted the Hells Angels and their allies against the Rock Machine and their allies, did not begin until after Cazzetta was out of the picture.

He went down pretty much as you'd expect. Back in the summer of 1992, West End Gang member Billy McAllister got out of prison again. He'd spent 22 of his 50 years behind bars for several different convictions but still had a great deal of street credibility and many connections. When he heard there was 5,000 kilos of cocaine in Florida looking for a buyer in Montreal, he jumped at the chance.

Quickly, he recruited two old friends—Michael Dibben and Colombian-born, Spanish-speaking Ashley Castaneda—and a small-time dealer he'd previously supplied, named Paul Larue. For muscle, the team added Cazzetta and his closest friend in the Rock Machine, Nelson Fernandez.

What they did not know was that it was all a major sting operation put together by Montreal police, the RCMP and the DEA. In fact, McAllister's contacts in Florida were actually a pair of undercover DEA agents, John Burns and Ed Dickey. Burns met three times with Larue (once in Montreal and twice in the US) to set down the ground rules and for Larue to sample the product. Satisfied that it was good stuff, Larue, following Burns's orders, then raised $875,000 from members of the Alliance, including the Rock Machine, as a down payment.

Cazzetta and Fernandez brought the money to Burns in a Jacksonville, Florida, hotel room on March 19, 1993.

Two days later, the *Montreal Gazette* reported that RCMP officers arrested McAllister at his palatial chalet in the Laurentians. From a jail cell, he called the *Gazette* to correct and berate them after they printed an article that quoted him as saying that he believed he was set up by West End Gang boss Allan "the Weasel" Ross. "That's a total crock and a total falsehood, and you shouldn't write things like that," he told the paper. "I know that Allan Ross would never, ever do such a thing. When you write articles like that—I'm serious when I tell you, it's for your own good that I tell you this—there could be reprisals for yourself."

At about the same time the RCMP stormed McAllister's house, DEA agents nabbed Larue and Castaneda in a Burlington, Vermont, Denny's where they were expecting their first shipment of coke to arrive. It wasn't hard to recognize Larue, who stood out amongst the dour New England churchgoers with his $50,000 mink coat and $35,000 watch.

Dibben sent two flunkies, Francesco Rubbio and Sebastiano di Maria, to Jacksonville for his own order of 200 kilos. They were promptly arrested, as was he in Montreal.

Fernandez was already in jail in Canada, so the Americans were content to leave him there. Years later, he would switch sides to the Hells Angels just before succumbing to cancer in prison.

Cazzetta managed to escape the dragnet and even continued to run the Rock Machine through go-betweens. Acting on a tip, the OPP tracked him down at a pit bull breeding and fighting compound in Niagara Falls on May 6, 1994. He went first to Donnacona prison in Montreal, then to the US.

That's when the bodies started to fall. It was the Rock Machine who struck first and second.

The first victim was Pierre Daoust. A close friend of the Montreal Hells Angels, Daoust owned a Harley repair shop and often rode with the old-timers. On June 13, 1994, two men walked into the shop. When Daoust stood to address them, one of them pulled out a gun and killed him.

The following day, Hells Angel Normand "Norm" Robitaille was standing outside an east-end garage on Rue Rouen (minding his own business, as they say) when two masked men approached him and shot him. Robitaille—who was the godfather to two South Shore gangs, the Evil Ones and the Condors—survived and identified the shooter, to his friends not the cops, as Rock Machine full-patch Normand Baker.

That night, acting on a tip that the Rock Machine was planning an attack on the Evil Ones, the police raided a Boucherville hotel room. Inside, they found five men with two handguns, three remote-controlled bombs and 12 sticks of dynamite. Arrested were Montreal Rock Machine members Baker, André Sauvageau and Guy Langlois as well as Quebec City full-patches Martin "Blue" Blouin and Fred Faucher. All five were convicted, but only Blouin, who claimed it was all his plan and equipment, received a long sentence.

While the beginnings of the suddenly hot war were rumbling among the bikers, big changes were happening with the Mafia at about the same time.

The Calabrians were still around, although not making the biggest of headlines. Paolo Cotroni and his old pal Vincenzo "Jimmy Rent-a-Gun" De Santis were accused by the local tabloid press, including *Allo Police!*, of setting fire to the Oscar nightclub on the night of December 17, 1992. Oscar's owner had, perhaps not entirely coincidentally, fired Paolo's girlfriend earlier that day. Neither was charged.

In comparison, Vito Rizzuto and his consigliere Joseph Di Maulo (Desjardins's brother-in-law and a Calabrian who had sided with the Sicilians after a bitter dispute with Frank Cotroni's brother-in-law Claude Faber over exactly who ran the hotel and restaurant workers' union) were implicated in a plot to liquidate $3 billion in gold bullion stolen from former Philippine dictator Ferdinand Marcos. Again, neither was charged. Not long after, Libertina Rizzuto, Nick's wife, was arrested in Switzerland for trying to withdraw $5 million in cash from one of her husband's bank accounts. Like a trouper, she kept her mouth shut and waited out the RCMP and Revenue Canada and was also never charged.

In May 1993, the family was reunited (and strengthened) when Nick Rizzuto was granted a surprise parole from authorities in Venezuela. At least, it surprised most people. A month earlier, Domenic Tozzi was having lunch with a person he thought was a money-laundering pal of his but who was actually an undercover RCMP officer, whom the force has told me I can identify as DR-374. Over lunch, the officer testified in court, Tozzi bragged to his friend that he personally had taken $800,000 in cash to an unnamed Venezuelan official in exchange for the old man's freedom.

Later, when Rizzuto lawyer Jean Salois was asked about the transaction, he denied it had ever happened. "Certainly, my clients would never have entrusted Mr. Tozzi with $800,000," he said. "You know, Mr. Tozzi had a very bad reputation in the milieu. It makes no sense, and it borders on comedy."

Be that as it may, when Nick stepped off the plane in Montreal, dozens of family memebers and other well-wishers were there to greet him, including Tozzi.

Another notable face among them was one of the Mafia's few bright lights, Raymond Fernandez. He certainly was tough—what we would, these days, recognize as a psychopath. At 21, he ordered a 17-year-old stripper to have sex with a fat, ugly friend of his. When she demurred, he punched her in the throat, killing her instantly.

That led to a prison sentence in which he was frequently written up for threatening and assaulting fellow inmates. In July 1985, a fellow inmate said Fernandez threatened to kill him over a minor disagreement. A few weeks later, another prisoner was caught trying to smuggle 138 grams of hashish into Archambault when he was returning from furlough. When he was caught, he said that Fernandez had threatened to kill him if he didn't do it. The following month, he beat another inmate nearly to death over a gambling debt. Over the same period, he also earned three complaints for threatening the lives of three prison employees.

Fernandez's ascent after he left prison was a prime example of a trend that made the Rizzutos a number of enemies among mafiosi in Montreal and around the world. He, like many other important Montreal mafiosi including Raynald Desjardins, was neither Sicilian nor Calabrian. In fact, neither man was even Italian. Fernandez was from Spain and Desjardins, among many other Rizzuto operatives, was French-Canadian. Many Italians in the Mafia believed non-Italians could not be trusted when push came to shove.

CHAPTER 9

THE WAR EXPANDS OUTSIDE MONTREAL

When the next mafioso did fall in Montreal, it wasn't to law enforcement. Sabatino "Sam" Nicolucci was a longtime Rizzuto associate who had just served 6 years of a 14-year sentence after being caught with 12.6 kilos of cocaine in Vancouver in September 1985. Once out, he started using and selling cocaine again. But, like so many before and after him, he did not pay his bills on time and something had to be done.

On a pleasant afternoon in August 1994, Nicolucci was relaxing at a Jean-Talon strip joint when four men surrounded him and forced him into their car. They then put him on a plane that stopped in Miami before taking him to Colombia. The Colombians let Montreal know that they would release Nicolucci once they were paid the $1.7 million he owed them. It's not known what Vito answered, but he didn't send them a penny to release his old friend.

It was probably just as well for Nicolucci. Soon after he was abducted, a huge RCMP money-laundering sting operation netted 47 arrests, including Rizzuto associates Vincenzo Di Maulo,

Domenic Tozzi, Emanuele Ragusa and Valentino Morielli. All four were convicted. Nicolucci had actually been the prime target and was charged in absentia with no fewer than 233 charges, including laundering $31 million and conspiring to import more than 400 kilograms of cocaine from Colombia.

While Canadian authorities convinced themselves Nicolucci had died in Colombia, he was still around and would soon resurface. After realizing they weren't going to be paid by his friends, the Colombian dealers handed him over to the police, who threw him in jail pending charges. When the Canadian authorities found out about his continued existence, they started the process to extradite him. There were newspaper reports that the Canadian embassy in Bogotá would be attacked if he was extradited, but those stories were probably launched by the dealers trying to re-interest Montreal in paying a ransom or by Montreal hoping that Nicolucci would stay in Colombia, rather than come to Canada and potentially shoot his mouth off.

In either event, his extradition went off without a hitch and he kept his mouth shut. Although he did manage to beat 61 of the charges against him, the other 172 put him behind bars for a very long time.

While the Rizzutos were having trouble with the Colombians, the Cotronis were making profoundly important friends in that country. After the Colombian military killed Pablo Escobar on December 2, 1993, the landscape rapidly changed in Colombia. His Medellín Cartel immediately started to fragment, and many of his best people changed sides and aligned with the rival Cali Cartel, which quickly became even more powerful, with a near-monopoly on Colombian cocaine.

The Cotronis got in there first. Francesco Jr., who was acting boss while Frank was behind bars, flew to Cali to meet with Gilberto "the Chess Player" Rodriguez Orejuela and Miguel "the

Master" Rodriguez Orejuela, the founders and leaders of the cartel, at Miguel's castle-like mansion compound. After a long and, one would assume, productive meeting, Francesco Jr. flew to Acapulco and met with Mexican middlemen at a hotel co-owned by his father.

By the time Frank got out of jail on September 28, 1995, the Cotronis had moved back up in the world.

Just as the Mafia used Latin America as a means to increase their dominance, so did the bikers. While the Hells Angels had not gone so far as to declare war on the Rock Machine or the Alliance, they did come to a consensus that Baker would have to be punished for killing Daoust and trying to kill Robitaille.

For New Year's 1995, Baker and fellow Rock Machine member Robert "Tout Tout" Léger decided to take their wives on vacation in Acapulco. Baker spotted some Hells Angels on their plane, but Léger told him to think nothing of it. On the night of January 4, Baker took his wife to the Hard Rock Cafe. Léger and his wife were going to go, but backed out at the last minute. While he was enjoying his date, Baker was approached by a man he did not recognize, but at least one unidentified witness told the CBC that the man had said "Happy New Year" in French before shooting him dead.

The man fled on foot, but a number of other bar patrons caught him and held him down until the police arrived. They could have saved their efforts. There was a quick lack-of-sufficient-evidence acquittal for the accused, François Hinse, who was a prospect of the Hells Angels Trois-Rivières chapter.

While the Hells Angels were not yet that concerned about the Rock Machine threat, there were major internal rumblings that would change their future. Many of them came from Stadnick.

He had stepped down as national president to take over a more profitable position. He'd created the Nomads, an elite chapter of the Hells Angels who answered to no one and had no clubhouse.

The idea was that they were to be welcomed as members by any clubhouse. The Nomads' all-star roster included Stadnick, his pal Pup Stockford, Mom Boucher, Biff Hamel, Gilles "Trooper" Matthieu and Denis "Pas Fiable" Houle from Montreal, Louis "Mélou" Roy and Richard "Rick" Vallée from Trois-Rivières and Wolf Carroll from Halifax. The existence of the Nomads gave its members another level of insulation from law enforcement.

Each member had his territory and responsibilities. For example, Roy was the Nomads' point man with the Italians, a position that made him exceedingly wealthy. It was Stadnick's responsibility to expand sales in the area between Montreal and British Columbia. It wasn't an easy job—many people I have spoken to remember him being on the telephone constantly—but the potential benefits were astronomical.

Stadnick used several methods. The primary way he got his message (and product) across was to form friendships with existing clubs or their individual members. On any given night, Stadnick could be seen with members of Satan's Choice at a strip joint in Oshawa or cutting into thick steaks with the Grim Reapers at the finest restaurants in Edmonton. Of course, supplying clubs or even individual members with cocaine and hashish also went a long way toward making good friends.

Constantly at his side throughout his travels in those days was Donald "Bam Bam" Magnussen. Huge, strong and more than happy to start throwing punches, Magnussen acted as Stadnick's bodyguard and as something of an executive assistant. In the early 1990s, the preternaturally wily Stadnick was actually arrested twice in Winnipeg—once with Magnussen, once without. The first arrest was a silly one. While trying to board an airplane from Winnipeg to Hamilton, Stadnick was frisked and found to have $81,000 hidden in his belt. He was arrested on a proceeds-of-crime charge. Two months later, Stadnick, Magnussen and some local bikers known as Los Brovos beat up two drunken undercover cops who interrupted one of their parties and even climbed onto one of the bikers' Harleys, according to the Winnipeg police complaint.

While cops in Hamilton and Montreal, who had fairly accurate suspicions of Stadnick's status and operations, were celebrating, they were being overly optimistic. Judges threw out both cases. For one thing, there's no law against carrying $81,000 and police have no right to demand to know how you got it. And when a couple of pissed-up cops crash a private party and then start climbing all over private property, at least one Winnipeg judge believed they should expect a brutal beating.

As flamboyant as Stadnick was elsewhere, he was careful, even stealthy, in Ontario. His first moves were not unlike the Cotroni-Simard plan to gain a foothold in Toronto. But Stadnick didn't ask for Papalia's permission (and he wouldn't have gotten it, anyway). Instead he moved strippers—his pal Pup Stockford had a talent agency—mostly into remote Ontario communities. While the dancers themselves were not always dealing, they did do a very effective job of sorting out who was who as far as potential dealers and customers were, and also worked as mules, rotating back and forth from Montreal to various Ontario towns.

Emboldened, Stadnick used another method to get boots on the ground in Ontario. He started his own club in, of all places, Toronto. It was Papalia's territory to be sure, but by 1994, Johnny Pops wasn't what he used to be. Not only was he old, and, according to many, suffering from the early signs of dementia, but he had lost a great deal of power in the area because of his abrasive personality, the increasing weakness of the Magaddinos and his own group through arrests and deaths, and the emergence of many other criminal groups. His grip on Toronto was becoming increasingly weak as his family—by then effectively headed by Niagara Falls–based underboss Carmen Barillaro—concentrated its efforts on border crossings and became increasingly dependent on the Outlaws as dealers and muscle.

Toronto—despite its size and the amount of commerce that goes through it—had never really had a dominant Mafia family while Papalia held sway. Under his not-always-watchful eye, seven major 'Ndrangheta families—Coluccio, Tavernese, DeMaria, Figliomeni, Ruso, Commisso and Racco—operated in the city, with none of them really distinguishing themselves above the others and none of them ever seriously encroaching on Cosa Nostra operations.

Toronto did have one "star" mafioso in Paul "the Fox" Volpe, but he had a bad habit of making important people very angry. He never endeared himself to the Magaddinos, he cheated the Commissos on real-estate deals, he owed money to the Philadelphia mob and to the notorious Duvalier family of Haiti, but, more important, he appeared on a CBC documentary that reported all of those details and on which he all but admitted he was a Mafia bigwig, even pointing out that "you got to get rid of" informants.

It was too much. On November 14, 1983, an innocent bystander called the cops about a BMW parked at the Toronto airport with blood leaking from its trunk. Police found Volpe inside, shot in the back of the head. Although the Commissos had once hired a biker named Cecil Kirby to take Volpe out (Kirby backed out and turned informant), most people actually believe that he was killed on Papalia's orders.

By 1994, Papalia wasn't ordering anything other than his lunch. Toronto wasn't quite an open city for criminals the way Las Vegas has always been, but there was more than enough room for anyone bold enough to make a name for themselves.

There was a much-ballyhooed alliance of bikers dedicated to keeping the Hells Angels out of Ontario, but, aside from the Outlaws, they had lost a lot of their will to fight. In fact, some—like the Kitchener Satan's Choice—had become friends and clients of his on the sly.

So when Stadnick started a club in Toronto, there was little to stop him. It would have worked too, but for his choice of leader and manpower. For a leader, he settled on Dany Kane.

Just a few years removed from being a skinny kid working in a thread factory, Kane was a steroid-enhanced tough who trafficked drugs and firearms, had been to prison for torturing a thief and had blown up a Rock Machine–aligned bar. He'd been a full-patch member of the Condors, a South Shore puppet club. When a command decision from Sorel ordered the Evil Ones to absorb the Condors, Kane was offered a full-patch Evil Ones membership but instead asked to join the Hells Angels as a prospect.

Wolf Carroll sponsored him, and took a strong liking to the capable young soldier. Eventually, he introduced him to Stadnick, who found his experiences as a dealer and an enforcer to be ideal prerequisites for promotion. Stadnick's big mistake was to put the Toronto club in Kane's hands, after outlining the general idea. Immature, vain and secretive, Kane would later become the Montreal Hells Angels' worst headache.

On January 29, 1994, Kane unveiled the gang—the Demon Keepers, which he named after his own initials—and its patch. Kane fancied himself something of a graphic designer, and his logo featured a chain ring with crossed assault rifles, which were superimposed by the scowling face of what appears to me to be Bela Lugosi as Dracula.

Many of Kane's other strategic decisions were also questionable. Rather than recruiting at least one guy who spoke English or had any familiarity with Ontario at all, Kane drew the Demon Keepers from an array of South Shore tough guys, some of whom had already been discarded by the Evil Ones.

When they got to Toronto, they immediately set up shop in a

luxury high-rise near the corner of Yonge and Eglinton. It was an indefensible location; parking was limited, it was impossible to set up surveillance equipment and its proximity to neighbors and its paper-thin walls made the Demon Keepers' members and guests highly visible and their conversations almost public. At least they were in French.

Stadnick's plan was for the Demon Keepers to visit bars in Toronto and other Canadian cities (not Hamilton) and offer cocaine, hashish and meth at lower prices than the competition. But even on the rare occasions that the dullards under Kane's command could communicate their plan to likely customers, their crude tactics did not inspire confidence. Not a single sale was made.

However, the Toronto police—tipped off by the RCMP and Sûreté du Québec as to the Demon Keepers' identity, location, vehicles and travel patterns—followed them constantly and arrested or ticketed them for any tiny infraction they could. Since many of them had warrants or at least previous records, the cops gave them a choice: Leave Ontario and we won't prosecute. Quickly, 11 of the 18 original members took them up on it.

The ax finally fell on the ill-fated gang when a car with Kane and two other members was stopped and searched by the Ontario Provincial Police just off the 401 in Belleville on April 1, 1994. They found two handguns (one had been reported as stolen), a rifle, ammunition, gloves with lead sewn into the fingers (for use as brass knuckles), Demon Keepers jackets and paraphernalia and a gram of hashish. Since one of the men, Michel Scheffer, had no criminal record, and another, Denis Cournoyer, was an accomplished meth cook, it was decided that the Demon Keepers would be folded and that Kane should take the rap, he later told the RCMP. Scheffer was released and Cournoyer fined. Kane spent only four months behind bars, but this prison stint would change his life and have a profound effect on the Hells Angels.

While Stadnick was exporting the Hells Angels' ways (and drugs) westward, Boucher and the other Sorel members had plenty to take care of at home. The feud with the Alliance had evolved into an all-out war. It started, according to my police and biker sources, in August 1994 when Robert "Ti-Maigre" Richard, the Hells Angels new national president, dropped a letter off at Rock Machine headquarters asking them to stop referring to themselves as a motorcycle club.

In the post-Cazzetta era, they had done exactly that, realizing that the legal protections available to them far outweighed the fact that few of them had anything more than a passing interest in motorcycles, let alone owned one.

Ignored, the Hells Angels unleashed their war machine. Their first major hit crippled the opposition. In Repentigny, on the morning of October 28, 1994—nine days after a Hells Angels–associated dealer named Maurice Lavoie was shot dead just blocks away—Sylvain Pelletier got into his brand-new Jeep Cherokee. His girlfriend, seven months pregnant at the time, had just stepped out of the car to get something she had forgotten when Sylvain turned the key. That ignited a firebomb that engulfed the car in flames and tore the guy in the driver's seat to shreds. He wasn't just any guy, he was the undisputed leader of the Pelletier gang, the largest drug-dealing network in Montreal that was not affiliated with the Hells Angels.

With Sylvain out of the picture, leadership of the Pelletiers defaulted to his brother Harold. Although an assassin by trade, Harold was horrified by his brother's murder and was unable to lead the gang effectively. In October 1995, he called it quits and approached the Sûreté du Québec for some level of immunity in exchange for information.

Harold admitted to 17 murders between offing dealer Michel Beaulieu in 1983 when his debts to the Pelletiers grew unmanageable until his arrest in 1995. In exchange for naming names and essentially destroying the family business, Harold was given a light sentence, $140 a month in prison and $450 a week afterward. Not the $20,000 a week he was making as a hit man, but certainly enough to get by on.

One of the people he was tasked with killing, but never did, was Mom Boucher. Harold was actually just one would-be assassin in a long line of them. Boucher, who courted media coverage in much the same way Stadnick avoided it, was Public Enemy Number One for a number of groups.

The killing of rival bikers had become commonplace in many Quebec communities. There were some places where it was greeted with outrage, particularly in Quebec City and its suburbs, but in Montreal the frequent shootings and firebombings were greeted with an almost blasé attitude, as long as it was only drug dealers killing other drug dealers. Keep in mind that it was a city that had seen almost uninterrupted gang wars—though never before quite this intense—for more than 20 years.

In the midst of the fighting, both sides went on something of a recruiting drive. One of the most prized recruits was a tough guy named Scott Steinert. Born in Wisconsin, he had come to Montreal at age eight, when his father was transferred by the paper company he worked for. Big, strong and armed with the power of persuasion, Steinert was quickly gathering a great deal of support among the Hells Angels. Richard, the new president, sponsored him as a prospect, but his impulsive, aggressive ways did not endear him to everyone.

Steinert's power as an earner could not be discounted. The owner of three stripper agencies and an escort service, Steinert brought a lot of money into the club. He was also proving very valuable as a bomb-maker for the war against the Alliance.

One of the people drawn to him was Kane. But he wasn't the same Kane whom Stadnick had anointed as leader of the Demon

Keepers. Already psychologically fragile, the steroid-addled Kane had two epiphanies while he was in the Quinte Detention Centre. The first was that he was bisexual. A tryst with another inmate led Kane to realize he was attracted to other men and really wanted to act on it. In the milieu Kane found himself in, that could have resulted in a death sentence, so he was forced to start a secret life.

Actually, two secret lives. While behind bars, he came to the conclusion that the Demon Keepers' failure could not have been his fault. The blame had to lay elsewhere. As he contemplated the question over and over again, Kane came up with the only answer. Stadnick—for reasons unknown, unexplained and, to Kane, immaterial—had set him up to fail. Although it didn't really add up, it made sense to Kane and prompted him to act. While still in jail, he agreed to work as an undercover agent for the RCMP, reporting everything he knew and would learn in exchange for cash.

But none of the Hells Angels knew that. When Kane was released, he returned to Sorel. Reactions were mixed, but generally positive. Stadnick, overwhelmed with work, had little to say to him, aside from assuring him he did not blame him for the Toronto disaster. Carroll, his original sponsor, was little help. Despite his prestigious status as a member of the Nomads, he had a drinking problem and frequently cried poor when called upon for dues or contributions to parties or business ideas. Richard, the new president, didn't have any interest in him.

Boucher, also busy, was distant. On one occasion, he was with Kane and two other young wannabes when he spoke with a man in a black Mustang. After he finished, he told them "that's my pig," explaining that the driver was a police officer on his payroll. While there is no doubt that the Hells Angels paid off at least a few cops, the Mustang guy actually turned out to be a ruse. Boucher was checking their reactions in an effort to determine if any of them were informants. It didn't work; he didn't catch Kane.

The one Hells Angel who did really like Kane was Steinert. While still a prospect, Steinert had become one of the biggest earners in the club. In fact, when Michael "l'Animal" Lajoie-Smith went to jail for firebombing Le Gascon, a Rock Machine–associated strip club, Steinert took over as godfather of the Evil Ones, a very lucrative position. He told Kane that he was wasting his time in Sorel, that the way to get ahead was to go to Laval and join the Rockers.

The Rockers were a club like no other. While other puppet clubs replicated the Hells Angels' activities in far-flung territories, the Rockers had more specific tasks. The Hells Angels had plenty of dealers in Montreal, but what they needed was muscle. The Rockers supplied it. By the time the war against the Rock Machine was in full swing, the Rockers had divided into two distinct groups: the baseball team, which used baseball bats and other usually-not-lethal weapons for assault and intimidation, and the football team, which used guns and firebombs to kill.

The makeup of the Rockers didn't resemble that of the Hells Angels either. Although founded by ex-SS member Mom Boucher—and featuring his son, Francis, who had hosted Aryan Fest 1992, a celebration of neo-Nazi ideals—the Rockers had a black member. Somewhere along the line, Mom Boucher met and began to work with Gregory "Picasso" Wooley, who was a big player in a street gang named Master B. Boucher grew to like, respect and even trust Wooley. While Boucher and his well-documented racism might have warmed up to Wooley, Hells Angels bylaws forbade him from becoming a member. Boucher sidestepped that by making him a member of the Rockers. He appears to have been right about Wooley, who became a very big earner (he became wealthier, in fact, than many Hells Angels and several Nomads), an enthusiastic intimidator and a loyal member who never informed on anyone.

Kane did join the Rockers, even though he knew it meant trafficking, assault or murder. Because that's what the Rockers did.

While Kane was getting away with his double-double life, other problems were gripping the Hells Angels. The war against the Rock Machine was not going as easily as many thought it would. Casualties were mounting on both sides, and the resistance to the Hells Angels was not appearing to get any weaker no matter how many on either side were killed.

At the end of March 1995, one of their big weapons started to unravel. A small-time dealer named Michel "Pit" Caron was arrested and quickly made a deal. He gave up Serge Quesnel, one of the Hells Angels' most prolific hit men, whom he had once helped out on a job. After he was arrested on April 1, facing the rap for at least four first-degree murder charges, Quesnel gave up everyone he knew in the Trois-Rivières chapter to the SQ in exchange for a chance at parole after 12 years and $390,000 in cash as a paid police informant. The Hells Angels were hurt more by the loss of an effective hit man than they were by his testimony. Although he was trotted out in case after case, Quesnel's recollections did little to damage the club, because judges and juries found him unreliable.

That was nothing, however, compared to the blow that hit them that summer. During the war against the Rock Machine, firebombings were commonplace. Since ineffective ones left useful evidence behind, it became standard operating procedure to take credit only for the successful jobs and keep the others quiet.

A little after noon on August 9, 1995, a Jeep Wrangler containing drug dealers Jean Côte and Marc Dubé exploded on a busy Montreal downtown corner, sending a shower of body parts and pieces of the car into the area. The targeted men in the car were killed, and a cylindrical chunk of metal shot from the blast and embedded itself into the skull of an 11-year-old boy playing with his friend nearby. Daniel Desrochers died in a nearby hospital a few days later.

Any sympathy—or even ambivalence—the bikers had among the community disappeared as news of the boy's death spread. That meant more cops, more informants and a greater chance of winding up behind bars.

More important, the incident caused dissension within the ranks of the bikers. While the Montreal Hells Angels may have included pimps, extortionists, drug traffickers and cold-blooded killers in their ranks, they could not abide the killing of innocent children. At first, many believed the Rock Machine was behind the bomb because Côte and Dubé were affiliated with the Hells Angels. That hope quickly dissipated as it was learned that both men were in debt to the club. When it was also learned that the bomb had a remote timer that meant the person responsible for triggering it must have also seen the children, tensions and suspicions flared.

Fingers were pointed in every direction, but no one received as much suspicion as Steinert. Not only was he a master bomb-maker, but his normally loud and ebullient manner changed to sullen and near silent after Desrochers died.

He had made some enemies within the club who would be more than happy to see him go down. Steinert earned an incredible amount of money from his sex-trade businesses and even more as godfather of the Wild Ones, and he was not afraid to show it off. He rather audaciously purchased the infamous Lavigueur Mansion on Laval's Île aux Pruches and was well known for using it as a set for porn films, in which he sometimes participated.

Nobody had more reason to hate him than Stadnick. Steinert had no problem stepping all over Stadnick's territory, and he was hardly quiet about it. A fluent English speaker, Steinert was cultivating his own network in Ontario and Winnipeg. He even bragged that he was planning on establishing his own gang, in Belleville, Ontario—the same town where Kane had been arrested, dooming the Demon Keepers—since he was due to become a full-patch, sponsored by Richard, soon. That must have enraged the proud Stadnick.

Also, he stole Stadnick's aide-de-camp, Magnussen. The tall English speaker now ran drugs westward for Steinert, not Stadnick. In fact, they had become so close that Magnussen actually lived in the guesthouse on Steinert's compound.

The point of no return happened in May 1996. Stadnick knew that there was no way to get to Canada's west without passing through Winnipeg, so he worked long and hard to win over the bikers in the Peg. For years, he had wooed the two major clubs there—Los Brovos and the Spartans—and had even started a small club of his own. After years of deliberation, he had decided on Los Brovos to become the Prairie provinces' first Hells Angels chapter.

It was more than just a formality. While the leadership was all for the patch-over, not everyone in the club was so gung ho. They knew that the Hells Angels in Quebec were fighting a bloody war against the Rock Machine and others, and that, after Desrochers was killed, they looked like villains. Some members voiced fears that they would be recruited for the war. Or that it would spread west.

Those suspicions turned to accusations that spring. Just days after Stadnick had told Los Brovos president Ernie Dew that the club had earned their Hells Angels' prospective status, Mike McRea, Carroll's replacement as president of the Halifax chapter, invited much-respected former Los Brovos president David Boyko out east for a party. He was reluctant to go, but McRea insisted.

Magnussen burst into the party and grabbed Boyko, screaming that he owed him money. The big man was turfed, but the next day Boyko's body was found in nearby Dartmouth.

Back in Montreal, the subject of what to do with Magnussen, who many thought was an undercover cop, became something of a hot potato. According to Kane's reports to the RCMP, Carroll offered to kill him. Since Boyko's murder occurred had in his territory, he had some responsibility. But he wasn't up for it.

Instead, Boucher selected his personal driver/bodyguard, André "Toots" Tousignant, for the job. After a few weeks went by, Tousignant had proven too busy for the job, so it was offered—it wasn't clear by whom—to Kane for $10,000.

Kane desperately did not want to kill Magnussen, whom he considered a friend, and told the RCMP as much. Then two things happened that moved the hit up the Nomads' agenda. First, they learned that Magnussen had been nominated as a prospect for the Sorel chapter, and then they found out that he had gotten into a bar fight and had beaten the crap out of the wrong person—Vito Rizzuto's son Leonardo.

Steinert, meanwhile, had his own problems. While in jail on a weapons charge, Boucher was taunted by a Sûreté du Québec officer who told him there was a top-level rat in his inner circle. Boucher, with plenty of time to think, narrowed the number of candidates to six. One of them was Kane, another was Steinert.

The Nomads relieved Kane of his responsibility to kill Magnussen. After his release, Boucher said that it would be bad for morale if a Rockers prospect were to kill someone so close to so many in the Montreal chapter. Now that Steinert was on the Hells Angels' death row, there was no way such a low-level functionary (and potential rat) as Kane could take down a full-patch member like Steinert. Instead, Kane said, he nominated Stadnick for the job. It made sense: Magnussen had turned his back on him for Steinert, and the Boyko murder had endangered his plan of westward expansion.

Not long after, the bodies of both Steinert and Magnussen were recovered from the St. Lawrence. While no charges were ever laid, it's probably significant that the two were beaten to death with hammers, well known in the underworld to be the trademark of the city of Hamilton.

They were not the only Hells Angels with prices on their heads. Acting on a tip, on May 16, 1997, police arrested Gilles Lambert, Yvon Roy, Martin Simard, Serge Boutin, René Pelletier, Martin Pellerin, Bruno Lévesque, Hubert Lanteigne, Richard Lariviere and Jean-René Dufresne—all Rock Machine members or associates—for plotting to assassinate Boucher. After their convictions, Lambert claimed that their reasoning was that if they killed Boucher, less bellicose Hells Angels would take over, and the two clubs could negotiate some kind of peace, or at least divide up Montreal.

Less than a week later, Rock Machine Quebec City chapter president Claude "Ti-Loup" Vézina was dragged out his bed after police lured his guard dogs into a cube van. He and second-in-command Dany "le Gros" Légaré were charged with trafficking after an undercover RCMP officer negotiated seven separate drug deals with the two. As well as a PCP lab and $1.5 million worth of several types of drugs, police seized a small arsenal consisting of 325 kilograms of explosives, detonators, seven handguns, two submachine guns, three assault rifles and a silencer. Both Vézina and Légaré were convicted of trafficking.

While the Hells Angels were engaged in an all-out war with the Rock Machine, they were also neck deep in internal problems. People needed to be murdered, rats were in their midst and police were making mass arrests. While both Stadnick and Boucher were capable leaders, they were becoming overwhelmed by the ambitions they had established for themselves and their gang.

CHAPTER 10

ENTER A NEW PLAYER

It was clear that the Rock Machine were not just losing the war, they were losing their leadership. That prompted a move that profoundly changed the war in Quebec and the cold war in the rest of Canada. Traditionally, organized crime in Canada works in a sort of equilibrium until someone upsets the apple cart. First it was the Calabrian faction of the Cosa Nostra, which brought the French Connection and heroin to Canada. Then they were usurped by the Sicilian faction of the Cosa Nostra, fueled by cocaine. They empowered the Hells Angels to claim Canada as their own, and that's when the shooting and firebombings started. That's because while the Sicilians and their friends in the Hells Angels may try to corner the market on illegal drugs and vice in Canada, there's always someone who won't play ball. Over the years, that has meant groups like the Rock Machine, the Dark Circle, the West End Gang, the Pelletier Clan, the Dubois brothers, various 'Ndrangheta families, the Outlaws and many others. But in the summer of 1997, another international player was added to the mix.

The Bandidos were formed in Eastern Texas in 1966. Over the years, they had grown into the Hells Angels' number-one rivals—displacing the Outlaws—and dominated much of Texas and the southwestern states. Much less xenophobic than the Hells Angels or Outlaws, they had accepted many Hispanic members and established chapters in many Western European nations, quickly making great sums of money and recruiting lots of manpower very quickly.

Aware of this, new Rock Machine Quebec City president Frédéric Faucher and new Montreal president Johnny Plescio reached out to the Bandidos. The club's top people in Texas were not that interested, but the Europeans were. The two of them, along with Tout Tout Léger, headed to Sweden to attend the Bandidos' pan-European Helsingborg run on June 18, 1997, but were turned back by Swedish authorities who were aware of their criminal records. About a month later, Faucher and Plescio (this time with mammoth Paul "Sasquatch" Porter instead of Léger) managed to meet with the Bandidos European brass at a bike show in Luxembourg. Together, they agreed in principle to have the Rock Machine patch over to the Bandidos.

That was of little import to either Boucher or Stadnick, both of whom had bigger plans and other things on their minds. Boucher, who greatly admired the cartels of Colombia, decided to use one of their tactics. After having come to the conclusion that law enforcement was a much bigger threat to his empire than the Rock Machine or any other competitive organization, he had come up with a plan to intimidate the authorities. He decided to kill or threaten every cop, prosecutor, judge or anyone else who stood in their way. He began with the ones he hated the most, prison guards. It made sense to him to start there. A great deal of business, recruiting and score settling among bikers in Canada is done behind bars, and the more corrections officers look the other way, the more effective it is.

Under orders from an impatient Boucher, Rockers hanga-round Stéphane "Godasse" Gagné and the man he reported to, Toots Tousignant, waited just outside the parking lot of Bordeaux Prison on June 26, 1997. Both men had stayed in the prison before, and Gagné had earned his stripes inside by fighting constantly with Rock Machine members and associates after he refused to deface a photo they had of Boucher or renounce his loyalty to the Hells Angels.

At Bordeaux, their job was to kill the first guard they could. Tousignant hatched a plan in which the pair would be on a stolen Suzuki Katana (a very un-Harley-like motorcycle) and shoot the guard on the Pont Viau bridge, then speed off into Laval, dump the bike in a mall parking lot and get away in a car they had waiting. It would be almost impossible for the cops to catch them.

They followed one guard driving a battered Jeep Cherokee, but when he turned away from the bridge, they turned around. When they arrived back at Bordeaux, they saw a white minivan pull out of the lot. They followed it onto Pont Viau, came up even with it, and Gagné shot the driver several times before Tousignant twisted the accelerator and sped away. The white minivan, its driver dead, came to a stop on the shoulder after it rolled to a stop.

Much to Boucher's amusement, the victim was a woman, prison guard Diane Lavigne. Toots was made a Nomads prospect, and Gagné was made a Rockers prospect.

Boucher then planned a second prison-guard hit, this time at Rivière-des-Prairies, and with Paul "Fon Fon" Fontaine—Toots Tousignant's right-hand man and the son of a Dubois brothers enforcer—to go along with triggerman Gagné. On their first attempt, Fontaine told Gagné, "Killing a Rock Machine—that does not bother me, they are our enemies," before pointing out he had no grudge against the guards and reminding Gagné that killing a prison guard meant a 25-year sentence without parole. With that, he aborted the mission, telling Gagné that the escape route had not been properly thought out.

Boucher wouldn't have it. He told Fontaine that not only was he going to have to go through with the job, he was also now the triggerman.

On September 8, 1997, the two flagged down a prison bus that was empty except for its driver and another prison guard. Once it stopped, the pair blasted it with gunshots, killing driver Pierre Rondeau, but completely missing passenger Robert Corriveau. The two men fled in a minivan, which they abandoned in a parking lot after setting it on fire, and made their getaway in a tiny Mazda.

Once they had gotten back to Boucher, Fontaine was told he was a Nomads prospect but that he had to stand guard at the bedside of Mélou Roy. The Trois-Rivières boss—who had been one of several important Hells Angels suspects to walk after a series of juries and judges found Serge Quesnel to be an unreliable witness—had been shot four times while visiting his father in Jonquière. The primary suspect was Rock Machine heavy-hitter Faucher.

Gagné, who now had his hand in two killings, was handed $5,000 and told to take his wife and son on vacation. They chose Boucher's favorite spot, the Dominican Republic. When he returned, Boucher (who was dealing with both Montreal Mafia factions) gave Gagné another job—spying on the Cotronis.

Just as things were looking up for the young killer, Gagné was arrested. On December 4, 1997, Steve Boies was arrested for trafficking and gave Gagné up immediately in exchange for having his trafficking charges dropped. In fact, he attempted to collect the $100,000 reward posted for information regarding the identity of the prison-guard murderer or murderers. They cops wouldn't go for it, and he was convicted of trafficking.

When Gagné was picked up, he too started negotiating immediately. He knew he wouldn't get the reward, but he wanted at least the same deal Quesnel got. The cops agreed. He was convicted of murder but agreed to talk.

Not long afterward, Boucher was picked up after a throat cancer treatment at Notre Dame Hospital. He was charged with two counts of first-degree murder and conspiracy. Having prepared for this day for a very long time, the cops took Boucher to a specially designed maximum-security cell located within Tanguay prison for women. He was not given bail.

Warrants were issued for Tousignant and Fontaine, but neither could be found. Both turned up eventually. Tousignant's charred remains were found by a guy walking his dog. The corpse was so badly burned that its sex could not be determined upon first examination. Later, investigators not only identified it as Tousignant, but figured out that he had been shot in the head and chest before he was set aflame. It's not coincidental that Boucher was not sure he wasn't a rat.

It took longer to track down Fontaine. Living under the pseudonym Jean Goyer—complete with a birth certificate taken from a child who died in 1956 and an Alberta driver's license—he managed to get by with support from several high-placed Hells Angels. Until May 27, 2004, that is. A passing Quebec City cop named Gaston Thomas just happened to recognize him on a street corner. "It was outside a parking lot of a duplex on Rue Bélanger in Quebec City. He was accompanied by a lady named Manon Pruneau," Thomas said in a press release that was quoted in several newspapers. "I read him his rights and said: 'Paul Fontaine, you are accused of murder and attempted murder of prison guards.' Then he rode in the back of my police car toward the SQ headquarters in Montreal. It was 6:50 p.m." In February 2009, Fontaine was found guilty of the murder of Rondeau and the attempted murder of Corriveau.

Gagné didn't have much dirt on Stadnick. Well, at least nothing that could be used to make any arrests. But he did quote Stadnick's master plan—something far more important than Boucher's somewhat ridiculous plan to terrorize the state into backing down. He told police that Stadnick wanted to see "just one patch all across Canada." His plan was to spread the Hells Angels' dominance and doctrine from coast to coast—one gang to control everything, operating above the law and without any competition.

While all the craziness was going down in Montreal, he was actually succeeding. On July 23, 1997, he threw a huge party in Alberta to announce that two chapters of the Grim Reapers had been patched over as Hells Angels Edmonton and Hells Angels Calgary. The Rebels—a Calgary-based club that almost went to war with the Grim Reapers—were made a prospective chapter, contingent on relocation, and another club, the King's Crew, became a puppet club holding down the Hells Angels' interests in Red Deer. As would become commonplace when the Hells Angels moved into town, police found a few dead dealers—those who wouldn't cooperate with the area's new overlords—before everything settled down.

On October 18, 1997—Los Brovos' 30th anniversary—the Stadnick-led Hells Angels rolled into Winnipeg's Elmwood district to party. At the end of the party, Los Brovos were no more. Their members now wore the winged skull on their backs with rockers that read HELLS ANGELS and MANITOBA.

Embittered, Spartans president Darwin Sylvester reached out to the Rock Machine. His plan died when he went missing—the long-running rumor is that he was shot then fed to hogs on May 29, 1998. Still, the Rock Machine found an appreciation for the Gateway City and would continue to be interested in expanding there.

Stadnick's westward expansion had taken hold. Just a few years removed from hand-delivering drugs with Magnussen, he now was the godfather of three new chapters and a number of puppet gangs to do his bidding out there. The territory between

Ontario and British Columbia was essentially his with the only opposition coming from a few disorganized, mainly First Nations, street gangs and law enforcement, which had never faced serious organized crime before.

As huge a success as taking over the Prairie provinces was, it paled next to the real prize. Not only is their combined population significantly less than half of Ontario's, they don't even begin to approach the drug-buying market in the Toronto area all by itself. While Stadnick was winning the West, something happened in the middle part of Canada that would change organized crime in the country forever.

One of the 'Ndrangheta families that had worked under Papalia's Cosa Nostra in Hamilton for decades were the Musitanos. More patchwork low-level crooks and thugs than organized unit, the crew originated in 1937 when Angelo "the Beast" Musitano fled to Hamilton from his small Calabrian hometown after murdering his sister. Leadership later transferred to Angelo's nephew Dominic Musitano, a bitter and belligerent man who resented operating under Papalia but who knew enough to keep quiet about it. Unlike the big man, he had no problem working with bikers, including the Outlaws.

In 1985, he had a severe heart attack that reduced his ability to lead the 'ndrina, and in 1991, he died after a stroke. His brother, Antonio, was deemed unfit to be a boss, so leadership fell to Dominic's sons, Angelo and Pasquale "Fat Pat" Musitano.

They represented a new kind of gangster, ones who had grown up watching *The Godfather*, *Goodfellas* and, sadly (because it is so roughly hewn and cartoonish), *Scarface*. They were loud and flashy, largely ignorant of the old customs that had kept the Mafia so strong for so many years.

They had tired of kowtowing to doddering old Johnny Pops, so they decided to do something about it. They knew a guy, Ken

Murdock, who could help. Their father's old driver, Murdock had three strong qualifications for the job they had in mind: He mistakenly believed himself to be part of the family, he was a coke addict who could easily be convinced to do just about anything for a bag and, finally, he had killed before. While there's a huge difference between knocking off some laid-off steelworker who'd gotten behind in his gambling debts and assassinating Ontario's godfather, Murdock took the job for $10,000 and a bag of cocaine.

In fact, Murdock told police that the Musitanos gave him a list of four targets. Papalia was at the top of the list. On May 31, 1997, while Johnny was walking from his condo to his center of operations on Railway Street two blocks away, Murdock ran up behind him, shoved his handgun into the back of the old man's head and pulled the trigger. He ran away, leaving the big boss lying face down in a growing pool of his own blood.

It was an incredible affront. Nobody in Buffalo had given the Musitanos the go-ahead to kill the old man. Since Murdock shot him in the back of the head, it prevented Johnny from making peace with his God and from having an open-casket funeral. Those sorts of violations would have led to a war only a few years earlier.

In fact, they might have done so in 1997, but Murdock also killed the second man on his list, Carmen Barillaro, who was the real power behind Papalia's crew anyway, on July 22. Without its leaders, the Cosa Nostra was paralyzed.

The third name on the list was Ion "Johnny K-9" Croitoru, a former professional wrestler and small-time crook who had reestablished a Satan's Choice chapter in the city. Murdock, friends with Johnny K-9, went to the big man's door and told him about the list. Croitoru thanked him, and Murdock left.

The fourth name on the list was, I have been told by several reliable sources, Outlaws president Mario "the Wop" Parente. But Murdock had given up by then.

The Musitanos paid him just $2,000.

Unable to stay out of trouble, Murdock was arrested for extortion in the autumn of 1998. He was, as usual, prepared to keep his mouth shut, until the police played him a recording of Fat Pat and Ang laughing at him, calling him, according to the evidence put forth by the Crown at their trial, a "low-life" and casually plotting to have him killed. Finally realizing that his years of unquestioning loyalty to the Musitano family had been profoundly misspent, in exchange for a 13-year sentence and a changed identity, Murdock told the cops everything.

The Musitanos then started negotiating. If the cops would drop all other charges, they would plead guilty to the one they would have the hardest time fighting. They each received a 10-year sentence for conspiring to kill Barillaro.

With the Mafia out of the picture, there was little to stop Stadnick from swooping in and taking over Ontario in the same way he had the Prairies.

While the Mafia was self-immolating in Hamilton, they were still fighting it out on the streets of Montreal. In the summer of 1998, Frank and Francesco Jr. were both behind bars, leaving the family in the hands of Paolo "Paul" Cotroni, the second-oldest of Frank's five sons. More than any other Cotroni, Paolo was involved with the Hells Angels, Rockers and Death Riders.

On August 23, just as he was arriving home after having had dinner at his younger brother Jimmy's house, two men burst from behind the hedges and shot him six times as he was still halfway in his car. A neighbor saw what happened and, unbelievably, chased the two men. He watched as the pair of assassins rounded a corner then hopped into the back of an already-running car before speeding off.

Paolo was rushed to Sacré-Coeur hospital but was too far gone. His family took him off life support two days later. Just before his funeral was to begin, a Connecticut-based mafioso named Vincent Melia was shot in the face in Montreal's Ital bar. He was said to have close ties with the Rizzutos. He survived.

Although Paolo's assassination and a May 20, 1998, mass arrest of 26 Death Riders and their associates may have appeared to help the Rock Machine's cause, they were clearly still losing the war. Founding member Richard "Bam Bam" Lagacé was gunned down on July 30. Another Rock Machine heavy-hitter, Peter "Buddy" Paradis, was shot on August 19. He survived but was badly injured, and his extensive Verdun drug network was slowed down to the point that some of his dealers switched sides. He was arrested the following month, along with full-patch Daniel Leclerc, on trafficking and weapons charges. Both were convicted. Even more crippling was a raid of a Rock Machine dinner meeting at a posh downtown hotel on October 28. Of the 25 men arrested, many took the police up on their offer to release them the following day on the condition that they no longer associate or communicate with known Rock Machine members or associates.

Worse was still to come. On September 8, 1998, two men snuck into the backyard of Johnny Plescio's Laval home. One stood on a lawn chair, peeking into Plescio's living room as the Rock Machine president watched television. His accomplice then cut the cable wire. When Plescio stood up to see what was the matter with the TV, the gunmen pulled out their Cobray submachine guns and shot at him 27 times. Sixteen of those shots actually entered his body, killing him instantly. His younger brother, Tony, was shot to death in a McDonald's parking lot in front of his wife and baby less than a year later.

With so many of the leadership of the Rock Machine dead or sidelined by injury or arrest, the club fell more and more under the sway of Faucher. His desperation to have the Rock Machine patch over to the Bandidos became even more urgent.

Although severely crippled, the Rock Machine still had some bite. Nomads and Death Riders godfather Biff Hamel was taking his wife and son to a pediatrician in Laval on April 17, 2000. After he dropped them off and was walking toward his car in the parking lot, he noticed two masked men following him. He broke into a sprint but couldn't outrun their bullets. Hamel was the 135th victim of the Quebec Biker War and the highest-ranking Hells Angel to die.

His death prompted a move that was actually overdue. The Death Riders were reorganized as the Rockers North chapter and relocated to Blainville, at the foot of the Laurentians. Under the auspices of Montreal Hells Angels Stéphane "Fesses" Plouffe and Benoit Frenette, their territory would include the North Shore and the Laurentian ski resorts, which had formerly been serviced by the increasingly ineffective Wolf Carroll.

After Papalia and Barillaro were killed and the Musitanos went to prison, Stadnick came to Ontario meaning business. Although short on free time—he had already anointed yet another new chapter in Saskatoon on September 18, 1998—he made it a point to meet with and interview almost every notable biker in Ontario. Sometimes renting entire hotels, Stadnick interviewed many non-aligned clubs as units, and members of avowedly anti–Hells Angels clubs, like the Outlaws, individually.

As word spread, many of the 1%ers who did not agree with the way Stadnick and the Hells Angels went about their business, or had been rejected or snubbed by him, were approached by the Rock Machine. Somehow, they managed to set up three chapters in Ontario—in Kingston, Toronto and London (although the London chapter never completely materialized). I have been told that expansion to Ontario was a prerequisite to the Rock Machine becoming Bandidos. In fact, although they kept the eagle's head logo, their patch changed from black and silver to the Bandidos' red and gold.

Their three shaky chapters didn't slow Stadnick down a bit. If anything, they gave him more incentive to take over Ontario. He offered Hells Angels patches—something that had been hard-won in the past—in exchange for almost any other patch in the province. He even extended the offer to certain individual members of the Outlaws and the new Rock Machine.

It all came down in Sorel on December 29, 2000. Cops watching the place were shocked to see Harleys with license plates from British Columbia, Alberta, Saskatchewan, Manitoba and Nova Scotia. They were even more shocked to see no fewer than 168 from Ontario, their riders wearing such divergent patches as Satan's Choice, Para-Dice Riders and even a few sporting Charlie, the Outlaws' famous grinning skull, on their backs. The most notable guest was Paul "Sasquatch" Porter, a founding member of the Rock Machine who had survived at least three attempts by the Hells Angels to kill him. At the party's end, all of them were wearing Hells Angels patches, and there was a huge bonfire of old leather jackets and vests. Satan's Choice and Para-Dice Riders—two of Canada's oldest and most-established clubs—ceased to exist. Besides Edmonton, Calgary, Saskatoon and Winnipeg, Stadnick had created new chapters in Keswick, Kitchener, Oshawa, Simcoe County, downtown Toronto, east Toronto, north Toronto, west Toronto, Windsor and Woodbridge. He also created an Ontario Nomads chapter and within months would add new chapters in Niagara, Ottawa and Regina, Saskatchewan.

It was a wildly divergent group. Some were hardened drug traffickers and tough guy bikers, others were inexperienced but looking for a piece of the action and some were just drug dealers who actually had to be taught how to ride a Harley. But it didn't matter; Stadnick was now in charge of Ontario. There was no more Mafia to keep him out, and there was little the remains of the Outlaws and the tiny band of rejects who had called themselves the Ontario Rock Machine could do about it.

While Stadnick was on top of the world, however, his counterpart on the other side was not. Faucher, along with fellow full-patch Marcel "le Maire" Demers, was caught in an RCMP sting. Despite plea bargaining, Faucher received a 12-year sentence for trafficking. He was done. So, too, was the Rock Machine. On December 1, 2000—less than a week before Faucher's arrest—there was a huge party in Woodbridge at which the 45 men who still made up the Rock Machine handed in their eagle's head patches and exchanged them for Bandidos "fat Mexican" probationary patches. A longtime Bandido who had established their first Oklahoma chapter, Edward "Connecticut Ed" Winterhalder, was sent up to oversee the assimilation. Standing guard outside were the members of the Woodbridge-based Loners, who had not taken Stadnick up on his offer.

They picked as their president Alain Brunette, a young but commanding figure who had befriended many Bandidos in Europe as well as Winterhalder, one of the few Americans with any interest in the Canadian operation, who describes the events in his book, *The Assimiliation*. Brunette had earned his stripes working under Sasquatch Porter. But unlike Porter, when he saw things going south for the Rock Machine in Montreal, he didn't turn his back on the club and change sides. "They killed all my friends, my brother bikers," he told Benoît Roberge, a Montreal police investigator, according to Winterhalder. "And now they want me to change sides? I'm not a prostitute." Still, he did make it clear to the Hells Angels that he was interested in peaceful coexistence.

Twenty-three years, almost to the day, after the Hells Angels had arrived in Montreal, there were no major Canadian-based motorcycle clubs left. After several small wars and one big one, hundreds of dead bodies and tons of wheeling and dealing, there were three important clubs in Canada—the Hells Angels, the Outlaws and the Bandidos—and all of them answered to bosses south of the border.

After the change of colors and names, Winterhalder and the American Bandidos were surprised to learn that the club they had patched over was still on the losing side of a major war. Réal "Tin Tin" Dupont had been a South Shore drug dealer with links to the West End Gang. He had dominated the drug trade in Chambly and also organized the town's annual regatta. He was not a founding or very vocal member of the Rock Machine, but he was one of those drug dealers who refused to work with the Hells Angels and soon found himself a full-patch member. He was arrested for trafficking cocaine and hashish and on weapons charges. While the SQ were investigating him, they noted that he and his associates frequently met with the local police force (since amalgamated into la Régie intermunicipale de police Richelieu-Saint-Laurent), and that he bragged about "protection" and "privileged information." Still, he got only six months.

Not long after he got out, the police tagged him again. This time he was caught with $125 million in counterfeit cash. According to the indictment, he was selling $100 bills for 25 bucks from the back of a van in a shopping mall parking lot. It was the biggest counterfeiting bust in Canadian history, and it netted Dupont 98 months in the slammer.

He was released on parole in 2000 under the stipulations that he not wear his colors or associate with known members of the Rock Machine (which now applied to the Bandidos). Dupont did his best to lie low. So it was something of a surprise when he was shot while seated in his car on January 18, 2001, while parked outside of a store in Saint-Laurent's Quartier Bonaventure.

While the choice of victims left a few Canadians scratching their heads (Dupont's prison stints had robbed him of his status as top dog in Chambly), the Americans were literally shocked to find out they were suddenly at war with the Hells Angels in a predominantly French-speaking region more than 2,000 miles away from their headquarters in San Leon, Texas. Winterhalder was aghast. "Tin Tin was the first Canadian Bandido to die. For Bandidos worldwide, this was a very serious situation," he writes in *The Assimilation*. "We had anticipated that our arrival would keep the peace, not provoke more violence. The turf war with the Hells Angels was anything but over."

According to Winterhalder, the Americans couldn't understand what was going on in Canada. He claims—and it would be in his best interest to do so—that the Bandidos were intended to be a motorcycle enthusiast club, not a drug trafficking ring. He says he and his peers back in the US were shocked that the Canadian Bandidos were more interested in selling drugs and fighting the Hells Angels than they were in motorcycles and that he himself has not been convicted of a Bandidos-related crime. He called a meeting to explain that Bandidos were supposed to be bikers first and have real day jobs; they were not to be full-time gangsters.

He was talking to the wrong guys. The Rock Machine was never really a motorcycle club. Its members were nothing more than drug dealers who posed as motorcycle enthusiasts for legal reasons. Sure, some had bikes and a few members really took them seriously, but that's not why they were formed, nor why they stuck together, nor why they went to war with the Hells Angels.

When Winterhalder told the new Bandidos what their bosses expected of them, they packed up and left. At least, many of them did. The Toronto Bandidos chapter collapsed after ten of its members, including president Billy Miller, chose to join the Hells Angels Ottawa chapter, which was led by Sasquatch Porter, one of the few Rock Machine founders still alive.

Whether Americans liked it or not, the remaining Canadian Bandidos were still at war. That fact hit home on February 13, 2001, when Brunette and Bandido prospect William "Bill" Ferguson were driving through the snowy Laurentians. Ferguson noticed that a car appeared to be following them at a discreet distance. Brunette told him it was probably the cops, that it happened all the time and they had nothing to worry about. He was wrong. The car began to accelerate and when it came even with Brunette's white Pontiac Grand Am, the front and rear windows on the passenger side slid down and the guys inside started shooting. Brunette took a bullet to the gut but somehow had the presence of mind to steer his bullet-riddled car into oncoming traffic. That either scared off the would-be assassins or convinced them they had killed him.

The Hells Angels had no plan to slow down their pursuit of the old Rock Machine just because they had changed jackets. The Montreal cops were tipped off to a February 15, 2001, meeting at the Holiday Inn on Rue Sherbrooke in which the Hells Angels were going over war plans. Inside, they arrested Nomads full-patches Denis "Pas Fiable" Houle, Normand Robitaille, Trooper Mathieu, Dick Mayrand, Michel Rose, Nomads prospects Jean-Richard "Race" Larivière and Luc Bordeleau and Rocker full-patch Kenny Bédard for trafficking. Confiscated were pictures of several Bandidos—most notably Serge "Merlin" Cyr, who was acting as president of the Montreal chapter and whose 1997 plot to assassinate Boucher had been foiled when the truck he loaded with dynamite was towed away. All eight of the men had handguns on them. Making a deal to plead guilty to weapons charges in exchange for having conspiracy and gangsterism charges dropped, each of them was sentenced to a year in prison.

While that arrest did hamper the Nomads, it was nothing compared to what happened next. The Nomads' leadership made two critical mistakes—one was trusting the wrong person, the other was allowing someone to fall through the cracks.

The person they trusted was Kane. An RCMP agent since the days before Stadnick's grand westward expansion, Kane was by early 2000 a full-fledged Rocker. Like most Rockers, he earned his stripes in the war. After Kane was relieved of the task of killing Magnussen, the Nomads, in particular Wolf Carroll, had another job for him. Robert MacFarlane had been smart enough to open one of the first cell phone stores in Halifax, and it had made him rich. He also allegedly dealt cocaine, and that made him a lot richer. Like a lot of coke users and dealers, he felt he was above anyone else's rules and he had pissed off the Nomads by selling in their territory, often undercutting their prices. Carroll wanted him dead.

He recruited Kane. For $25,000, Kane agreed to fly to Halifax and make the hit, but on the condition that his best friend—Rockers prospect Aimé "Ace" Simard—be part of the operation. Carroll agreed but did not know that Kane and Simard were also secretly lovers. When the time came, the MacFarlane hit was a comedy of errors that included a misfiring gun and Simard's pants falling down, but the fat Haligonian did die—at Simard's hand. Kane fired four shots but intentionally missed every time.

The two were caught and eventually brought before a judge, who dismissed the case.

As Carroll's star began to wane, Kane found himself working more and more often for Norm Robitaille, mostly as a driver and bodyguard. It was one day when Kane was driving Robitaille, the most clean-cut of the Nomads, around that he was entrusted with his boss's briefcase. While Robitaille was busy, Kane spirited the briefcase to his police contact, who photocopied everything inside.

The cops had the Nomads' ledgers, which reflected millions in transactions, but the buyers and sellers and even the products were in code. They would never stand up in court.

That's when the second person, the one who fell through the cracks, came onto the stage. For decades, both sides of the Mafia, and others, relied on a wheeler-dealer from Candiac named Raymond Craig for some of their cocaine. Over the years, Craig—who had spent four years in Colombia and even married the daughter of a Bolivian drug lord—had made his own connections and had his own people. It had always been Craig's policy not to sell directly to bikers. He didn't trust them and liked the insulation provided by supplying the Mafia, who then sold to the bikers. "My husband did not want to work with the Hells Angels. He had never worked with them before and he never wanted to," his wife, the former Sandra Antelo, said, according to Crown attorney Madeleine Giauque. "My husband knew how these people worked. He said from the beginning they were not the kind of group he wanted to work with."

Sandra herself did not take his advice and began secretly supplying cocaine through her own connections to two Nomads, Michel Rose and André Chouinard (although, to her credit, Rose did not reveal his affiliation until after they had started doing business). It worked without a hitch for a couple of years, but in the spring of 2000, she supplied them with a 2,400-kilogram shipment, and they balked at the price. They argued, but could not reach a solution.

Sandra went to Raymond for help, coming clean with him. He then went to Mom Boucher to get his men to live up to their deal. Instead, Boucher, who had long resented Craig because he would not sell directly to him, said that now that Rose and Chouinard were in possession of the cocaine, it was up to them to decide what to pay Sandra.

Sandra, perhaps wiser for the experience, was driving down Autoroute 15 in June 2000, when a car came even with hers and a masked man in the passenger seat opened fire. Although her car was terribly shot up, she was hit with nothing worse than a few cubes of shattered safety glass.

That wasn't the end of it. On August 29, 2000, Raymond and Sandra Craig were coming home from dinner and drinks after Claude Faber's golf tournament in Saint-Adèle when their car was approached by a Suzuki Sidekick mini-SUV. Again, a masked man in the passenger seat opened fire, but this time, his aim was true. Well, sort of. Raymond was killed immediately, but Sandra again was unharmed. The murder sent shock waves through the drug trafficking community, among which Craig had many friends. According to *The Globe and Mail*, a "well-informed source" told the paper, "No one could have taken out a guy so close to the head of the family without having obtained permission."

As that was happening, the police were getting closer and closer to the Nomads. Kane had died—the official word is suicide, but many disagree—on August 9, 2000, but he had not only handed over Robitaille's ledgers, he had given them the name of one of his most important operatives, Nomads prospect Jean-Richard "Race" Larivière. Tailing him led to the discovery of what the cops called the "Nomads National Bank"—a treasure trove of cash and records in a high-rise apartment. Since it was still all in code, they didn't have enough evidence to arrest anyone other than Larivière. Rather than blow the operation by taking him in, the police decided to wait for a miracle.

It happened when Sandra Craig walked into the RCMP's Montreal headquarters on January 24, 2001. Mourning her husband and fearing for her life, she agreed to talk in exchange for immunity. After several discussions, she was given the ledgers and asked if she recognized any of the code names. She knew them all. One account, named "Gertrude," saw $10,158,110 in sales between March 30, 1999, and December 15, 2000. She identified it as Stadnick's.

That was enough for the police to assemble a small army of 2,000 cops to pull off Operation Printemps on March 25, 2001. In all, 142 Nomads, Hells Angels and their associates were arrested. Some, like Francis Boucher, were already in jail when they were charged. His dad, Mom, was also already in jail for the prison-guard murders.

All of the Nomads were arrested on the first day except Stadnick, who was arrested the following day while he was vacationing in Jamaica, and Carroll, who, as the official version goes, eluded capture and went on the lam.

The arrests marked the end of an era, but it was not, as many naive observers believed, the end of the bikers in Canada or even in Montreal. It was a setback, to be sure, but just as the Lennoxville Massacre and its aftermath had flushed out the first wave of Hells Angels in Canada, the Great Quebec Biker War and Operation Printemps took out the second. And things were hardly going well for the other side. The few Bandidos who were still alive, out of jail and had not yet switched sides to the Hells Angels trod very lightly. The Outlaws, who had not been having much luck recruiting in the face of all the new Hells Angels in Ontario, were mostly old and many of them had so many court-ordered restrictions they barely qualified as a club by that point.

As the Hells Angels were regrouping in Montreal, they were virtually untouched in the rest of Canada. While there would always be a strong Hells Angels presence in and around Montreal, strategic and financial leadership shifted westward. It would be the very bikers whom Stadnick had brought into the fold—in places like Alberta, Manitoba and Ontario—who would be running things for the Hells Angels. Their opposition would be made up of those in the Bandidos—who would later be known again as the Rock Machine—in the same places, and even a reinvigorated set of Outlaws.

While it's true that the Great Quebec Biker War with its near-daily shootings and bombings was over, the cold war between the Hells Angels and their allies against their collected adversaries was far from finished. It just spread to the rest of the country.

CHAPTER 11

THE FIGHT FOR WINNIPEG

There's not much here. Just rocks and trees and a bumpy, poorly maintained two-lane highway. There's a big blue sign shaped like a map of Manitoba that reads BIENVENUE AU MANITOBA WELCOMES YOU. About a quarter-mile later, there's another sign that reads (in English only) RADAR DETECTORS ARE ILLEGAL IN MANITOBA. But the sign is almost superfluous, as all traffic is coming in from Ontario, where radar detectors are also illegal. There are no cops around anyway. None for miles.

Despite the rough pavement, the narrowness of the road and its location in the middle of nowhere, traffic is steady, even bustling, on the Trans-Canada Highway at the Ontario-Manitoba border, both night and day. It's mostly tractor-trailers, but there are always a few private vehicles and passenger buses mixed in. Any of them could be carrying cocaine. That's because this piece of road is widely known as something of a drug-trafficking superhighway.

To find out why, I spoke with a number of law enforcement officers and Greg, a Toronto man who had worked extensively as a drug smuggler over the same route for several years. "I just needed some quick cash after university," Greg told me, almost, but not quite, apologetically. "I never carried anything but weed." He explained that a guy he knew in Toronto (a friend of a friend) would give him a knapsack full of weed, which he would take on a bus to Winnipeg. There, he'd wait for a contact, usually at a Tim Hortons doughnut shop or a Harvey's burger joint, walk into the parking lot, get into his contact's car, then exchange the knapsack for an envelope or bag full of cash. Done deal.

After a while, he'd earned enough to buy a car to make his trips into Manitoba, a move hastened in July 2008 after a carnival worker was beheaded and partially cannibalized on a Greyhound bus on the Trans-Canada Highway just outside Portage la Prairie, Manitoba, no more than an hour down the road from Winnipeg. "I had seen some nasty characters on the bus before," Greg told me. "But that was just too much for me."

Greg eventually stopped making deliveries after his career in media relations and product publicity began to take off. He didn't really know who he was working for at the time, just some guys, friends of friends. The whole thing seemed "pretty innocent" in his opinion, because he considered marijuana to be virtually harmless and the laws against it wrong and obsolete.

He never worried about getting caught by police—at least after his first couple of trips. "I never even saw one [cop] on the bus or anywhere near the bus stations," he said. "And once I was driving, all I had to do was stay around the speed limit and they'd leave me alone."

Everyone I asked about why that stretch of highway was so important for drug trafficking directed me to a map. Drugs come into western Canada from a variety of sources. Although a great deal of marijuana is actually grown in Canada, almost all of it is cultivated in British Columbia and southern Ontario, and even more comes to western Canada from places like California and Mexico. With methamphetamine, there are a few small-time cottage industry–style meth cooks in Canada, but their production is absolutely dwarfed by the amount that comes from south of the border, mainly under the control of giant Mexican drug cartels and their cronies. Cocaine and heroin, of course, usually come from Montreal.

Drugs are not the only products trafficked into western Canada. Prostitutes and strippers—obviously stripping is not illegal, but the profession is inextricably linked to organized crime in this country—traditionally come from Quebec, but their numbers are increasingly being augmented by women from Eastern Europe and East Asian countries, especially South Korea and Taiwan.

Although the US-Canadian border is more than 3,000 miles long, the RCMP and United Nations maintain that almost all cross-border drug trafficking takes place at Ontario's Great Lakes crossings (Sault Ste. Marie, Sarnia, Windsor, Fort Erie and Niagara Falls) and British Columbia (primarily Douglas). Drugs and people imported to Canada from other places, according to Canadian Security Intelligence Service reports, arrive predominantly through Canada's six major deep-water ports—Vancouver; Montreal; Quebec City; Saint John, New Brunswick; Halifax and St. John's, Newfoundland. Traditionally, small amounts of drugs have been flown into Canada, mainly by tourists from Mexico, South America and, especially, the Caribbean, but increased airport security since the September 11, 2001, attacks on New York City and Washington, DC, has put a damper on that, according to FBI annual reports.

That leaves organized crime groups in Canada with a major logistical challenge—getting their product to customers in western Canada. Lucrative markets for drugs and vice exist in Calgary and Edmonton (both with populations around 1.1 million); Fort

McMurray, Alberta (a fuel-oil boomtown full of young, mostly male nonresident workers known to many as "Fort McMoney"); Winnipeg (with 700,000 residents) and the cities of Saskatchewan, Regina and Saskatoon, each with a population of about 250,000. There is simply too much money to be made in these places for organized crime groups to ignore them.

Other than some locally grown marijuana, almost no product comes to the western provinces from British Columbia. The mountains are a real, physical barrier, the markets on the West Coast are very lucrative and, according to the United Nations Office on Drugs and Crime, more drugs are actually exported from British Columbia to higher-profit markets like the US, Australia and Japan than to the rest of Canada.

Instead, western Canadian drug and vice markets are served almost entirely by Ontario and Quebec. Air travel is out. Security is just too tight these days. Likewise, looping into the United States is also out of the question. Heightened security concerns, sophisticated detection methods and severe penalties make border crossings far too dangerous for all but the most foolhardy trafficker to risk.

Which leads back to the map. The border between Manitoba and Ontario is almost 1,000 miles long, reaching from icy Hudson Bay in the north to Lake of the Woods and Minnesota in the south. It is crossed by just one road, the two-lane Trans-Canada Highway. The vast territory encompassed by Manitoba, Saskatchewan, Alberta, Yukon, Northwest Territories and Nunavut—an area bigger than all but six countries in the entire world and home to more than six million people—is effectively supplied with drugs and other forms of vice by that single two-lane highway. In western Canada, drugs and other vice come through just one city—Winnipeg—where the road from the east leads and branches into different directions.

That status as a choke point between Canada's east and west has historically led to growth and prosperity for Winnipeg. The French and English knew it in historic times. More recently, the Hells Angels and others have come to recognize how valuable Winnipeg is for trade between eastern and western Canada.

Crime had always been a big problem for Winnipeg, but it got a lot worse once the Hells Angels arrived. The lure of supplying drugs to the West was too great for them to ignore. Enacting his own version of Manifest Destiny, Stadnick anointed Los Brovos as Hells Angels Winnipeg. They also took over an existing gang, the Zig Zag Crew, to work the streets for them. The Hells Angels filled the Zig Zag Crew with their own people, designed a new logo and established it as a motorcycle club with a patch featuring the initials ZZC in flames.

The Zig Zag Crew, in turn, had a number of street-level dealers working with them, many of them aboriginals. They were not traditional puppet gangs but autonomous organizations supplied by the Hells Angels. The alliances were loose at best, but common goals and common enemies kept them together. Through them, the Zig Zag Crew (and, by extension, the Hells Angels) built alliances with aboriginal gangs including the Indian Posse, Redd Alert and the Native Syndicate.

As is always the case though, the Hells Angels weren't the only act in town, no matter how hard they tried. There are always drug dealers who either won't or can't work with the Hells Angels. And in Winnipeg, there were plenty of them.

The primary opposition came in the form of another aboriginal gang, the Manitoba Warriors. Founded in the Headingley Correctional Centre just west of Winnipeg in 1992, the Manitoba Warriors began as an organization to protect aboriginal inmates from Hells Angels and their supporters, who dominated the prison. Once outside, the members of the gang organized in much the same paramilitary way as a biker gang, with officers, members and prospective members, who were known (just as they are in many motorcycle gangs) as strikers.

The Warriors had a brutal reputation and their members were quickly accused of the rape and murder of 16-year-old Brigitte Grenier at an outdoor rock concert and the murder of one of their own members, Bernard Cook, after he tried to leave the gang. Two men, Kyle Unger and Timothy Houlahan, were accused of and charged with Grenier's rape and murder but not convicted. Unger spent 19 years in prison before he was acquitted after a reexamination of the evidence, while Houlahan committed suicide during the investigative phase of the case.

It wasn't until 1996 that the Manitoba Warriors made their presence known in the national consciousness.

At the time, according to Canadian government studies and several media reports, the Headingley Correctional Centre was dominated by the Indian Posse. The reports say that the institution's guards were very relaxed about discipline when it came to Indian Posse members, allowing them to congregate in the building's basement, make trades, enforce their own discipline through beatings and even have sex in the prison's yard.

Every day, the members of the Indian Posse would meet for prayer sessions with what they called the "burning of sweet grass," though guards later admitted in court that they knew the group was actually smoking smuggled-in marijuana and considered the chapel as something of a clubhouse.

The gang was so prevalent that new inmates, aboriginal or not, were often branded with the initials IP with unsterilized needles—normally little more than heated paper clips—almost as soon as the doors locked behind them. As one contemporary inmate told a CBC reporter, "If you are not a Posse member when you go into Headingley, you soon will be."

The Manitoba Warriors had had enough. On the morning of April 26, they fought back. Inmates took whatever they could from the prison's workshop and kitchen to use as weapons. For 18 hours, armed groups controlled the institution, fighting, breaking glass and starting fires. No guards were taken hostage, but a few had the severed fingers of four prisoners thrown at them—media reports identified the tortured men as either "sex offenders" or "informants," depending on the source. Other guards were attacked, according to the RCMP. Eight of them required hospitalization after the riot, and one, Earl William Deobald, was said in the subsequent inquest to have had "his scalp hanging off" after being attacked by an inmate wielding a fire extinguisher.

When it was finally put down, the riot had caused $3.5 million in damages and resulted in 19 arrests. The CBC reported that investigators found that the gang had built a still that supplied them with home-brewed alcohol for at least 18 months. The guards had long known of its existence but were powerless to do anything about it because there were far too few of them, and they were intimidated by the gang's members.

Most of the arrested accepted plea bargains, but ringleader Anthony Joseph Zerdin went to trial. The Crown reported that rioters acted like "a pack of stoned, crazed animals" and that the members of the Manitoba Warriors had turned Headingley's Block 1 into a "torture chamber." Zerdin laughed openly at some of the testimony, according to the *Winnipeg Free Press*. When rebuked, he explained that he found the recollections of the victims to be "funny." Not surprisingly, he was convicted.

The riot put the Manitoba Warriors on the map. With their newfound prominence, the Manitoba Warriors—often bedecked in blue bandannas and blue vests in opposition to the Hells Angels' red—began to sell drugs openly in and around Winnipeg. They even operated in areas known to be the territory of the Hells Angels, represented in the area by their allies the Zig Zag Crew, Indian Posse and Native Syndicate—all of whom wore red. But, lacking a cohesive conduit to large quantities of high-profit drugs like cocaine and meth, the Warriors remained small time—outside of prison, at least.

The two groups also competed in the sex trade, both sides fielding teams of prostitutes vying for the same customers. That competition immediately led to violence, even before Los Brovos patched over to the Hells Angels. At approximately eight o'clock on the morning of August 6, 1996, Mattias Zurstegge went to his son's unassuming house on Semple Avenue in the West Kildonan neighborhood of Winnipeg and was surprised to find the front door unlocked.

Inside, he found his son, Stefan Heinz Zurstegge, who had been shot twice and stabbed 34 times, including in his left eye, which had been completely removed from his head.

Following a trail of blood into the laundry room, Zurstegge then discovered Jason Joseph Gross. His head had been bashed in by what was most likely a baseball bat and he had been stabbed 10 times in the face and chest.

Both men were barely clinging to life.

More blood led down the basement stairs. According to the CBC, at the bottom of the stairs, Zurstegge found the mangled remains of well-known Hells Angels associate Thomas Russell Krowetz. The 250-pound, tattooed and "unnaturally muscled" body of Krowetz was in the fetal position. He had been shot in the chest, buttocks and right thigh, stabbed 36 times over his entire body and had been repeatedly beaten on the head with a blunt object. The elder Zurstegge was shocked at the sight of a slash—more than five inches long—on Krowetz's throat that had severed his jugular vein.

Unlike the other two, Krowetz—who had been known as an enforcer for a prostitution ring operated by Quebec-based Hells Angels long-distance—was definitely dead. Zurstegge called an ambulance, but his son and Gross were too far gone. They both died on the scene.

Forensic experts determined that the men had been brutally tortured for a long period before the fatal wounds were delivered. Using evidence and interviews with witnesses, police came up with a solid case.

They determined that a few weeks before the murders, a man named James Delorme had accepted $1,000 from a Los Brovos prospect named Robert Sanderson for the right to have Taisa Marunchak (who had just graduated from Immaculate Heart of Mary High School) work for him as a prostitute. At the time, Los Brovos were an independent club, aligned with the Manitoba Warriors against the Indian Posse, who already had ties with the Hells Angels. The Hells Angels had no official presence in the city but had a network of associates like Krowetz who took direction from members in Quebec, including Stadnick.

Marunchak testified that she worked for Sanderson and lived with him at the seedy Stock Exchange Hotel. Before the murders, Marunchak overheard Sanderson call a Manitoba Warriors hangout (referred to in court documents as "the booze can") and ask, "Is the Big Goof there? Okay, we'll be down in a bit." She then said that Sanderson and his friend Robert Tews left with two guns and a large knife, which they hid in a paper bag.

Her evidence was corroborated by others. Brent Stevenson said he saw Roger Sanderson (no relation to Robert) talking to Krowetz (Marunchak identified him as the "Big Goof") at the booze can. After Krowetz left, Stevenson saw Robert Sanderson and Tews arrive. They met with Roger Sanderson, wrapped up their knife and guns and left together.

On the day of the murder, Stevenson received a phone call from Roger Sanderson telling him to watch the news on TV that night. He did. The lead story, of course, was the triple murder. Stevenson called Roger Sanderson back and testified that he told him, "Robert Sanderson walked into the house and capped them like it was nothing."

Marunchak testified that the trio arrived back at the hotel after the time of the murders and that she saw Tews without his shirt and shoes. When she asked about them, he told her that he had gotten blood on them. The men also discussed a need to clean some blood out of Robert Sanderson's car—a 1988 Mercury Cougar—and to burn or bury something else, although she did not hear what it was. Later, she noticed that Robert Sanderson was wearing some jewelry that she recognized as having belonged to Krowetz. When she asked about it, he replied: "Looks good on me. Besides, Russ won't need it anymore."

On the strength of her testimony and physical evidence including oil stains, the victims' hair and blood as well as a bloodstained baseball bat in Robert Sanderson's car, all three were convicted and sentenced to life imprisonment. Robert Sanderson appealed his conviction twice on the grounds that the juries were not apprised of Stevenson's criminal record (which Sanderson's legal team claimed compromised his credibility as a witness) and his conviction was actually overturned on his second appeal, after he had served nine years in prison, due to the weakness of other evidence aginst him.

A month after Krowetz, Gross and Zurstegge were murdered, the Manitoba Warriors targeted a Hells Angels–associated cocaine dealer named John Henry Bear. According to witnesses, three armed men wearing blue bandannas over their faces burst into a rooming house Bear had been living in and terrorized the residents until they told them where Bear was hiding. He was pulled out of a closet and executed, witnesses said, for selling in Manitoba Warriors' territory and undercutting their prices.

Although the violence may have brought the Manitoba Warriors credibility among their drug-dealing and prostitution-running peers, it also attracted the attention of politicians and law enforcement. Aboriginal leaders like Ovide Mercredi and Elijah Harper negotiated with gang members and sponsored a truce between the Indian Posse, the Manitoba Warriors and their new puppet gang, the Deuce. The truce was quickly threatened when eight Manitoba Warriors allegedly beat 18-year-old Indian Posse associate Terry Acoby to death with baseball bats during a blizzard, but war did not erupt. Instead, both gangs went on recruiting drives (the Deuce were said to have targeted elementary schools), continued expansion to the communities of northwestern Ontario and strengthened their ties with biker gangs.

Tensions from this new front in the cold war continued to mount until law enforcement stepped in. On November 4, 1998, a combined force of 150 RCMP and Winnipeg police officers raided the homes of fifty members of the Manitoba Warriors. They laid 260 charges ranging from gangsterism to murder against thirty-five of them, including thirty-two aboriginal men, one aboriginal woman, one white man and one black man. The police also seized ten assault rifles, five handguns and a significant amount of drugs, mostly cocaine.

Their trial caused a sensation. None of the arrested were granted bail, and critics quickly pointed out that members of alleged Asian and Russian gangs arrested under similar circumstances were. Eric Robinson, an NDP member of provincial Parliament from the northern riding of Rupertsland (now known as Kewatinook) and outspoken activist on aboriginal issues, was particularly vocal. He shared a mother, who had died at the age of 31 from alcoholism, with one of the accused, alleged Manitoba

Warriors treasurer Isadore "Izzy" Vermette, he said, in an interview with the *Winnipeg Free Press*. "This trial won't better relations between aboriginal people and whites," Robinson told reporters. "If I joined four Indians outside, we'd be called a gang."

At the biggest trial in Manitoba's history, the accused Manitoba Warriors required a new courthouse with Plexiglas protecting the witnesses and the accused. Again, extraordinary treatment of the accused led critics to make claims of racism. "They [the province] have constructed this super-courthouse, there's super-security, the accused are shackled to the floor and, in my view, it's all completely unnecessary," said Phil Fontaine, former national chief of the Assembly of First Nations, to the CBC. "Where has this been done to anyone before?"

Lawyers for the accused focused their defense efforts on proving that the members of the Manitoba Warriors were small time. "This case will never get to verdict," said David Phillip, who represented five of the accused. "The Crown can barely justify this, given the expense. The allegations are that the Manitoba Warriors were trafficking in cocaine at the street level in various hotels in Winnipeg, at the quarter-gram, or $20, level. It's not alleged they were importing or trafficking in kilos," Phillip told the *Free Press*.

He also strove to convince the court that the Manitoba Warriors were not members of a sophisticated crime organization but rather just a number of friends in a loose association characterized by media and law enforcement as a street gang. "There is a huge qualitative difference between a street gang and an organized crime syndicate," he pointed out to the CBC. "The alleged president of the gang was driving a 1982 Chevy Malibu, for heaven's sake. Of the 35 arrested, no one had more than $100 on them. There is no application to seize the proceeds of crime. Some of these guys are charged with welfare fraud. If you weren't a Manitoba Warrior you'd be looking at six to nine months on these charges."

One by one, the accused Manitoba Warriors accepted plea bargains for lesser crimes. That did not prevent sordid details of their activities from coming out. There was testimony that one of them, 20-year-old Steven Darren Traverse, forced a rival drug dealer to bark like a dog while Traverse sliced into his flesh with a large knife, then kicked him in the face with a steel-toed boot for "not barking loud enough," according to the Crown. The witness claimed that he and others present did not intervene because they knew Traverse was a member of the Manitoba Warriors and feared retribution from the gang if they stopped him. The victim, who required 83 stitches, refused to testify and fled the province. Traverse pleaded guilty to trafficking; he was not charged with assault.

The arrests dealt a crippling blow to the Manitoba Warriors and news of the accuseds' poverty and poor decision making led to a severe loss of credibility on the streets. They were pushed aside, and their old allies in Los Brovos turned their backs on them, throwing their lot in with their old enemies, the Hells Angels, and eventually winning Stadnick's favor.

That began a period of near-hegemony in Winnipeg's organized crime by the Hells Angels through their allies, the Zig Zag Crew and the Indian Posse—at least on the streets. A sudden infusion of pro–Manitoba Warriors manpower, though, changed the complexion of how things worked behind bars, especially in hardcore places like Headingley. In blocks and whole institutions where any dissent against the Indian Posse or their allies would have been quickly and violently put down in the past, the Manitoba Warriors walked unmolested and even dominated some areas. And while they were there, they were making friends, making connections and learning the trade.

The Manitoba Warriors did not completely disappear from the streets of Winnipeg, either. They were simply pushed farther down the organized crime food chain. They found it harder to find product to sell and harder to find territory to sell it in. The Manitoba Warriors—basically alone and far outnumbered—lived off the crumbs the Hells Angels and their allies didn't find important enough to pursue.

They kept running into trouble. In October 2006, 10 men involved with the Manitoba Warriors were arrested on weapons charges. A few months later, an investigation at the Paa Pii Wak—a government-funded halfway house dedicated to, among other things, getting aboriginal people off drugs and out of gangs—resulted in a raid. According to police, the management of Paa Pii Wak hired staff from local gangs affiliated with the Manitoba Warriors, who then recruited the former convicts to—or reacquainted them with—the Manitoba Warriors. "They were actively pursuing their criminal lifestyle," Winnipeg police constable Jacqueline Chaput told the CBC of the staff. "They were not trying to get out of that lifestyle."

Police had set up an intense surveillance operation and were prepared for months of evidence gathering but ended the project after just four days because they felt they had gathered enough evidence to arrest most of the staff.

The first thing they noticed was that Paa Pii Wak did not fulfill one of its primary mandates, providing shelter for the homeless regardless of ethnicity or affiliation. Despite agreeing to house anyone and to allow a minimum of 1,200 person-beds per year, the staff of Paa Pii Wak regularly turned away all but a few who came to their doors, no matter what the weather conditions. "It was like, sorry, unless you're a friend of the Manitoba Warriors, you're not staying here. If you're just some cold homeless guy, beat it," said Winnipeg police detective Wes Law to the Free Press. "This was a multimillion-dollar corporation, over the course of its lifespan, being run by the Manitoba Warriors. The Manitoba Warriors were using Paa Pii Wak to further their criminal enterprise."

The police recorded numerous drinking parties (although alcohol was officially banned at the facility) and several cocaine deals. "When you have a situation when you're empowering gang members or gang-member associates to conduct supervision of people who are released from our courts, clearly that's a flawed concept," Sergeant James Jewell of the Winnipeg police's Organized Crime Unit told Global News. "Evidence of drinking on site, we also have what we believe are cocaine dial-a-dealers attending to the premise and things of that nature." He even came up with the perfect sound bite, calling the situation "gangs gone wild in Winnipeg."

Seven people involved were charged with obstruction of justice. Although supporters and (unindicted) staff members protested, claiming that Paa Pii Wak supported only healthy lifestyles and that racism had motivated the police raid, the government cut off all funding, effectively closing the center. Criminal charges were then dropped.

The Manitoba Warriors—at least the important ones—were all behind bars again. The Hells Angels were free to operate on the streets without major opposition. Their dominance was made obvious on social media. While bikers and their supporters and fans do use sites like Facebook and Twitter, more often they air their opinions in the guestbooks on one another's Web sites. Law enforcement often uses this Internet chatter to determine who is in charge in a specific place, and who is the opposition. During the period in which the Hells Angels held absolute sway in Winnipeg, the guestbooks of many of their rivals in other places—gangs like the Bandidos, the Outlaws, the Mongols, the Vagos and others—would frequently be filled with requests from Winnipeg and other Hells Angels–dominated areas of Canada asking for a "real club" to come and oust the Hells Angels.

CHAPTER 12

AN OPPOSITION RISES

No matter how powerful the Hells Angels are in any given area, there is always an opposition, there are people who want to sell drugs but don't want to be part of a motorcycle gang, recruits who fail the grueling and often humiliating probationary period and those the Hells Angels either rejected or had no interest in anyway. Over the years that meant that the Hells Angels did their best to absorb the competition—like Satan's Choice, the Para-Dice Riders and countless others—or go to war with them—as they did with the Outlaws and the Rock Machine—and either force them into submission or exterminate them altogether.

In Winnipeg, the opposition coalesced around one man—one strange, untrustworthy man. Small with a hateful stare, Michael Sandham didn't look like a theology student, and he didn't last very long as one either. Later, he enlisted in the military, serving in the 2nd Battalion of the Princess Patricia's Canadian Light Infantry—a highly regarded mechanized infantry unit—from February 1991 to June 1994. Although he often claimed he had been on dangerous missions in far-off locations, he never saw any active duty and was never stationed overseas.

After his discharge, he served as an auxiliary police officer in Sainte-Anne-des-Chênes, a quiet little town commonly known as Ste. Anne, just off the Trans-Canada Highway, whose economy is dominated by a rather large senior citizens' residence. The force's personnel profile listed his nickname as "Poo-Bear" and his "technical skills" as "martial arts (sixth-dan black belt), demolitions/explosives, riot control, internal security/antiterrorism and parachute training." Most of that wasn't true, according to the Crown. He also claimed to have invented a new martial arts fighting style he modestly named "Sando."

On the strength of his performance at Ste. Anne and his military experience, Sandham was accepted into the Winnipeg Police Training Academy, graduating in June 2002. He was trained, according to his official transcript, in "police vehicle operations, firearms, use of force/subject control tactics, first aid [and] CPR."

He was then quickly hired as a constable by the police force of East St. Paul, Manitoba. It was a slightly tougher job than he had seen in Ste. Anne. A bigger community adjacent to Winnipeg, St. Paul is still very sedate and mostly free of the large-scale crime seen throughout Winnipeg and many of its suburbs.

Sandham served without incident in East St. Paul until an OPP officer spotted him at a party with the Outlaws in Woodstock, Ontario. The officer called Sandham's boss and filled him in.

Unable to convincingly deny his involvement, Sandham accepted the force's offer to resign on October 15, 2002. He received a letter of recommendation from the chief of police, David Grant. "It was just a letter of reference stating that his on-duty performance was up to standards," Grant later told the *Free Press*. "I don't have any qualms about writing the letter at all. Like I said, it was to deal with his on-duty performance, which was good. He performed his job well. There were no complaints from the public, no complaints from officers, myself or council about him. And up to the point he resigned, he was a good officer."

When a veteran biker heard that Sandham was an ex-cop and spread the word, he was finished with the Outlaws. They wanted nothing to do with him.

Unemployed, he opened a martial arts school and, through the magic of steroids, eventually looked the part of a fighting-skills teacher. Even so, he could not attract enough pupils to keep the school running, according to the Crown. As his business failed, his marriage deteriorated. He later said that the steroids made him abusive toward his family. He threatened his wife's life as she was leaving with their children.

Although he told people that he was a spy during this period, he was actually selling vacuum cleaners. He was not very good at it, eventually declaring bankruptcy.

Dejected professionally and personally, Sandham started looking for work and for a place to belong. He had enjoyed his week with the Outlaws, but since they wouldn't have him, he started looking for a different motorcycle gang to belong to.

He found one in the Bandidos.

When the police began Project Amigo in 2001, it was intended to investigate 27 cases of arson in Hells Angels–dominated bars in Montreal. By the time it finished in June 2002, they had collected enough evidence to effectively destroy what was left of the Rock Machine-turned-Bandidos in Quebec after the war with the Hells Angels. When the smoke finally cleared, the gang was almost extinct. Law enforcement had managed to do what the Hells Angels had tried, but couldn't pull off. Discounting those behind bars and those who had been driven into hiding, there was not a single member of the old Rock Machine left on the streets of Quebec and maybe 15 left in Ontario.

Since the investigation that had led to Project Amigo was directed at the Rock Machine, only those Bandidos who had been Rock Machine members were actually affected. Those who remained were collectively known officially as the Bandidos Toronto and Bandidos Canada, as they were both the local and only national chapter. They had no official clubhouse, instead meeting in the basement of a restaurant in Toronto's then-still-sketchy Riverdale neighborhood (the building now houses the trendy Prohibition Gastrohouse).

They were a strange and disparate group. "I thought Walter [Stadnick] had scraped the bottom of the barrel with some of the guys he patched over," a police officer familiar with the situation told me. "But these guys made them look professional." Many of them were poor, some still lived with their parents and few even knew how to ride motorcycles, let alone owned Harley-Davidsons. And there were major cultural and philosophical differences between them—while two members openly espoused Nazism, they also had a generally well-liked Jewish prospect.

Despite the Canadian Bandidos' lowly status, the Hells Angels—eager to control all bikers in the country—offered to let them patch over as prospects or hangarounds depending on their experience. The understanding was that if their offer was not accepted, the Bandidos would eventually be shut down, perhaps by force. For several reasons, including the fact that some of them had been targeted for assassination by the Hells Angels in the recent past, the Bandidos refused. Defiantly, the Canadian Bandidos began to call themselves the No Surrender Crew (while still identifying themselves as Bandidos) and came up with a logo and patch they sewed onto their jackets.

With Bandidos Canada's relatively capable national president ("el Presidente," in the gang's pidgin Spanish parlance) Alain Brunette behind bars after Project Amigo, they needed a new top man.

As their focus also turned from Quebec to Ontario, there was a power struggle as to who would emerge on top. The remaining Bandidos had a natural leader. Wayne "Weiner" Kellestine had founded a gang called the Annihilators and had been their president during the patch-overs to the Loners, the Rock Machine and the Bandidos. But since he happened to be in prison on drug and weapons charges related to an incident in which he was shot at by a pair of Hells Angels associates, he was ineligible for the job.

Instead, the title was assumed by his friend, Giovanni "Boxer" Muscadere, who had been recruited to the Annihilators just a few years earlier. Better known as John, Muscadere was an Italian immigrant who had grown up in Windsor, Ontario, and turned to boxing early in his life to combat local bullies who taunted him for his accent. He was, by many accounts, a friendly and approachable man who was well known among his friends and coworkers (he worked as a forklift operator at a since-closed truck-parts manufacturing plant in Tilbury, Ontario) for instructing young men in boxing and for flashing his smile, which—since all four of his top front incisors had been knocked out—struck some as amusing and others as grotesque.

When Kellestine was released from prison in August of 2004, he rejoined the Bandidos, but Muscadere remained el Presidente. Many sources have reported to me that Kellestine was deeply embittered by the fact that his one-time protégé—a man who had been a biker for less than five years—was now his boss. Grudgingly, Kellestine took the title of sargento de armas (sergeant at arms).

In January 2003, while Kellestine was still in prison, Toronto Bandido Francesco "Bam Bam" Salerno was in Edmonton visiting some friends when he ran into Joey "Crazy Horse" Campbell. Under his birth name of Joe Morin, Campbell had been a member of the Rebels, a fiercely independent gang that folded in 1997 after their secretary-treasurer Scott Jamieson was arrested for running

Police surveillance tapes showed construction boss Nicolo "Mr. Sidewalk" Milioto (*left*) stuffing cash he received from Mafia boss Nicolo Rizzuto into his socks. —*Gouvernement du Québec*

Gilles Surprenant, a former City of Montreal engineer, admitted to taking more than $700,000 in bribes. But because he had spent more than $200,000 at the Casino de Montréal, he said he felt he had helped the city's economy. —*Gouvernement du Québec*

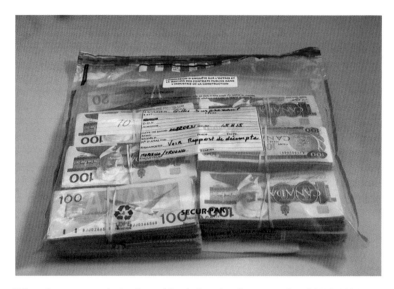

When Surprenant admitted to taking bribes, he also surrendered $122,800 in cash to the City of Montreal. —*Gouvernement du Québec*

Construction boss Lino Zambito, who had been charged with influencing an election, told the Charbonneau Commission that construction projects in Montreal were required to pay 2.5 percent of their budgets to the Rizzuto family, 3 percent to the Union Montreal party of Mayor Gérald Tremblay and 1 percent to Surprenant. —*Gouvernement du Québec*

The original membership of the Hells Angels Nomads chapter posed for this photo at a wedding. In the front row is national president Walter Stadnick on the far left and Montreal president Mom Boucher on the far right. —*RCMP*

The Demon Keepers were an ill-fated attempt by the Hells Angels to establish a puppet gang in Toronto in 1994. Their leader, Dany Kane, turned RCMP informant after the gang went under. He designed the gang's logo.
—*Ontario Provincial Police*

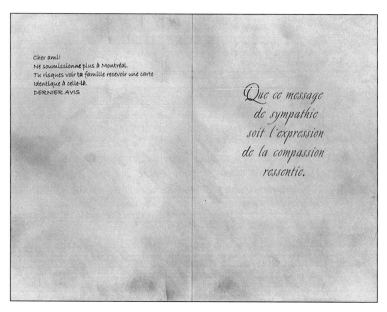

Cher ami!
Ne soumissionne plus à Montréal.
Tu risques voir ta famille recevoir une carte
identique à celle-là.
DERNIER AVIS

Que ce message
de sympathie
soit l'expression
de la compassion
ressentie.

After he was threatened over the phone, Quebec City contractor Martin Carrier received this condolence card with a warning that his family would receive another one if he continued to bid on government construction contracts.
—*Gouvernement du Québec*

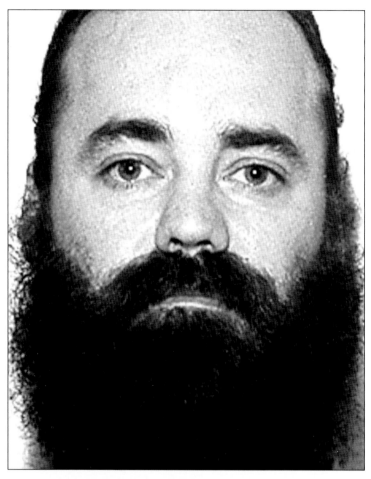

Darwin Sylvester was the founder and president of the Spartans. While his Winnipeg rivals Los Brovos were becoming Hells Angels, he was negotiating with the Rock Machine. He went missing in 1998, and many people believe he was murdered and his corpse was fed to pigs. —*Winnipeg Police Service*

Mayor Gérald Tremblay resigned from office in 2012, stoutly denying any links to organized crime. —*Ville de Montréal*

Michael Applebaum, Tremblay's replacement as mayor of Montreal, was arrested not long after taking office. He was Montreal's first Anglophone mayor since 1912. —*Ville de Montréal*

Despite not having had an official clubhouse since 2007, the Hells Angels Downtown Toronto chapter opened a store in 2013. Because non-members are strictly forbidden to wear the club's name or logo, the clothes carry the Hells Angels' nicknames—81 or the Big Red Machine. —*Tonia Cowan*

Forensic investigators search the house and barn of Wayne Kellestine near Shedden, Ontario, after eight members of the Bandidos were murdered there in 2006. —*Ontario Provincial Police*

The United Nations gang attended the funeral of one of their own, Duane Meyer, in 2008. Their leader, Clay Roueche (*front row, center*) thought it would cool if they dressed like gangsters. —*U.S. Customs and Border Protection*

Stanley "Tookie" Williams was the co-founder with Raymond Lee Washington of the original Crips street gang in 1969. Since then, the Crips and their rivals, the Bloods, have spread through the United States and Canada, but their links are tenuous at best, unlike the Mafia or biker gangs. —*California Department of Corrections and Rehabilitation*

an illegal after-hours bar at the Rebels' Edmonton clubhouse at the intersection of 115th Avenue and 85th Street. He had changed his name after an argument with his father.

Campbell nonetheless had a great deal of value to biker gangs. He owned Independent Artists, a talent agency for strippers that served much of western Canada. The industry was dominated in Canada by the Hells Angels. As soon as they had arrived in Edmonton, the Hells Angels recruited Campbell. As a veteran biker with much to offer, his time as a prospect was very short and he became a full-patch member very quickly. However, tensions with old rivals, major disagreements over how things should be done and how wealth should be divided led to his quitting the club peacefully, if not amicably.

Eager to align with another group to protect himself from the Hells Angels, Campbell visited the Bandidos in Toronto that spring. In a meeting with el Secretario Glenn Atkinson (variously known as "Wrongway" or "Irish"), Campbell ironed out the details of setting up a Bandidos chapter in Edmonton. On May 25, 2003, Campbell was given probationary-member status in the Toronto chapter with the understanding that he would recruit more members out west and eventually set up a chapter there.

Confident after their minor success in Edmonton (and other larval enterprises elsewhere in the West), the No Surrender Crew started shooting their mouths off, bragging about their westward expansion and intimating that the drug-soaked shores of British Columbia were their next target.

Complicating matters for the Canadian Bandidos was the fact that the Washington State Bandidos had established a working agreement with the Hells Angels in British Columbia to exchange highly potent BC Bud marijuana for cocaine and other drugs. Although the two parent gangs were officially enemies, the chapters on the West Coast near the border put their differences aside for the sake of commerce. Having these upstart, bedraggled Ontario Bandidos (who had few, if any, friends south of the border anyway) set up stake in Edmonton was bad enough for that relationship, but having them in British Columbia would just be too much for the relationship to bear. The idea that these Bandidos—with no friends, no connections, no infrastructure, no clout and no money—could replace the Hells Angels and supply their "brothers" in Washington State was absurd.

Unaware of the tensions his efforts were creating on the West Coast, Campbell had effectively recruited about a dozen new members (mostly from his old gang, the Rebels) and it looked as though he would succeed in establishing a Bandidos chapter there. But late on a Friday night—January 30, 2004—Campbell and his friend Robert Charles Simpson were gunned down as they exited Campbell's pickup truck in the parking lot of Saint Pete's, a client of Campbell's Independent Artists that describes itself as "the Heavenly Men's Club." Police characterized the killings as assassinations because of the efficiency with which they were pulled off. "Two guys, maximum four bullets, that's a professional hit and if the whole place was sprayed, then it was either done by really frightened amateurs or by another group trying to make a very serious point," an investigator told Global News.

The bar's owner, Pete Bodenberger, denied any knowledge of gang affiliations between the dead men, the assailants or any of his customers or suppliers despite the fact that the murders occurred a stone's throw from the establishment's front door at one of its busiest times of the week. "We, as a club, had no involvement with the incident," he told the *Edmonton Journal*. "We don't even get fights in the bar, so this is very unusual. The staff is pretty upset."

Simpson's father, Sparky Simpson, denied that his son had any connection whatsoever to motorcycle gangs, but the Bandidos

Canada Web site had a photo of him and identified him by name as a hangaround, the step below a prospect.

Without Campbell and Simpson, the Edmonton Bandidos project failed. The men they had collected changed allegiances and became Hells Angels hangarounds. Other clubs that the Bandidos had ridden and partied with and hoped to recruit, like Death's Hand in Calgary, also abandoned them. It was clearly too dangerous to defy the Hells Angels in Alberta.

There was, however, one place in western Canada where the Bandidos had taken root—Winnipeg. It started when Muscadere and his pals toured the West searching for recruits and met Sandham. They were impressed not only with his (mostly imaginary) military experiences and skills with weapons and explosives, but also his well-muscled physique and (again, made-up) martial arts prowess. He seemed to be everything they wanted in a biker. They recruited him and his friends to their club, giving the Winnipeg chapter prospect status in November 2004. They just didn't know that he was also a former police officer and compulsive liar.

Actually, one had an inkling. Veteran biker Frank "Cisco" Lenti had heard from friends in the Outlaws that Sandham may have been a cop and he told Kellestine. Kellestine assured him that he'd take care of it. He would, he said, interview Sandham in such a way that it would be impossible for him to hide his past. When Lenti returned, he found the two men laughing over beers. Sandham was in, over Lenti's protests.

After the failed martial arts school and bankruptcy, Sandham established two companies, ACRT Tactical Systems (the acronym was for Applied Control Response Tactics, making the name both redundant and awkward) and Sabre Inc., which offered police-style security training. Near the end of Sandham's stint with the East St. Paul force but before his dalliances with bikers became known, the man he reported to, Constable Norm Carter, recommended he apply to Prairie Bylaw Enforcement (PBLE), a private company contracted to assist police in rural Manitoba communities. Sandham pitched them his services.

Although Sandham's actual qualifications were probably more than enough to get him hired, he felt a need to seriously pad his résumé again. In an investigation made public by the Crown, it was revealed that Sandham made several claims that were either dubious or completely untrue. When it came to martial arts, he said he was "a 27 year veteran and Grand Master in Martial Arts," having earned a "6th Dan Black Belt in HwaRang Kempo and a 4th in Dan Taekwon Do," along with another black belt in Brazilian jujitsu and a "red sash" in Wing Chun Kung Fu. He said he had attended seminars and demonstrations by "such famous people as Chuck Norris, Steven Seagal, Bill 'Superfoot' Wallace and Dan Inosanto (the only person certified by Bruce Lee)." Most outrageously, he claimed to have participated in "full contact fights" throughout the world, earning a remarkable record of 12 wins (11 by knockout) without a single loss. None of that was close to being true.

He also claimed that he was a "VIP Protection Specialist and has protected such persons as former Chief of Staff General DeChastelane, former Prime Minister Brian Molruney, Princess Patricia and various other higher military staff." There were some obvious problems there. Besides spelling John de Chastelain's and Brian Mulroney's names incorrectly, Sandham claimed to have protected Princess Patricia even though she died in 1974 when he was just four years old. He may actually have been referring to her daughter—Patricia Edwina Victoria Knatchbull, Second Countess Mountbatten of Burma—also known as Lady Patricia, but that's unlikely. He also claimed to be a paratrooper and a commando, which were complete fantasies.

Dave Prud'Homme, founder and owner of PBLE, either didn't notice or didn't care because he hired him anyway. "When Mike came over, after he left East St. Paul police, he came over with a great letter of recommendation from the chief from there," he told the CBC. "So that's all I needed."

According to all reports, Sandham did his job well and was well liked among his peers. If anything, he had a reputation for being just a bit too enthusiastic. Prud'Homme attended a few of Sandham's training sessions and was said to find them—particularly one in which Sandham taught his students how to reload and fire a shotgun with one hand in case the other was injured—somewhat excessive. "It was beyond what we required," he later told the CBC. One other event indicated that this new officer had something of a past. "I remember when the Hells Angels came through one day, and he knew all of them by name," said one of the PBLE officers he trained.

After taking Sandham on full time, Prud'Homme noticed some changes. He was acting erratically. Then Sandham sent him an e-mail telling him that the job was "too stressful" and that he was having "mental problems." Those revelations surprised Prud'Homme, who noted that Sandham set his own hours, defined his own territory and was paid very well by the standards of the place and profession. It surprised him that a paratrooper and commando who had protected world leaders, royalty and celebrities would find giving out tickets in rural Manitoba too much to bear. "I couldn't see where the stressful part came in," Prud'Homme said in the same interview with the CBC.

After just a few months on the job, Sandham quit. Prud'Homme had no problem with that, but was somewhat disturbed by how much personal property Sandham had left behind. Prud'Homme called him about it. Sandham told him he wanted his stuff back or to be paid $4,000. Convinced that Sandham's stuff wasn't worth anything close to $4,000, Prud'Homme called him back to tell him he wanted to return his belongings. Sandham instructed his former boss to take his stuff to the alley beside his house and throw it over the fence so his wife could collect it.

His stress came from a double life as a bylaw-enforcement officer called "Poo-Bear" and a biker known as "Taz." It was a tough time to be a Bandido in Canada. Kellestine, who had befriended Sandham, was in trouble with the rest of the gang for his unilateral involvement with a number of meth makers and dealers (effectively excluding the club) and, far more importantly, he had not paid his dues or his mounting debts. There was a push in Toronto, especially among those members who had not been members of Kellestine's Annihilators, to strip him of his patch. They stopped inviting him to parties, then stopped calling him altogether.

Sandham himself was at odds with another powerful Bandido. Luis Manny "Chopper" Raposo (also known as "Porkchop") was el Secretario of the club, and it was his duty to, among other things, collect dues from members. While other members had also fallen into arrears, none were quite as flagrant as Kellestine, a man Raposo had never gotten along with. Things got far worse. On June 25, 2005, Sandham attended a Bandidos party at Kellestine's farm just outside Iona Station, Ontario.

Unable to get the No Surrender Crew to commit to a plan to make the Winnipeg guys a full Bandidos chapter, Sandham and his own men—made up mostly of his workout buddies—stopped paying their dues, which they considered too high anyway. Raposo was enraged. He campaigned against granting the Winnipeg prospects chapter status and for turfing Kellestine.

Without their dues, Raposo was unable to remit mandatory payment to the Bandidos international headquarters in Texas. Like many debtors, the No Surrender Crew began to avoid contact with the Texans, leaving telephone calls and e-mails unanswered. "You can't come here, we can't come there, but you do not want to answer any questions," wrote Bill Sartelle, el Secretario of the Bandidos worldwide. "There are issues that need to be resolved. I have made attempts to get these answers, but have not [received any]."

Raposo found his job so frustrating that he quit, instead assuming the title of road captain. George "Crash" Kriarakis took over as el Secretario. Nothing changed. Kellestine and Winnipeg refused to pay, and the Canadian Bandidos were too afraid to speak to their bosses in Texas. That prompted the Texans to pull the plug. Sartelle made it known in a mass e-mail on December 28, 2005, presented by the Crown.

> *To whom it may concern: For the past year or more, we, BMC USA, have attempted to make communications with Canada. We have directed face to face visits from whoever is in charge up there. Up till now there has been no visit from the proper person. It has been decided that due to lack of participation, Canada's Charter is being pulled. Effective immediately: Return all Bandido patches and property to the following address: Bill Sartelle 511 Gleneagles dr.Friendswood, Tx. 77546 In approximately 30 days we will make notification to all that we no longer have a Chapter in Canada and that any person wearing our Patch, in Canada, is not sanctioned.*
>
> *Bill 1%er*

More than anything before it, the public defrocking split the Canadian Bandidos into two separate and adversarial sides: the official Canadian Bandidos, who rallied behind Muscadere and begged the Texans to reconsider their decision and for Bandidos from other countries to come to their aid, and the upstarts, led by Kellestine and Sandham, who secretly communicated with the Texans to allow them to reform the club in Winnipeg without the Torontonians.

Frustrated with the Canadians' lack of communication and money, the Texans made one last-ditch offer to the No Surrender Crew, according to the Crown. They would allow them to remain Bandidos on the condition that Muscadere (whom they considered stupid, pompous and cowardly) step down as president and that the more stable Kriarakis take over the club's reins.

The Crown claimed that Muscadere responded cryptically.

> my name is bandido-boxer i speak for the no surrender crew canada bandidos my phone number is [redacted] reverse charges i will pay for it my enemy have treated all of us with respect you're a peace of work.

Something had to be done. The Texans were out of patience. They wanted their patches back. They wanted to be done with Canada. But it wouldn't be easy. Since most of their membership—certainly any who could handle the task of forcibly depatching an entire chapter, including Sartelle—had felony convictions, they could not cross the border into Canada. Desperate for a solution, the Texans took Sandham up on his offer of a face-to-face meeting, which both sides hoped could lead to a separate peace.

The only place the two groups could meet was at the Peace Arch Park, which is in both Douglas, British Columbia, and Blaine, Washington. The Canadian contingent was made up of Kellestine, his friend David "Concrete Dave" Weiche and Sandham, representing Winnipeg. Kellestine had wanted to bring another friend—Cameron Acorn, a full-patch Bandido from Keswick, Ontario, just north of Toronto—but he was serving time on a robbery conviction.

The Americans sent Peter "Mongo" Price, said the Crown. A monster of a man at six four and 350 pounds with a huge mop of hair dyed bright orange, Price was well known for appearing at meetings well armed (if not ridiculously over-armed) and wearing a bulletproof vest.

They came up with a solution. If Kellestine, Sandham and their allies could take the patches of the No Surrender Crew, they could remain Bandidos. Two chapters would be established—Winnipeg, under Sandham's leadership, and London, under Kellestine's. Kellestine would be in charge of the operation and, if he succeeded, would be national president. If he failed or balked, he too would be stripped of his patch and Sandham would be national president and president of Winnipeg, which would be Canada's only Bandido chapter. Weiche, perhaps sensing the impending danger of the plan, went into hiding immediately after the meeting.

Kellestine stalled, and the Texans and Sandham pushed him, holding the threat of his own patch over his head. Pressed into action, Kellestine invited the No Surrender Crew to a party at his farm on April 7, 2006. Most of the No Surrender Crew attended. Acorn was in jail. His alleged accomplices in the December 2005 murder of Keswick, Ontario, drug dealer Shawn Douse—Pierre "Carlitto" Aragon, Randolph Brown and Bobby Quinn—were lying low and did not make the trip. Veteran bikers Bob "Peterborough Bob" Pammett, Pietro Barilla, Frank "Cisco" Lenti and James "Ripper" Fullager didn't attend, but their status was excuse enough. Besides, Lenti walked with a cane after losing much of his leg to a car bomb years earlier and Fullager was terribly ill with cancer.

Most of the other members of the No Surrender Crew— George "Pony" Jessome, George "Crash" Kriarakis, Luis Manny "Chopper" Raposo, Francesco "Bam Bam" Salerno, John "Boxer" Muscedere, Paul "Big Paulie" Sinopoli, Jamie "Goldberg" Flanz, Michael "Little Mikey" Trotta—made the drive down the 401 from Toronto to Iona Station. Flanz was the only prospect invited. Jessome had cancer too, but he was much younger and stronger than Fullager.

Waiting for them were Kellestine, his friend Frank "Frankie" Mather and the Winnipeg crew—Brett "Bull" Gardiner, Dwight "Big D" Mushey, Marcello "Fat Ass" Aravena, Sandham and another prospective Bandido who the judge ruled could be identified only by his initials, MH. A former member of a Hells Angels puppet gang, he had been kicked out after a series of what they considered avoidable arrests before being recruited by the Bandidos.

Although both sides spoke of reconciliation at the party, each wanted to pull the other's patches. When Sandham and his men arrived, Kellestine told them that the Toronto Bandidos had sent two men to assassinate "the boss" in Winnipeg.

The Toronto Bandidos were followed to the farm by OPP officers in relation to the Douse murder. They turned back when the bikers arrived at Kellestine's. Not only were they sure it was just a party, but they had no search warrants.

Kellestine led the No Surrender Crew into the barn. Sandham—in the loft and smart enough to be wearing a bulletproof vest—and Raposo locked eyes. Both shot. Raposo died. Sandham was knocked down, but his vest had absorbed the pellets from Raposo's sawed-off shotgun. Kellestine demanded to know who had shot first. Sandham assured him it was Chopper.

The remainder of the No Surrender Crew were then disarmed and shot one by one. Their bodies were discovered the following morning in their cars in a farmer's field about nine miles away from Kellestine's residence.

After the slaughter, Sandham drove MH, Mushey and Aravena back home to Winnipeg. It was a quiet, paranoid ride even though Sandham had switched the Manitoba plates on his red GMC Jimmy SUV to Ontario ones to avoid drawing attention. They received a troubling phone call on the ride home. Three Bandidos—two from Ontario and one from Winnipeg who had a beef with Sandham— had arrived unannounced at the home of Sandham's in-laws, looking for him. It looked like getting caught by police wasn't the boys' only problem.

Meanwhile, back at Kellestine's ranch, the OPP immediately suspected Kellestine of the killings. They descended upon the farm and eventually arrested those inside, including Kellestine, Mather, Gardiner and two friends—Erik Niessen (variously described as a Bandidos hangaround or supporter) and his common-law wife, Kerry Morris—who had arrived after the massacre. Despite a hasty clean-up attempt, police discovered an immense amount of evidence and charged all five with eight counts of first-degree murder. Kellestine, Sandham and Mushey were each found guilty of eight counts of first-degree murder. Mather and Aravena were both found guilty of seven counts of first-degree murder and one count of manslaughter. Gardiner was found guilty of six counts of first-degree murder and two counts of manslaughter. The murder charges against Niessen and Morris were later dropped, replaced by eight counts of their being accessories after the fact. Niessen pleaded guilty to obstruction of justice, while charges against Morris were dropped.

With the No Surrender Crew exterminated and Kellestine and his cronies behind bars, Sandham began to build the Winnipeg Bandidos as his own gang. He took the Jimmy to a detailing shop where he had it thoroughly cleaned. An organized crime unit officer just happened to be in the shop at the same time and recognized him. He followed him and watched as Sandham changed the car's tires on a roadside, throwing the old ones into a ravine.

Sandham had brand-new vests made for MH, Aravena and Mushey. Things were looking up. But what he didn't know was that he hadn't gotten away with murder. MH, feeling guilt over the murders and eager to start a new life, accepted an offer from combined law enforcement to become a paid informant, wearing a wire to meetings in exchange for protection and cash.

Sandham reached out to Texas, and they agreed to listen. Things got ugly quickly when Aragon decided that he should actually be the head of the new Canadian Bandidos. He publicly accused Sandham of being an ex-cop, which would have made membership in the Bandidos forbidden to him. Sandham fired back that many of the Toronto guys didn't have Harleys (or even know how to ride a motorcycle), which made them inadmissible to the club. According to the Crown, then he sent e-mails—fraudulently using the name of prospect Big D Mushey—to Toronto and the Americans swearing that the sender had known Sandham for years and that he had never been a cop. In one to Aragon, he wrote:

> Hey Carlitto, it's D here. Things are really fucked up. For one thing, Taz is not a cop nor has he ever been one. Two of us have known him since he was in the Army a total of 16 years. We back him 100% and have good reasons too. He doesn't keep anything from us.

In another to Carlton "Pervert" Bare, a senior member in Texas who had raised concerns about Sandham, he wrote:

> Hello Bandido Pervert, what just happened? Taz is not a cop nor was he ever a real one, VERY FAR from it. Two of us have known him since he was in the Army, he is not a cop!

The responses from the Texans indicated confusion, annoyance and a lack of interest.

None the wiser, Sandham sought a blessing from his superiors in Texas. On June 6, 2006, he drove down—telling US Customs and Immigration officers alerted to his identity that he was just going to South Dakota to check out Sturgis, the site of a massive annual bikers' rally.

The details of the initial meeting were not decisive, but things began to unravel for Sandham less than a day later. The man he met with, Bandidos international el Presidente Jeff Pike, wrote in a mass e-mail made public by the Crown:

> *Taz was here in Houston last week. Within 10 hours of meeting him, the OPP and Biker Enforcement Unit from Canada was at my door. As it turns out, Taz is or was a police officer in Winnipeg. When asked about it, he said 'Everybody in Toronto knew about it and didn't have a problem with it.' we do not have or never will have cops or ex-cops in our club!!!*

Sandham's network of lies was beginning to catch up with him. After years of consistently lying about having been a cop, when presented with the undeniable truth, Sandham lied again— to the same people—telling them that it was a well-known fact and that his peers "didn't have a problem with it."

Despondent, Sandham drove back to Winnipeg. At 6:33 on the morning of June 16, 2006, Sandham was arrested for his part in the massacre by Winnipeg police and OPP officers. His first response, the Winnipeg police told the CBC, was "bullshit." Then he complained that the officers could simply have "knocked on the door" rather than "throwing a hammer through the window." He claimed "I wasn't there!" then appealed to the officer, saying: "I was one of you!" admitting he was a police officer. Then he shouted: "I'm not even a fuckin' member! I wasn't even fuckin' there!" Aravena and Mushey had been arrested earlier in the evening.

In the interrogation room, Sandham tried to make a deal with the police, offering testimony in exchange for either a reinstatement to the military or an appointment as an undercover police officer. They asked him what he knew. He spilled everything but was careful not to mention anything that would have even remotely incriminated himself. But the mountains of physical evidence, MH's testimony and Sandham's inability to explain why he was hiding in a sniper's position wearing a bulletproof vest and surgical gloves at a peaceful meeting prompted them to turn the poor, deluded man down.

He and the Bandidos had run out of even hard luck. Sandham, Kellestine, Mushey, Gardiner, Mather and Aravena were all sentenced to life in prison with no chance at parole for 25 years.

Their sentences, along with the deaths of Flanz, Trotta, Raposo, Salerno, Sinapoli, Jessome and Muscadere left very few Bandidos—if you could still call them that after Texas disowned them—on the streets in Canada. MH was in witness protection. Weiche was still in hiding. Acorn, Aragon, Brown and Quinn all went to prison for the murder of Douse (Flanz was also a suspect, but he was already dead by the time the trial took place). Fullager died of cancer. And the mercurial Lenti, who had been in a long list of motorcycle gangs, went to prison after he shot and killed a Hells Angels full-patch at a seedy Toronto strip joint in December 2006.

In August 2007, Jason Pellicore, a man with ties to the Mafia and a former Hells Angels prospect, said he was hoping to start a Bandidos chapter in his hometown of King City, Ontario, just north of Toronto. He was murdered outside a health club days later. Another former member, Carl Bursey, left the Bandidos and was arrested for and convicted of a variety of offenses, including uttering threats and parole violations.

It looked like the end. Even to those on the inside. On October 17, 2007, while he was in jail awaiting trial for his murder charge, Lenti posted on the Bandidos Canada Web site: "There isn't no more Bandidos MC membership in Canada, Cisco 13. 1%er Canada."

But it wasn't the end. That message was followed by a brief note explaining that the site would be up for "a while" to honor the "Shedden Eight." The domain had been prepaid, so it would have stayed up without maintenance until the account expired, but it didn't just peter out. In February 2008, the site was redesigned into a single page with the message: "Big changes coming soon . . . stay tuned." It was signed "NSCC," which law enforcement interpreted as standing for No Surrender Crew Canada.

It was never clear who spoke for the No Surrender Crew at that point. Most of those who were still alive were behind bars or in hiding. A source who claimed to be close to what remained of the No Surrender Crew told media that they were regrouping and hoping to reestablish themselves in Winnipeg and Toronto, but he didn't want to be identified. "They want the word to get out about their reopening," he said to several sources, including the *Toronto Star*. "They don't want any misconceptions because of what was listed on the site . . . about being closed down. They did close down for a short period of time. It's been years since . . . Shedden. What they've gone through, and the odds that they were up against, basically shook the club apart. But these guys have reassembled. A lot of the strongest members of the No Surrender Crew have come back together. They're just not willing to give it up and they've reopened the Bandidos back up in Canada again."

A police source, who also chose anonymity, said that the group were fairly well established in Winnipeg, and were hoping to make inroads in Ontario, which had recently seen the Hells Angels hit by a number of high-profile arrests. "You got Ontario chapters of the HA weakened by the recent investigations, you got this other trial [Shedden] going on where you have a bunch of people charged with killing," he said. "So you have that bad publicity coming out of that, that they don't exist anymore, so they want to prove to people they do. But you know what? I think their success rate will be a zero."

The actual Bandidos, the Texans who considered the word "Canada" to be something of a curse, were having none of it. All references to Canada were stricken from the Bandidos' international Web site (even the guestbook), and the club's leadership—who were generally more likely to talk with the media than most bikers—would not answer questions on the subject other than to deny any involvement with the massacre. The only statement they made was particularly damning of biker culture in Canada. "We were sick and tired of the fucking gangster mentality in Canada," said Bare, according to the Crown. "All it was was 'fuck the Hells Angels! Fuck the Hells Angels! Fuck the Hells Angels!' Down here, we don't have that. That's why we don't have any problems."

He had a point. Other than the March 2006 murder of Anthony Benesh, who had wanted to start a Hells Angels chapter in Austin, Texas, and had been warned by the Bandidos not to wear his colors in the Lone Star State, the clubs have largely been at peace in the US.

When the Web domain finally expired, the Bandidos Canada site went down. It was the end of the Bandidos in Canada. "It appears they are abandoning it," Connecticut Ed Winterhalder, who was in charge of managing the patch-over in 2001, says in his book, referring to any plan the Americans had to have Bandidos chapters in Canada. "The bottom line is that the Bandidos were just sick of the whole thing up there."

CHAPTER 13

LIFE AFTER THE SHEDDEN MASSACRE

Smart observers realized it was not the end of an organized opposition to the Hells Angels. "There is always someone out there," a veteran biker cop told me. "It's just a matter of [which] flag they march under." The bikers who had hoped to be the second incarnation of the Bandidos in Canada found themselves looking for a flag.

Many thought it would be that of the Mongols, a powerful and violent biker gang founded in southern California by Hispanics who were denied entry to the Hells Angels because of their ethnicity. The Mongols—who have supplanted the Hells Angels as the dominant biker gang in large sections of southern California and enjoy nothing better than annoying the Big Red Machine (which is what the Hells Angels like to call themselves)—played the part. Although the club claimed to have three full chapters in Ontario alone, law enforcement could not identify a single Mongol in Canada at the time.

The flag that was actually raised stunned many. In July 2007, an ad appeared in a Winnipeg newspaper announcing that—of all things—a Rock Machine clubhouse would be opening in the city on September 15. Few took the new Rock Machine seriously, even though the news was followed up by an expansive amount of Internet chatter. I asked a veteran biker cop I knew what he thought, and he dismissed the new gang by saying, "Internet bikers? LOL," although he also told me that anything could happen and reminded me that the original Rock Machine had started with even less.

In a situation remarkably similar to what had happened in Quebec a generation before, the Hells Angels in Winnipeg lost a number of associates and a great deal of support on the streets by turning on their own and putting money before anything else. "It got cold," a former Winnipeg Hells Angels prospect who quit the biker game entirely told me. "It was more about business than it was brotherhood; getting paid was all that mattered." And indeed it did appear that the Hells Angels in Winnipeg were as cold-blooded as those in Quebec had ever been.

After the Hells Angels took over Winnipeg in 2000, patching over Los Brovos, disbanding the Redliners and chasing off what remained of the Spartans, the first to fall was baby-faced drug dealer Benjamin Metcalf Marshall. The 20-year-old had been associated with both the Deuce and the Zig Zag Crew. It was a dangerous mix as the two clubs were on different sides of the Hells Angels alliance. On November 23, 2001, Marshall's mother, Shelley, called police to report him missing. They told her that her son had not been missing long enough to be considered a missing person. But 15 hours earlier, an unidentified body that fit Benjamin's description had been discovered just outside the River Oaks Golf Course. Wrapped in a clear plastic tarp duct-taped together, the victim had been killed somewhere else and dumped at the site. The following day, RCMP officers informed Shelley Marshall that her only child had been murdered.

Eight months later—using evidence from a witness who spotted a pickup truck speeding away from the crime scene—police arrested Derik Joel Zarichanski, 19, who had attended the same schools as Marshall since they were little more than toddlers, and his friend Luke Paul Pujol, 18, and charged each with first-degree murder. The investigation determined that the pair intended to kill another man as well, chop him to pieces and feed his remains to the hogs on a nearby farm and that Zarichanski had robbed two local caisse populaires (credit unions). A third man was also said to be involved, but police could not find enough evidence to charge him.

The boys considered themselves tough guys. Three months before the murder, Pujol had gotten into a bar fight. At the Palladium nightclub at the Four Points hotel, a group of men began chasing Pujol for reasons unknown. Pujol pulled a handgun and shot at them, grazing one of his pursuers in the thigh. At his trial, Justice Brenda Keyser told him, "You're very lucky a flesh wound was all that happened, or you'd be facing a much more serious charge."

While waiting for trial in Headingley, Zarichanski (whose first name has also been spelled "Derek" and "Derick" in the media) injured his hand. On November 6, 2002, he was transported to Misericordia Health Centre in Winnipeg by two corrections officers for treatment. When the van carrying him stopped in front of the hospital, Zarichanski (who had somehow obtained a key to his leg shackles, smuggled it into the van and freed himself without the guards noticing) kicked the doors open and ran away.

The media went wild. Not only had an accused murderer escaped from custody, but a close friend of his had been arrested a few days earlier with a frightening array of military-style weapons, some fully automatic, stolen from a Winnipeg-area gun collector. "That makes him [Zarichanski] frighteningly dangerous," a police source told me. "He appears to be sufficiently connected to access these weapons."

Zarichanski was at large for almost three weeks until police received a tip that he was staying at his girlfriend's apartment on St. Mary Avenue in downtown Winnipeg. At 11:20 on the morning of November 25, Zarichanski—tipped off and dressed only in his boxer shorts—climbed down to the ground from the seventh-floor balcony, then ran through traffic, first down St. Mary Avenue, then down Portage (Winnipeg's main drag). He attempted to open the driver's side doors of stopped cars but had no luck.

Witnesses reported that they saw a pickup truck chasing Zarichanski, attempting to run him down. When Zarichanski made an abrupt change of direction, the driver performed a sharp U-turn in traffic and went after him again, finally colliding with him. "The truck hit him. He just flew. He hit the ground and I didn't think he'd get up, but he did," one of them told the *Winnipeg Free Press*. "It was just crazy. It looked like the people in the truck were trying to kill him. It hit him hard. The hood was dented. The bumper was dented and the lights were broken."

Still fleeing on a broken ankle, Zarichanski punched through the driver's side window of a black Pontiac Sunbird and, after a struggle, its driver fled through the passenger door.

The terrified driver left behind his two sons—aged eleven months and five years—who rode along with Zarichanski on a high-speed chase through downtown Winnipeg that ran several red lights.

Although every cop in Winnipeg had been alerted, police lost contact with the speeding Sunbird until it showed up in front of E'Clips Hair Design at 12:37. Zarichanski then abandoned the car and the terrified children before getting into another car, a Pontiac Grand Am, and being driven away by the car's occupant.

Police then stormed the area. One cop car rammed the Grand Am as it was attempting to exit a strip-mall parking lot, stopping it. A shot was fired by one officer, but it didn't hit anyone. "I saw a vehicle trying to get out of the parking lot," a witness told CBC News. "I saw a bunch of heavily armed officers swarm the car. They swarmed onto that car like a bunch of flies on doo-doo."

Zarichanski, his grandmother, Jean Gartner, who was driving the Grand Am, and another man who was in the car were arrested at the scene. Obstruction of justice charges against Gartner were eventually dropped.

His trial was nearly as dramatic. Defense lawyers for both Zarichanski and Pujol quit. Then the Crown attorney quit. In September 2006—almost five years after Marshall's murder—the defense filed a motion to dismiss the charges because the trial had been delayed too long. It was denied. A month later, Pujol agreed to a deal. He pled guilty to conspiracy and avoided an actual murder charge. Somehow, Zarichanski managed to make a deal too, bringing his charge down to second-degree murder. When the gavel finally, mercifully, came down on October 19, 2006, Pujol got seven years (minus two years for time served and plus one year for the Palladium shooting) and Zarichanski got life with no chance of parole for twelve years.

Neither man has found prison easy. Pujol waived his right to apply for parole because incidents behind bars made it unlikely, while Zarichanski has been transferred twice, once for assaulting a guard and later for his involvement in a gang brawl.

People were still talking about Marshall's murder in the spring of 2002, when a street-level dealer named Daniel Tokarchuk, who worked the River Heights neighborhood for the Zig Zag Crew, ran into a problem. He'd become addicted to the cocaine he was supposed to be selling and had run up a debt of more than $15,000 to his supplier, Zig Zig Crew bigwig Trevor "Boss" Savoie. Aware of the Hells Angels' propensity for killing recalcitrant debtors, and unwilling to let that happen, Tokarchuk waited outside Savoie's house on the morning of May 12. When Savoie emerged,

Tokarchuk fired three bullets into his chest. Savoie, just 25, was dead, and Tokarchuk was quickly taken into custody. Savoie's funeral was attended by members of the Zig Zag Crew and the Hells Angels. Tokarchuk claimed the killing was in self-defense but was convicted of second-degree murder.

Savoie's murder did not sit well with the Zig Zag Crew or the Hells Angels. A year to the day after Savoie's murder, Tokarchuk's younger brother Kevin, 24, was shot once in the head outside his family's home on Churchill Drive in Fort Rouge. At the same time, a group of unidentified men visited Savoie's grave in Saint Boniface, leaving behind an unopened bottle of champagne and glasses. An ambulance arrived at 8:50 p.m., and Kevin Tokarchuk died on his way to a nearby hospital.

It later surfaced that a paid informant had told Winnipeg police that members of the Tokarchuk family could be in mortal danger, but they had not passed on the information to the family, according to CBC News. A number of officers, one of whom was a deputy chief, were suspended and investigated, but were not found to have acted improperly, as they successfully argued that they had consulted with a Crown attorney and decided together that the tip's source was not always credible and that the tip itself was just too vague.

In between the two incidents involving the Tokarchuk family, another Hells Angels–associated street-level dealer also found himself in severe money trouble. On the cold, clear morning of December 15, 2002, a passerby spotted an old Jeep stopped at the side of a farm access road near Rosser, an agricultural community about a half hour northwest of Winnipeg. As he approached, the witness saw a body just outside the still-open driver's side door. It was that of Vitalijus "VT" Kilikevicius, who had emigrated from Lithuania in 1995, leaving his then-six-year-old daughter behind. He had trouble finding steady work in Winnipeg until he became a drug dealer. Like many others, he got behind in his payments.

His punishment was a single bullet to the back of his head. It was a loud and clear statement that the Hells Angels would be paid or the debtor would die.

There were also minor turf battles when it came to street-level dealers who were associated with clubs on either side of the Hells Angels. Sirak "Shaggy" Okbazion's father, Rezene, left war-torn Eritrea for Winnipeg when Sirak was just 6 and finally saved enough money to bring the family to Canada when Sirak was 10. Unable to fit in with Canadian kids, Sirak had left school and was selling crack on downtown streets by the time he was 14.

Okbazion (whose last name has appeared in police press releases and the media as "Okbazion," "Okbasion," "Rezene" and "Resene") worked for the Mad Cowz, a gang made up almost exclusively of African immigrants, who had bad blood with many native Canadian gangs, particularly the B-Side (also known as the Broadway Boys). The boys involved with Mad Cowz had often witnessed massacres in their home countries and some had even served in ad hoc military units. Not surprisingly, they often found fitting into Winnipeg's culture difficult. "They barely speak English. There's nothing they can relate to. They walk around like little zombies. It's only a matter of time before they get drawn in," said a former Mad Cowz member to the CBC. "We watch them. Once it looks like they're ready, we go to them. We have fancy cars and gold chains—we sell dreams."

It wasn't uncommon for African kids Sirak's age to be working for the Mad Cowz, who lured boys into their organization with gifts and promises of a future and status. "They would give them sports clothes, flash the cash around and say, 'Hey, look what's available to you,'" said Harry Lehotsky, an outspoken minister in a region of Winnipeg with many such families. "And for many of them, they were no strangers to violence given the background of where they had come from and gone through in their home countries."

At 4:30 on the morning of August 27, 2004, Sirak's body was found in front of a reputed crack house on Sherbrook Street. The 14-year-old was lying in a full fetal position and had three bullets in his chest.

Residents of the area told police they had heard a foot chase prior to the sound of gunshots and identified four likely assailants. Police arrested two minors and 18-year-old Lance Laquette that day. They arrested 22-year-old Royce Berens two days later after tips from the public led them to a cheap motel. All the arrested were members of B-Side. Berens was also under investigation at the time for the theft of a shotgun from a police cruiser the previous summer. All four were convicted.

Okbazion's body was sent back to Africa for burial. Speaking for many in the community, Lehotsky warned that street gang violence rarely wanes and usually escalates. "Has nobody learned anything?" he asked in an interview with the *Free Press*. "The kid that pulled the trigger could just as easily be the next target. Nobody deserves to die this way. It's no way to die."

After Okbazion's murder, the Mad Cowz split into two very distinct groups. One faction, who had long been tired of the organization's strong-arm tactics, was outraged that their leadership did not exact revenge and left the gang. They founded a new gang called the African Mafia. Looking for a powerful ally in the region, the African Mafia reached a working agreement with the primarily aboriginal Native Syndicate, which made them—albeit loosely— aligned with the Hells Angels and Zig Zag Crew.

Other gangs were also fighting for drug-selling turf. Two Winnipeg men who sold drugs on a very small-time basis—in association with a group of friends called the MIR gang—came up with a plan. Clayton Thomas Korski and his roommate/ drug-selling partner, Aaron Shellrude, called up a friend named Wilson Martinez and offered to pay $12,000 for 13 ounces of cocaine. Twenty-year-old Martinez was a member of the LHS gang—an acronym for Loyalty, Honor and Silence—who controlled the drug sales in a few Winnipeg neighborhoods (but were much more powerful in other cities, especially Thompson) and also dabbled in extortion and identity theft. They agreed to meet at 11:00 p.m. on September 16, 2004, at the usual place— the play structure behind the Heritage School for grades one through five, according to court proceedings.

Martinez arrived with a friend, who remained in their car. The friend said he saw Martinez approached by two men wearing dark hoodies with their faces obscured. Then he heard a shot and fled. Someone called an ambulance, but Martinez died shortly after arriving at a nearby hospital.

Initially, police arrested both Korski and Shellrude. After charges were dropped against Shellrude, he became a cooperating witness and testified that Korski told him after the fact that it was his plan all along to kill and rob Martinez. Shellrude then left Manitoba. Korski was convicted of first-degree murder.

The death of Martinez raised tensions in the Winnipeg underworld. And nowhere did violence loom more ominously than in the prisons, where allies of the Hells Angels were living in close quarters with their sworn enemies.

At 9:30 on the morning of March 13, 2005, corrections officer Vincent LaRoche and his partner escorted a small group of prisoners to the recreation area of the federal maximum-security Stony Mountain Institution, about 11 miles north of Winnipeg. The guards left the gymnasium for about 50 minutes, leaving the inmates unsupervised. Upon their return, LaRoche discovered "bloody drag marks" which he followed into a washroom. Inside, he saw a body he described in his court-ordered statement as "inert." "His face had sustained so much injuries I did not recognize the person at first," LaRoche later testified. He checked for a pulse, found none and called for assistance. The inmate, 40-year-old David Tavares, was declared dead in the prison's medical unit.

Because he was a well-known member of the Native Syndicate, rumors quickly spread that Tavares was the victim of a targeted assassination. A witness, however, testified that it was an internal affair—another example of a Hells Angels–aligned organization killing one of its own members over a financial matter.

Inmate Steven Courchene testified that on the morning of the murder, Tavares had been drinking "home brew" (prison moonshine) and become aggressive, bothering other inmates about debts he said they owed him for cigarettes. One of the men he confronted was Alvin Cote, a higher-ranking member of the Native Syndicate, and the two almost came to blows. Courchene and another member, Victor Ryle, broke the squabble up. Cote, Courchene and Ryle agreed that Tavares deserved a "deboard"—prison slang for a disciplinary beating. Courchene's own role, he claimed, was to time the assault for exactly two minutes. Another member, Charles Coaster (who was serving time for manslaughter), was recruited to take part.

The beating quickly intensified, and Tavares hit the ground hard. "I knew it was getting out of hand. I pretty much said 'Holy shit, you guys are overdoing it,'" Courchene testified. "I think they all looked at him after and knew . . . he wasn't moving at all."

Cote, Coaster and Ryle were convicted of manslaughter.

Not long after, on the afternoon of June 2, 2005, a Winnipeg man named Aaron Hannibal told his common-law wife, Michelle Cockerill, something that disturbed her a great deal. He had been on and off the phone all day with someone she knew only as "Banger" and the two had been arguing. She considered Banger to be bad news. "He would talk about Banger in particular," she said. "He would be angry. They fought a lot." Hannibal told her he had to meet with Banger.

Hannibal had a dangerous job. He was a drug dealer and full-patch member of the Zig Zag Crew. So was Banger, whose real name was Daniel Kachkan. The two had never liked each other and constantly argued over territory, customers and prices. It was widely believed that a physical confrontation between the two was imminent. Kachkan, sources have told me, was widely viewed as something of a loose cannon.

After hanging up on Banger, Hannibal called his friend, Travis Britsky, for a ride to the Elmwood 7-Eleven convenience store at the corner of Talbot Avenue and Watt Street. It was well known in the neighbourhood as the place where Hannibal conducted his transactions. In the car, the two talked about Kachkan and what a jerk he was. What Hannibal told Britsky led the latter to believe that Hannibal intended to confront Banger but did not believe himself to be in grave danger. "Usually I have a vest when I deal with this shit," Britsky claimed Hannibal told him as he was leaving the car, referring to protective body armor, then added, "I never lose."

At about six that evening, police and an ambulance responded to a 911 call reporting a stabbing behind the 7-Eleven. Hannibal was rushed to a nearby hospital but died soon after arriving. He had suffered nineteen wounds, including three that had penetrated far enough to tear into his heart. According to my sources, at least 15 people witnessed the actual stabbing, but none came forward to talk with police. No charges were ever laid.

At this point, people in Winnipeg's drug-trafficking community were openly questioning the behavior of the Hells Angels and their allies. While just a few years earlier, the club's arrival had sparked a massive street party in celebration, the Hells Angels were now reviled throughout much of the region. But it was generally only through the relative anonymity of the Internet that people dared to speak of it.

CHAPTER 14

LAW ENFORCEMENT TAKES OVER AS THE HELLS ANGELS' PRIMARY OPPOSITION

Indeed the Hells Angels were soaring to new heights in western Canada, as the oil boom brought tens of thousands of people to Alberta, and the new wealth truly jumped off in 2006. The Edmonton, Calgary and Alberta Nomads chapters were busy providing cocaine, methamphetamine, marijuana, strippers, prostitutes and other products to these new boomtowns, particularly Fort McMurray. Not only were they established in the province, but after the Shedden Massacre killed off the will of the Bandidos to challenge them, they were almost a monopoly.

At that point the Hells Angels' only major opposition in western Canada was law enforcement. Winnipeg police had managed to turn an informant. Like many informants in Canada, Franco Atanasovic agreed to work for the police after he fell into severe debt problems. A career criminal, Atanasovic sold drugs for Hells Angels full-patch Ian Grant. It had been a mutually profitable relationship until Grant decided Atanasovic owed him $60,000 from a 2002 drug deal gone wrong. Atanasovic—who had been threatened with a gun at his son's hockey game over the debt four years earlier—believed he had cleared the debt up back in 2002 by appealing to his friend, Winnipeg Hells Angels chapter president Ernie Dew, who told Grant to let it slide. But near the end of 2005, Grant changed his mind and told Atanasovic that he was back on the hook for the debt, and there was no way to wiggle out of it. Desperate, Atanasovic went to the police and agreed to work as an informant in exchange for cash, immunity and protection.

According to the CBC, the police fitted Atanasovic with a listening device and gave him $2,000 in cash to give to Grant toward the debt. Predictably, Grant was enraged. "I don't think you're taking this perhaps as fuckin' serious as you should be taking it," he told Atanasovic before threatening him physically. "I'll just beat the fuckin' snot out of you every time I see you." The beatings, he said, would continue until the debt was paid. "Normally, I'd be beating the shit outta you by now," Grant (who is about a foot taller than Atanosovic) told him, sounding very much like a middle-school bully. "I'm just not because you're fuckin' everybody's buddy. But I don't really give a fuck, right? If I have to, I will." When Atanasovic pointed out that $60,000 is a great deal of money and would be hard to raise quickly, Grant told him that didn't matter—he wanted his money immediately. "I don't really care what you gotta do, right? It's not my problem," he said. "I don't care if you shit gold bricks. It's up to you, right? Find it fucking somewhere."

That's when Atanasovic came up with a plan: If Grant would front him some drugs for a new deal, he could make back enough to pay off his debt. He mentioned cocaine and meth specifically. Grant turned him down, instead instructing him to go to other Hells Angels, in particular, chapter president Dew. "Look at all the people you know here. Go to Ernie. . . . I know for a stone-cold fact, Ernie can phone and get 25 or 30 pounds right now," Grant said on tape, according to a CBC documentary. "Fuck, you know, in a phone call, right . . . I don't care what the fuck . . . steal it or fucking rob it or go to Domo and do whatever you gotta do." The "Domo" he referred to was Dew. Atanasovic knew Dew well because they had both worked part time as snow clearers at the Winnipeg airport.

Finally, the two came up with a solution. Like many drug traffickers, Grant had no problem accessing cash but had trouble getting credit because of a lack of verifiable income. Grant told Atanasovic that he would call the debt even if Atanosovic would buy him a new Harley-Davidson, worth about $23,000, and about $13,000 in parts and accessories. Antanasovic nervously agreed. The police bought the bike and the extras, and Atanasovic signed them over to Grant.

After collecting enough evidence, the Manitoba Integrated Organized Crime Task Force (reinforced by 150 RCMP officers) launched Project Defence on February 15, 2006, arresting 13 people, including Grant, Dew, Jeff Peck (who was also a full-patch) and Dew's wife, Vera. Also seized were seven kilograms of cocaine and three kilos of meth. Atanasovic—who had recruited his teenage son to ferry cash to various contacts—was paid $525,000 for his trouble, and police repossessed the Harley he signed over to Grant, the CBC said, under proceeds-of-crime legislation.

The trials initially went poorly as defense attorneys attacked Atanasovic's credibility, characterizing him as a lowlife who would say or do anything to protect himself. It's a common and effective tactic for attorneys, and Atanasovic had some serious blotches on his credibility. He admitted to stealing $5,000 in police money that he told the cops was for a drug deal, to making unauthorized calls to some of the people on trial and even to pretending to call Dew when he was actually speaking to a dial tone—in effect, fabricating evidence. A parade of 43 witnesses and a wealth of damning audio and video evidence countered the defense's argument.

In fact, the jury actually laughed and, according to CBC News, high-fived one another when they found out that Grant himself would be the final witness. In the end, Grant was sentenced to fifteen years, with two years tacked on later when he failed to pay a $118,000 fine. Most of the others pleaded guilty to reduced charges and were sentenced to between three and seven years in prison. Vera Dew pleaded guilty to arranging the sale of cocaine and received five and a half years behind bars and was forced to forfeit her home in St. Andrew's to the government. One of the arrested, an associate and alleged coke dealer named David Sutherland, fled the country and is still believed to be hiding out in his native Jamaica.

Ernie Dew's trial took place just after Grant's sentencing. The courthouse was surrounded by SWAT team officers. Dew raised many eyebrows when he fired his court-appointed lawyer in order to represent himself. While Justice Brenda Keyser allowed that, she would not permit Dew to cross-examine his old friend-turned-snitch Atanasovic. Instead, she appointed a lawyer to take care of that. After several weeks of defending himself, Dew relented and hired the lawyer Keyser had appointed to question Atanasovic, Sarah Inness, to defend him. Despite her best efforts, the jury found Dew guilty of trafficking, and he was sentenced to 13 years in prison.

• • •

While the loss of leadership and manpower was a major hit, the Hells Angels were still on top in Winnipeg. There was, however, a problem a few hours to the north. The small city of Thompson—which calls itself "the Hub of the North"—was experiencing a miniboom at the time, with both its nickel mines and hydroelectric dam project hiring large numbers of workers. As with many such towns attracting lots of young men, Thompson had a thirst for drugs and women.

Anybody who was anybody knew where to go for drugs in Thompson. Bekim Zeneli was born to Albanian immigrants in Thompson but had moved to Vancouver. Although he lived primarily on the West Coast, Zeneli ran the drug market in Thompson, sometimes in person at his rented townhouse, but usually through his gang, the LHS. The relationship the LHS had with the Hells Angels was complicated. Zeneli and his men were considered to be on good terms with the West Coast chapters and he had at least one full-patch friend in Winnipeg (Billy Bowden, who had gone to prison after stabbing romantic rival Jeff Engen in a bar), but he also associated with anti–Hells Angels gangs and was said to be despised by the Ontario Hells Angels, some of whom had their eyes on his territories.

An ambitious man, Zeneli actually registered LHS as a concert promotion company and planned to sell casual fashions under the name and logo, which featured the H and S intersected to form a dollar sign. He explained that his flashy cars and other signs of conspicuous consumption were acquired through his musical acts and smart investments.

Zeneli did not manage to convince law enforcement that he was just another businessman. While already fighting charges of kidnapping three men and a woman at gunpoint, Zeneli, his brother Mohammed and an associate named Donna "Mama Bear" Anderson were arrested and charged with a number of crimes, primarily cocaine trafficking, money laundering and conspiracy. In a rare move, the Crown won the right to forgo preliminary hearings after showing evidence that the LHS was indeed a criminal organization.

If the Crown hoped that would make their trial go quickly, they were wrong. It dragged on as Zeneli invoked all kinds of delaying tactics. While it was proceeding, and before he and his brother accepted plea bargains, the gang made something of a name for itself in underworld circles in October of 2003. After a particularly successful raid against the Indian Posse, a group of Winnipeg's antigang officers went to Earl's, a popular downtown restaurant, to celebrate. While the cops were enjoying themselves, a thief broke into one of their cars, making off with one officer's .40-caliber Glock semiautomatic handgun, ammunition, belt and holster, handcuffs and even his gang-unit jacket.

The cops eventually tracked it all down—when they raided a house on Flora Avenue, which involved shooting a dog named Shee Shee, who neighbors told the *Free Press* was half wolf—but the fact that the alleged thief was an LHS member gave the gang almost unprecedented credibility on the streets of Winnipeg. Shee Shee's reputation also gained in stature after she survived a direct gunshot wound.

At his trial in January 2004, Bekim Zeneli claimed that he was broke and applied for legal aid. Legal aid claimed he made too much money to qualify, so he came up with an ingenious plan that illustrated his almost unlimited chutzpah. Defending himself, he filed a motion to access $35,000 of the $43,000 seized when he was arrested, for use in his legal defense. The Crown countered that the money could not be released to him since it was covered in cocaine residue and, therefore, constituted evidence. The judge sided with Zeneli, pointing out that money was money and that he did not have to access the actual bills that had been seized.

In the meantime, Anderson, whom the *Winnipeg Sun* called a "crack-dealing granny," unsuccessfully fought her trafficking charges and erupted into a profanity-laced outburst at the Crown attorneys and her own defense attorney, David Guttman, when her sentence was passed down, shouting that they had gotten her "killed" because they had not made it clear enough that she had not cooperated with the investigation. "She has a hearing problem, and I don't know that she heard me correctly," Guttman told the *Sun*. "I don't think that she did."

Despite the influx of cash to their defense, the Zeneli brothers were sentenced to six years in prison. They were back on the streets in 2006, and Bekim, at least, regained his status as top dog in Thompson. His flamboyance did little to endear him to the Hells Angels, even those who were ostensibly his allies. That was made abundantly clear after a Winnipeg Hells Angels associate named Scotty "Taz" Robertson agreed to become a paid informant and allowed police to record his telephone calls.

Though never actually competent enough to be a full-patch member of any club, Robertson had a long history with bikers in Winnipeg, starting with the Spartans and then moving on to Stadnick's own Redliners and later the Hells Angels. Police sources said that few had much respect for Robertson because he was considered best friends with Spartans founder Darwin Sylvester. After Sylvester went missing on May 29, 1998, it surprised more than a few people when Robertson eagerly went to work for Stadnick's gang. A truck driver, Robertson was alleged to have couriered drugs from Winnipeg to Thompson regularly.

According to the RCMP, on December 12, 2006, Robertson received a call from a friend who described Zeneli as a "problem" that had to be dealt with. He agreed to meet with three full-patch Hells Angels at the Victoria Inn Hotel & Convention Centre by the airport. At the meeting, the men discussed Zeneli and one can even be heard on tape saying: "I'm going to get someone to whack him."

After listening to the tape, the police sent Zeneli a letter warning him that his life was in danger but giving no further details. It hardly took a brain surgeon to recognize that the threat came from the Hells Angels, even though another, similar letter was sent to his friend, Billy Bowden, a full-patch Hells Angel from Winnipeg.

Evidence gathered from other sources prompted the police in February 2007 to send yet another warning letter, to James Heickert, a high-ranking full-patch member of the notorious Oshawa chapter of the Hells Angels. By 2005, the Oshawa chapter were, according to a variety of sources, ferrying drugs from Ontario to Winnipeg (and points north and west, including Thompson) on routes and through contacts set up by Stadnick years earlier. Unlike the letter to Zeneli, the note to Heickert informed him that those plotting against his life were most likely members of the LHS. It was clear that Hells Angels and their allies were squabbling over drug money in Thompson and were prepared to kill over it.

It got uglier. In March 2007, Robertson told his police handlers that a Hells Angels–associated friend of his had let him know that he had called Zeneli's father and threatened his life. Robertson asked the man why. The man explained that Zeneli had threatened his wife, and he considered threatening Zeneli's parents to be fitting retribution.

The war of words calmed, but competition on the streets of Thompson was getting severe. Some complications were soon thrown into the mix. On July 1, 2007—Canada Day—police acting on a tip broke down the door of a Winnipeg hotel room to discover Zeneli hovering over a severely beaten and bloodied man in a chair. Although the cops believed Zeneli had spent hours beating the man—an LHS member who had fallen behind on his payments—charges were dropped after the victim declined to cooperate with police. The decision shocked Derek Coggan, a Crown attorney. "Obviously the intent here is to frustrate the justice system," he told the CBC. "I can't stress enough the danger these types of individuals pose to the community."

Then on November 6, 2007, another complication arose. Zeneli was arrested again and charged with possession of marijuana and failure to comply with court-ordered restrictions, imposed after the beating arrest, stipulating that he stay in British Columbia and report to a probation officer.

At his trial on November 28, his lawyer, Danny Gunn, argued that Zeneli had put his life of crime behind him. "He's trying to move his life forward in a direction that is separate and apart from what you see before you. He's moving in the right direction," said Gunn, pointing out that Zeneli was married, had two young children and a full-time job in Vancouver. The judge appeared to believe him, sentencing him to time served. Zeneli left the courtroom a free man.

Not long after, on November 11, 2007, young Devon Gurniak was working in an old industrial building his family operated as a pool hall when two men burst in. Gurniak recognized one as a local tough guy named Bruno Forest, but not the other. The man he didn't know was armed with a .45-caliber automatic handgun. The armed men were looking for Gurniak's brother Dean. The Gurniaks claimed that when Dean emerged, Forest and his partner accused the Gurniak brothers of being rats and ordered them to strip down to their underwear to reveal if they were wearing wires. It was clear at that point that the hit had been ordered by the Hells Angels, who knew there was an informant in their midst but had identified the wrong man.

The Gurniaks claimed that, even though they were not wearing listening devices, the gunman forced them to sit side by side. Then he opened fire, pointing the gun directly at Dean. Despite firing eight times, the would-be assassin missed Dean completely, instead hitting his portly brother Devon twice and nearly hitting another man who just happened to be in the building. The two assailants fled. Devon Gurniak was airlifted to a Winnipeg hospital and survived.

Forest was soon arrested and charged with attempted murder. Another man, Robert Colaciccio, was also arrested after a brief manhunt. Both were later acquitted of attempted murder charges due to inconsistencies in Devon Gurniak's story, a lack of meaningful physical evidence and uncooperative witnesses, but Colaciccio was convicted of discharging a firearm with intent to wound. Forest denied any involvement.

A few weeks later, the informant Robertson was invited to take part in a meeting in a room at the Holiday Inn to discuss the matter. He went and wore a wire. At the meeting, two Hells Angels associates discussed a plan for killing Zeneli. He was, they said, cutting into their business in Thompson. They described Zeneli, a Muslim, as a "terrorist." At one point, one of the men suggested they hire "a crackhead who would kill for $50."

Despite the fact that his handlers had instructed him to be a voice of reason ("he was to attempt to dissuade them from taking any action," one of them said), Robertson offered to kill Zeneli for $20,000 and asked them for a picture of Zeneli. They didn't have one but did give Robertson photos of some of his associates in Thompson.

After Robertson instructed the other two on how to get alibis for the time of the killing by going to bars, restaurants or movies and saving the receipts, one of the other men told him that there was another man in Thompson they wanted killed. It was Sean Heickert, a street-level dealer employed by Zeneli. They did not give a reason why. While it was widely reported in the media that James and Sean Heickert were brothers, they were not—their shared last name was just a coincidence.

Robertson jokingly asked them if they wanted a "two-for-one" deal, then told them that he'd knock off Sean Heickert—a job that would take less planning and presumably less risk—for the bargain-basement price of $2,000. Sean Heickert, he said, would be dead in a week, while Zeneli would live perhaps a week longer. The other men agreed, and told Robertson that their conversation had "never happened."

The police plan to prevent violence failed. On December 7, 2007—just more than a day after Robertson assured the Hells Angels he would kill Sean Heickert and Zeneli in a week or two—Zeneli was found shot to death in a townhouse he was renting on Brandon Crescent in the Eastwood section of Thompson. Surprised, the police brought Sean Heickert in for questioning. Police described him as "uncooperative" and released him after unproductive questioning. At the time, he was on parole from a sentence related to a 1994 manslaughter conviction in Ontario.

Desperate to prevent any retributive murders, police stopped their investigation and launched Project Drill, with the evidence they had against the Hells Angels and their associates, on December 11, 2007. In a series of raids from Vancouver Island to Winnipeg that included the Winnipeg clubhouse, Project Drill resulted in 18 arrests related to drug trafficking, gun smuggling and conspiracy to commit murder.

The most notable arrests were full-patch Dale Donovan (who had taken over presidency of the Winnipeg chapter after Dew was incarcerated), prospect Alain "Al" LeBras and most interestingly, Oshawa chapter full-patch James Heickert. James Heickert—along with Dean Gurniak and his Thompson friend Stanley Lucovic—were implicated in a murder conspiracy. Donovan and LeBras were found guilty of trafficking and organized crime charges. Heickert, Gurniak and Lucovic pleaded guilty to conspiracy charges. Heickert was sentenced to 25 years; Gurniak and Lucovic to 8.

Trafficking charges were laid against Hells Angels full-patch Lester Jones of the Kelowna chapter and Winnipeg hangaround Allen Raymond Morrison. Another man, 23-year-old Benjamin James Hamlin of Warroad, Minnesota, was charged with smuggling guns into Canada. Among the others charged with trafficking cocaine were Wayne Holmes, Zig Zag Crew full-patch Thomas Eric Anderson and Jason Pineda, all of Winnipeg. Stacy Jack Finch of nearby St-Pierre-Jolys, Manitoba, was charged with trafficking methamphetamine. Among the items seized were 11 kilograms of cocaine, 6 kilograms of marijuana, 2,000 hits of meth, 3 handguns and 5 submachine guns. Jones and Anderson were found guilty of cocaine trafficking, Morrison and Finch pleaded guilty to trafficking, Holmes and Pineda pleaded guilty to conspiracy and Hamlin pleaded guilty to weapons charges.

Two days after the raid, members of the RCMP's Emergency Response Team (ERT) surrounded the East Kelowna home of rap singer Madchild, a member of the group Swollen Members. Madchild (also known as Shane Bunting) demanded they produce a warrant. They didn't have one and told him all they wanted to know about was the Dodge Ram pickup truck in his driveway. Bunting told them he had borrowed it from a friend. Police asked if the friend was Lester Jones. Bunting assured them it wasn't.

After they left, Bunting told reporters that police had been harassing him since 2003 when a few members of the Hells Angels appeared in the video for his song "Heavy." Bunting, who later admitted to a severe OxyContin addiction in several published interviews, defended his right to associate with bikers. "I think that everybody knows that there's been people in our videos," he told the Kelowna News. "I have friends that are part of clubs, but this is supposed to be a free country and we can hang out with whoever we want."

Later that day, the ERT raided another Kelowna house—one of its neighbors said it was associated with the Independent Soldiers gang—and arrested Donald Lyons for trafficking cocaine. A search of the house uncovered five handguns, two assault rifles, a shotgun, a submachine gun and two Tasers. Despite the fact there was a two-year-old in the house, most of the weapons were loaded and easily accessible. When they discovered an improvised explosive device in a hidden floor safe, the cops called the RCMP Explosive Disposal Unit to defuse it. Finally, the RCMP said in a press release that a search of Lyons's car, a 2007 Cadillac Escalade, revealed a secret hydraulically powered compartment between the front seats that, when activated, popped open to provide access to five loaded .32-caliber handguns. Lyons pleaded guilty to trafficking and received an eight-and-a-half-year sentence.

Of all the arrests that came from Project Drill, the ones that caught the interest of media and public alike were those of James Heickert, Gurniak and Lucovic. While murder-related cases are always considered more fascinating than trafficking ones, what was really interesting was who the intended victim was.

After the Lennoxville Massacre (also known as the Sherbrooke Massacre), it was commonplace to hear that the Hells Angels had turned on their own brothers. Of course, those "brothers" were metaphorical. But the man James Heickert (along with bottom-feeders Gurniak and Lucovic) was accused of killing was Sean Heickert, whom many believed to be his real-life biological brother. That made lots of people in Manitoba consider the Hells Angels—particularly those in Ontario, who were already thought to be less-than-authentic Hells Angels because they all came from a massive patch over—inveterately cold-blooded.

While most people at the time believed that James Heickert ordered the attack in an effort to control the Thompson drug market, Zeneli's widow, Jennifer Collier, claimed it was because Sean had slept with James's wife.

Even with Zeneli dead and the others behind bars, the violence didn't stop in Thompson. On August 20, 2008, Sean Heickert was walking along a Thompson street when an SUV pulled up and its occupants opened fire. Heickert was airlifted to Winnipeg and survived but refused to talk with police on the matter.

On October 2, 2008, a body was discovered in a park in the Juniper section of Thompson. The neighborhood had been acquiring a reputation for wild youth, drugs and homelessness. The victim's tattoos—including one of a scorpion that covered much of the right side of his face—identified him as Christopher "the Scorpion King" Ponask. He was just 19 years old and left behind a pregnant girlfriend, Randi Duke. Though never convicted for a drug offense as an adult, Ponask was known to have friends in the Thompson drug trade. No arrests were made.

Less than a week later, police arrested Sean Heickert and charged him with Zeneli's killing. Perhaps coincidentally, James Heickert, Gurniak and Lucovic accepted a deal with the Crown and the next day pleaded guilty to conspiracy to commit aggravated assault against Sean Heickert. Sean Heickert was eventually convicted of first-degree murder.

Indeed, the Hells Angels had secured Thompson, but their reputation as money-hungry drug dealers who would kill their brothers—both metaphorical and biological—over debts led to a set of deeply disgruntled people in Winnipeg. And the long-talked-about opposition was about to become very real.

CHAPTER 15

GUESS WHO'S BACK

On September 19, 2008, two Australian men arrived at the Winnipeg airport. When questioned, Michael Xanthoudakis and Eneliko Sabine said that they planned to go fishing with a local man named "JD" they had met over the Internet. Previously alerted to look for any foreign visitors who could potentially be bikers, customs officials searched the pair's luggage. Inside, they found leather vests and other biker accessories, all emblazoned with the eagle's-head logo of the Rock Machine.

What the police had heard rumors of was true—the "new" Rock Machine had indeed formed and was planning a summit meeting in Gimli, a small town just north of Winnipeg. Both of the Australians had criminal records—Xanthoudakis had been convicted of assaulting a police officer—and were ordered deported as quickly as possible. Two men who had arrived to greet them at the airport were identified as area bikers; one was carrying a significant amount of marijuana.

At their immigration hearing, the lawyer for Xanthoudakis

and Sabine, Ed Rice, acknowledged that the Rock Machine had indeed re-formed in Winnipeg, and that their president was Ron "Sawed Off" Burling, who had been president of the rump version of the Winnipeg Bandidos after Sandham went down.

Burling, a small mountain of a tattoo-covered man, was something of a celebrity among area bikers. At his sentencing for convictions related to torturing a small-time Toronto drug dealer over a debt, the *Winnipeg Free Press* reported, Burling threatened the judge and court officers, tried to overturn a table, then feigned a heart attack. As he was being taken out of the courtroom on a stretcher, Burling asked a bailiff to retrieve his sunglasses.

Unable to avoid scrutiny after the Australian incident, the new Rock Machine came out to the media on October 1, 2008. In an effort to control what they wrote, a veteran Saskatchewan biker well known to police who wanted to be known simply as "JD" did something of a media tour talking to reporters about the new gang.

He told the same story repeatedly. The new Rock Machine was an "old-time" motorcycle club based on the virtues of riding, partying and brotherhood. Not only were they not an organized crime group, he said, they wanted nothing to do with criminals, indicating that drug dealers and others would not be welcome. "There's lots of money to be made legally. The real estate market is looking really good right now," he told several media outlets, including Global News. "We're just trying to be a law-abiding alternative to the Hells Angels. We're not going to be competing with anybody. If you get caught selling drugs, you're kicked out. Losers sell drugs."

When confronted with the nonsense of that statement in reference to the lawyer's assertion at the deportation hearing that Burling was in charge, JD claimed that Burling was not in charge, just a member. When pressed, JD said that the new Rock Machine, in the spirit of brotherhood, would never turn their backs on a member who had gotten into trouble. Of course, that didn't make sense because Burling was already in prison for drug-related offenses when the club was formed, but it was the best he could do.

JD also said that there were about 75 members of the new Rock Machine throughout Canada but that there were none in Quebec "out of respect for the Hells Angels" and because the new club did not want to inflame old hatreds there. Of course, if this new entity wanted to show respect for the Hells Angels, they certainly would not have named themselves the Rock Machine. If anything, the name was an upstretched middle finger to the Big Red Machine. It was almost as though these guys wanted to piss off the Hells Angels, but not enough to provoke any actual violence. At least for the time being.

JD spoke about Rock Machine chapters in Australia—where both the Hells Angels and Bandidos operate in large numbers—and the United States. One of the American organizers was veteran Daytona Beach, Florida–area biker "Crazy Eddie" Cicci, formerly of the Dead Rabbits MC. I spoke with some biker cops from the area. They were aware of the Rock Machine because of the war in Quebec but had not heard of their presence in Florida. When I mentioned Cicci's name, one cop said: "He's a nobody; this is Outlaws country, everybody else is small time."

A couple of days later, the much-anticipated Rock Machine summit—which JD said really was just a party to celebrate one member's engagement—did occur in Gimli under police sur-veillance. It was, as police anticipated, a patch presentation, but it was less than a momentous occasion. Not including the two Australians who were still being held, three people arrived. JD and another member from Alberta were given patches by another from Ontario; then the trio went to a Gimli bar to drink. When asked about anticipation that the meeting would be a major event, police were baffled by the low turnout at what they had heard was going to be a big deal. "This was their talk, but it didn't amount to much more than guys getting together to drink beer," Staff Sergeant Mike McTaggart of the RCMP Criminal Intelligence Section told the *Winnipeg Free Press*, pointing out that the Rock Machine had rented two cabins and bought lots of beer in Gimli. "Nobody came. It was a party where nobody came."

In the spring of 2009, the new Rock Machine set up a Web site, which made clear that the organizers behind the new club had descended from the ashes of the Bandidos' Canadian experiment. The Web site's tribute to fallen members named the Shedden Eight but none of the dozens of Rock Machine members who had died in the war against the Hells Angels in Quebec. These guys were obviously the old Bandidos. The site's "history" section gave a sanitized and wholly inaccurate account of how the Rock Machine came to be and why it had returned.

Clearly, they were positioning themselves as the opposition to the Hells Angels. In April 2009, they caught a break. Police in Quebec, New Brunswick, France and the Dominican Republic (long a haven and trafficking spot for Quebec Hells Angels) launched Operation SharQc, in which they arrested 150 Hells Angels and associates—many of them on charges related to the war with the original Rock Machine. It was a crippling blow, as 111 full-patch members were arrested, affecting the Hells Angels all over the country. And the Winnipeg Hells Angels—already weakened by Project Drill—were looking weaker.

That was followed by a set of surprise arrests that did not strengthen the Rock Machine but instead guaranteed that their center of power would be in Winnipeg, not Montreal or Toronto. The investigation started in 2001. DNA evidence left behind at the murder of Yvon Daigneault would prove key to finding his killer. The RCMP began to follow a few of the suspects. One of them, Gérald Gallant, fled to Europe in 2006 and was arrested in Switzerland for using a counterfeit credit card.

Under questioning and presented with the DNA evidence, Gallant admitted that he had been a contract killer for the Rock Machine during their war with the Hells Angels and also for the West End Gang. He admitted to the murders of 26 people, including Daigneault, a bar owner who had collaborated with the Hells Angels, and Paolo Cotroni. His information led to the arrests of Frédéric Faucher, a former leader of the Rock Machine, and Raymond Desfossés, a member of the West End Gang, as well as nine other members of the original Rock Machine.

Having Faucher and his Quebec-based allies behind bars for trafficking strengthened Winnipeg as the new Rock Machine's headquarters and distanced the club even further from the Bandidos.

As the Rock Machine grew in size and stature in Winnipeg, something of a war of words erupted on their Web site's guestbook. Starting in June 2009, threats and other saber rattling began to show up as support came in from around Canada and the world.

Despite the outpouring of support, the Winnipeg Rock Machine was still very much a small-time thing away from the Internet—rarely wearing colors out in the open—until law enforcement did something that almost guaranteed their continued existence, if not ascent.

Acting on a tip, the cops came to check out a bad dude. Michael Satsatin liked to hang out on weekends at the downtown Boston Pizza franchise. He'd sit at the bar, have a beer or two, watch the game and generally play the part of a friendly regular—like Norm from *Cheers*.

But it was more complicated than that. In a story recounted by the *Winnipeg Free Press*, members of Winnipeg's organized crime task force received tips in March 2009 not only that Satsatin was selling drugs at the Boston Pizza, but that he kept a loaded handgun in the glove compartment of his car. The complication was that

Satsatin was already working for the police as a paid informant.

He denied the accusations. All the cops could do was ask him to stop. Or at least stop being so obvious.

It hadn't always been a great relationship. In January 2009, officers spotted his car weaving in snowy traffic and stopped him. They charged him with drunk driving after he refused a Breathalyzer test, but he got off because of his valuable status as an informant.

In April 2009 Satsatin ran into more trouble. He told the cops that he owed a Hells Angel $15,000 and that the investigation would be compromised if he did not pay. The cops fronted him the money and he eventually paid $5,000 of it back.

Not long after, in June 2009, Satsatin got drunk at a Hells Angels party and wisely took a cab home. The only problem was that he left the cell phone the cops had given him to call in reports on the cab's backseat. Somehow, his cover was not blown.

A few days later, he ran two red lights. Police forced him to pay for one, but the other they forgave in the context of his position. Alcohol was never mentioned in the reports. After all, they were paying him about a half-million dollars.

That's because Satsatin was a paid informant, buying drugs and weapons while wearing a wire. He was even more valuable than previous informants. While they had been associates and hangers-on, Satsatin was a full-patch member of the Zig Zag Crew. It wasn't quite the same as a full-patch Hells Angel, but it was closer than police had ever gotten before.

It paid off. Satsatin recorded conversations about drugs (including cocaine, heroin, Ecstasy, methamphetamine, Oxy-Contin and marijuana) and weapons trafficking, about the Hells Angels' longtime rivalry with the Manitoba Warriors and even a plan to start a new Zig Zag Crew chapter in British Columbia to help out the Hells Angels there.

The wiretaps also detailed the relationship between the two

clubs. Each member of the Zig Zag Crew would pay $1,000 a month to the Hells Angels (at the time, there was also a $150 payment by each to settle a long-term debt) and do much of the Hells Angels' work for them, primarily the dangerous and illegal tasks. In exchange, the members of the Zig Zag Crew could eventually hope to become Hells Angels. In the law-abiding world, that's called a Ponzi scheme.

While Satsatin was collecting information, police were surprised by the murder of a well-known Winnipegger. At about 3:15 on the afternoon of Monday, November 1, 2009, police and an ambulance were called in response to reports of an injured man on Barber Street in the North Point Douglas neighborhood. When they arrived, the police had to control a viciously snapping dog to gain entry to the house. The front door was open with no signs of a break-in.

Inside was Daniel Kachkan, the Zig Zag Crew member who had previously been arrested for the murder of clubmate Aaron Hannibal but acquitted due to lack of evidence when no witnesses came forward and police were unable to find Kachkan's car or the murder weapon. The presence of the unleashed dog, likely to have attacked any stranger, and the unlocked door led amateur criminologists to believe Kachkan's killer was a friend or at least an acquaintance.

Satsatin's work came to fruition on December 1, 2009, when hundreds of officers from a number of forces launched Project Divide in Winnipeg and Brandon, Manitoba. On the first day, 24 arrests were made, but that soon grew to 34. Police also seized more than 10 pounds of cocaine, 12 ounces of methamphetamine, 12,000 Ecstasy pills, an ounce of heroin and 7 pounds of marijuana along with firearms and cash. More importantly, they managed to put every single member of the Zig Zag Crew and several Hells Angels behind bars. "We've hit the higher level of . . . members that are affiliated or prospects with the Zig Zag Crew as well as Hells Angels. And by doing so, we know that that's going to have a trickle-down effect. The impact is huge," said Jason Michalyshen, a Winnipeg police spokesman, to a crowded media scrum, including the CBC. "We're going to have less drugs on our streets, we're going to have less firearms, and ultimately making our community safer. That's really what it boils down to. We've hit the source." The few Hells Angels and their associates left on the streets were so paranoid about being arrested that they didn't seem to want to do anything even remotely illegal.

That had two major results in Winnipeg. The scarcity of drugs in the area caused prices to skyrocket, and the opponents of the Hells Angels began to feel like they could run the town. It didn't come out in the media until months later, but on the day of the arrests, a Rock Machine full-patch told a Winnipeg gang unit officer, according to CTV News, "Thanks for handing us the province."

Days after the arrests, the Rock Machine accepted a smaller Winnipeg club, the Vendettas MC, as their prospective support club. Primarily made up of nightclub bouncers, the Vendettas had pledged their allegiance to the Mongols earlier in the year.

At the same time, messages of support came from all over the world as anti–Hells Angels groups, including the Mongols and Outlaws, urged the Winnipeg Rock Machine to seize their opportunity.

Almost immediately the police began to pick up chatter and tips that the Rock Machine were emboldened by their rivals' misfortunes and would be more than happy to take advantage. The first and most obvious sign was that, for the first time in a decade, men could be seen on the streets proudly wearing the eagle's head of the Rock Machine—something they had not dared to do in public with the Hells Angels in charge. "The Rock Machine has been attempting to establish a foothold in the province of Manitoba due to the arrests in [Project] Divide," the Winnipeg police asserted. "Members of the Rock Machine have been capitalizing on the fact the Hells Angels members and supporters are low in number and have been 'flying' their colors throughout the city of Winnipeg, enraging members of the Manitoba Hells Angels."

Everybody in town knew that, while they were few in number and terrified of more arrests, the Hells Angels would not let such a vital stop on Canada's drug superhighway just fall from their grasp. "Tensions are extremely high . . . violence is imminent," a veteran Winnipeg organized crime officer told the media. He mentioned that he had knowledge that gang members on both sides were stockpiling weapons.

With the Zig Zag Crew eliminated and the Hells Angels under surveillance, boots were needed on the ground. With other chapters around the country under similar stresses, reinforcements would not come from outside. Instead, the Hells Angels gathered up a few men from Brandon and the Elmwood, Transcona and St. Vital neighborhoods of Winnipeg who had shown support for the Hells Angels in the past and organized them into a group called the Redlined Support Crew.

It was an interesting choice of name. When Stadnick first came to Winnipeg in 1995, he had collected a group of disparate men, whom he called the Redliners, to get a foothold in the city and provide him with information on Los Brovos and the Spartans. This new group, the hastily assembled and awkwardly named Redlined Support Crew, would be, for better or worse, the Hells Angels' representatives on the streets of Winnipeg.

The violence started right away. A guy named Fat Corey who had been kicked out the Zig Zag Crew and had latched on with the Rock Machine suddenly felt emboldened to start shooting his mouth off about how lame the Hells Angels were, according to Winnipeg police. In the middle of January, he was lured into the

Hells Angels–affiliated auto parts and repair shop DC Automotive, on St. Mary's Road, by an old friend on the premise that the arrests had led the Hells Angels to realize it was a mistake to have lost him and that they wanted to discuss his return.

It was a trap.

"He was attacked by several members of the Redlined Support Crew and suffered a vicious beating. Two members of the Hells Angels were also present," said a police spokesman. "As a result of this altercation, members of the Hells Angels, Redlined Support Crew and Rock Machine have all armed themselves as retribution is expected from both sides. There is imminent violence being planned . . . it is unknown at what time or place this violence could or would occur." The victim was in critical condition but survived. Fat Corey refused to cooperate with police in the investigation.

Quickly, news of the beating spread, and people expressed their indignation on the Rock Machine's Web site.

It didn't take long for an arrest. A SWAT team surrounded a house in Elmwood on February 3, 2010. They encountered major opposition in the form of a vicious dog. Once it was controlled, a search of a fenced-off section of the yard revealed a nine-millimeter handgun. Not only was it unregistered and loaded, but its serial number had been crudely altered. At about the same time, the police led one of the house's residents out in cuffs. A huge man, over 300 pounds, Justin MacLeod was well known in the neighborhood. Inside the house, the police found out why—a Redlined Support Crew vest and knit cap, a gold ring inscribed with the club's name and logo and a mounted picture of the entire Hells Angels Manitoba chapter. Later, they arrested his girlfriend and another man in the house.

MacLeod was charged with eight weapons offenses. His situation was more serious because he happened to be out on bail from charges related to an incident in which he was alleged to have sexually assaulted a woman and forced her to dance nude at a house party for hours on end. He was convicted on charges related to both arrests and sentenced to 66 months.

The police also accused him of participating in—or at least attending—the beating of the Rock Machine member Fat Corey. Sources tell me that as many as 20 men were present at the attack, including two of the few remaining free Hells Angels, despite the obvious danger of being there.

As provocative as the beating seemed to be, there was little gang-related violence in Winnipeg until spring. At about three in the afternoon on May 25, 2010, three teenagers were sitting on the porch of a house on Toronto Street. Two of the boys, 16-year-old Kyle Earl and 13-year-old Byron Cook, lived in separate apartments in the house, which had been converted into a triplex. The other, 19-year-old Marcus Payash, lived nearby. The whole neighborhood was talking about a recent drive-by shooting that had occurred a few blocks away on the night of May 20. Apparently, the shooter had intended to kill a person inside the house who had ties to the Manitoba Warriors, but proved a poor shot. Instead of the intended victim, the one bullet that hit flesh seared through the leg of a ten-year-old girl. Another girl, just eight, was also wounded by flying shards of glass.

Earl and Cook are black, and Payash is aboriginal. All were well known to police—who said they had been involved with the Native Syndicate—and proudly wore red bandannas and flashed gang signs for pictures. Earl had been in and out of foster homes but now lived with his mother and had quit school to sell drugs. He had been arrested three times between December 2008 and October 2009 on charges that included armed robbery. The *Winnipeg Free Press* reported that Payash sold crack and had been involved two years earlier in an incident in which 13-year-old Cody Shuya was killed when a shot from a pellet gun entered his eye and made its way to his brain. Sources also said he was known in the neighborhood for selling crack and for breaking into cars and homes. Neighbors had recently been complaining to police about a large group of teenage boys hanging out at the house, shouting gang slogans and harassing passing women.

The boys had something even more interesting than the recent shooting to talk about. Earl had made it known around the neighborhood that he was interested in leaving the Native Syndicate. Whether that meant he wanted to leave gang life altogether or not didn't matter to the Manitoba Warriors, who quickly sent a team out to recruit him. Shortly after that, on Saturday May 24, 2010, he was visited by three guys he didn't know who told him not to leave the Native Syndicate. To underline their command, they showed him that they were carrying a rather large handgun. "They didn't let any shots off," Cook later told the *Free Press*. "They just wanted to scare us, I guess—and they did."

The following day, someone did more than that. As the boys were sitting on the porch, a car drove up, parked and two men got out. They walked up to the house quietly, pulled out guns and opened fire. In a matter of seconds, they had rained down 18 shots on the unsuspecting boys.

"We were sitting on the steps and basically out of nowhere, shots," said Cook in the same interview. "They had it planned . . . they just started shooting. We didn't see the shooters or anything. Bullets just started flying."

As bullets flew at and past them, the boys clambered to get into the house. "The wood [from the porch] started flying everywhere and we start hearing bullets hitting glass," Cook recalled. "I just got up and started running upstairs and I looked at my hat [which was covered in gunpowder residue], and that's when I knew I could have died."

Cook didn't die. He received a shot to the right leg, but was out of the hospital the next day. Earl wasn't so lucky. Hit multiple times throughout his body, he died. Payash, unhurt, ran back out of the house brandishing his own gun. He chased the assailants around the corner to Agnes Street and opened fire. He missed his targets but managed to shoot a passing Dodge Neon, shocking but not injuring the three people inside, and a Pontiac Sunfire that was parked nearby.

After a lengthy investigation, the men who shot Earl and Cook were never found, but Payash and a 14-year-old associate were arrested for the earlier shooting incident that had wounded the two young girls.

Immediately, well-wishers made a Facebook page to commemorate Earl. Among the many posts was one by a person who identified herself as the girlfriend of an Indian Posse member. "I know the HA is all big," she wrote on the page. "You gotta remember they might run the insides [prison], but they don't run the outsides."

An inquiring Winnipeg blogger who goes by the name Black Rod found a post regarding Earl's murder on a forum on aq.com, a site for adventure gamers.

> *this is a very sad day for me, i just wanted to talk a little bit about it to make people aware. my best-friend (Kyle Earl) was killed last night, by another gang member. this is very sad because he was my best bud since i was 5. i remember 2 days ago i told him to leave the gang he was in. and he told me he was going to. and he was supposed to sleep over this weekend. it makes me very sad i lost my bestfriend/ my brother. this made me realize that their really is bad things going on out there and people should be more aware. and the thing that makes this all worse. they wouldn't let me see him. and the worst part of all they havent found his killer.*

Earlier posts by the same gamer claimed that he and Earl attended high school in Winnipeg with Justin Bieber (which was not true) and planned to "punch that faggot out."

The violence continued as spring transformed into summer. Darren Walsh was one of the tens of thousands of Newfoundlanders whose families had migrated to more prosperous parts of Canada. Walsh was an amiable, but goofy-looking guy—gangly with glasses, a shaved head and an oversized mustache.

On the Sunday afternoon of July 4, Walsh was waiting with his girlfriend and niece in a bus shelter near the corner of Euclid and Main (just across from the Elvis Pawnshop and the Economy Pawnshop). He was on his way downtown to pick up a prescription. A bus arrived going in the other direction and let off a man named Jheruel Mananghaya, who worked with Walsh and his brother Trevor at the Spring Air mattress factory. Mananghaya, who was carrying a Weedwacker box, spotted Walsh, crossed the street and began to argue with him. He produced a shotgun from the box and shot Walsh, who immediately hit the ground. Mananghaya fired two more times at the prone Walsh then fled, dropping the weapon. Six months earlier, a 17-year-old boy had been stabbed to death in the same shelter after witnessing a domestic scuffle.

A witness to the shooting followed Mananghaya from the scene, finally tackling and pinning him at the corner of Jarvis Avenue and Robinson Street and holding him until police arrived.

Initially the police reported the killing as a random incident, claiming the two men had never met. As more facts came out, it was clear that the two knew each other well from the factory and that Mananghaya had been banned from carrying a weapon after a 2005 armed robbery conviction. Eventually the fact that Mananghaya was a member of the Redlined Support Crew also came out. That prompted police to admit: "This was likely a targeted attack on the victim." Mananghaya was convicted of first-degree murder and sentenced to life. Whether Mananghaya killed Walsh on orders or for his own reasons is still a mystery.

Shortly before midnight on the following Thursday, a young man named Dylan "DCB" Ferland went outside to smoke. He was visiting friends on McKenzie Street in the city's north-end Luxton neighborhood. Ferland, 18, was well known to police, and his older brother, Harold, was a full-patch member of the Indian Posse who was serving time in prison after police raided a hotel room in Brandon and found him with 22 small packages of cocaine. Just a few months earlier, someone had shot at their home, causing only material damage.

As he puffed away on the quiet street, a car rolled up in front of him with the windows open. The three men inside fired a volley of shots and Ferland fell. He died before sunrise at a nearby hospital. His mother stressed that although he knew gang members, he wasn't one himself.

Police quickly arrested William Laporte, 21, and Dillon Lecoy, just 18, and issued a Canada-wide warrant for Stephan "Soldier Boy" McKay, 32. McKay was tracked down in Calgary and arrested by police there. Despite the flare-up of violence, things seemed to be going very much the Rock Machine's way on the streets of Winnipeg in 2010. They had been growing, particularly in Winnipeg, with high-profile recruits like Gregg Hannibal (younger brother of the murdered member of the Zig Zag Crew Aaron Hannibal) and Billy Bowden, a former full-patch Hells Angel and good friend of both the Hannibal brothers and the men who were shot in Thompson. Since he had been the only Hells Angel friendly with LHS, it also clarified which side that gang was on.

Both new members of the Rock Machine clearly had reason to distrust or, indeed, to hate the Hells Angels for turning on their own. In fact, many on the streets of Manitoba believed that Bowden had murdered Daniel Kachkan, the Zig Zag Crew member who had killed his "brother" Hannibal. Bowden had, after all, killed before, having pleaded guilty to manslaughter in the 2007 death of bodybuilder Jeff Engen.

The club's path wasn't without a few bumps. In March 2010, police were tipped off that a vacant warehouse on Sargent Avenue was being used for illegal purposes. Using that information, a judge allowed them to install hidden cameras and listening devices in the building. The police watched for months as people frequently came into the warehouse to process cocaine. That led to a July operation in which the police entered the building while it was empty, discovered bags of cocaine in the ceiling and photographed them. Using that as evidence, a judge issued a warrant that allowed them to listen in on the telephone calls of individuals they had seen working in the building and to secretly enter the homes of some of those involved, again taking pictures of cocaine and marijuana.

Later, police recorded people from the warehouse meeting with known members of the Rock Machine. On one occasion, they witnessed a bag change hands. They rushed to get a warrant. When they finally caught up with the suspect, Rock Machine member Ronald King, he was six hours down the Trans-Canada Highway just outside Indian Head, Saskatchewan. Tipped-off RCMP officers there stopped King's BMW and found $463,000 in cash inside. He was charged with proceeds-of-crime violations, but those charges were dropped.

Then, on September 23, 2010, police conducted raids on the warehouse, eight residences in Winnipeg and houses in Montreal and Langley, British Columbia, arresting nine people in Winnipeg, two in Montreal and one in Langley. They also issued a release that said they had seized 20 pounds of hashish, 15 pounds of marijuana, $500,000 in Canadian currency, $40,000 in jewelry and several vehicles. Since the alleged trafficking ringleaders were Winnipeg's Kosmas Dritsas and his 60-year-old Montreal-based father,

George, the media started referring to the group as the "Greek Mafia." Both Dritsas were convicted of trafficking and sentenced to four years in prison.

That was pretty minor compared to what happened to the Rock Machine internally in September. Until that time, the two major chapters—Manitoba and Ontario—had worked well with one another, but a rift occurred over a controversial issue. Most of the members of the Rock Machine—which were primarily those in Manitoba, but also smaller groups in Alberta, New Brunswick, Nova Scotia, the US and Australia—were very eager to expand to Quebec. They cited the fact that many of their friends who had shops related to motorcycles, leather and tattoos were being extorted by the Hells Angels and that the club's history began there. The fact that Montreal just also happened to be the nation's supermarket for drugs and prostitutes was a coincidence.

It was such a divisive issue that it led to frequent, heated arguments. The only prominent member in Manitoba who was against the expansion drive was a veteran who had seen violence firsthand. Years ago, Jamie "JC" Korne had been vice president of Sandham's Winnipeg Bandidos. He had found many of Sandham's managerial decisions unsound and began to deal directly with the leadership in Ontario, particularly Kriarakis and Raposo. Korne was in danger of being kicked out of the Bandidos at the time of the Shedden Massacre and was not invited on the fateful trip to Ontario. Later, it was revealed that he was one of the trio of Bandidos who had arrived ominously at Sandham's mother-in-law's house.

Korne wanted no part of Quebec. The rest of the Manitoba chapter, however, turned on their "brother" because of a desire to help out friends in Quebec. Or it may have been because of drug money. At any rate, Korne was turfed from the Rock Machine in bad standing on September 2, 2010.

There was opposition in Ontario too. The chapter there—many of whom were familiar with how things worked in Quebec and some of whom actually remembered the Great Quebec Biker War—were dead set against expansion to La Belle Province. The argument again became heated. Ontario chapter and national president Sean "Dog" Brown—some say the original founder of the new Rock Machine—was subject to a vote of non-confidence in November. He lost. Their media release (misspelling Brown's first name), which was posted on their site, read,

> *Each Chapter President carried the Chapter votes forward and it was an unanimous vote that Dog is to be removed from the National President position and put out of the Rock Machine Motorcycle Club in BAD STANDING. Furthermore it has been agreed among Chapter Presidents that the current Ontario Rock Machine members are also 86 d from the club.*
>
> *Effective on this day the 23rd of November 2010 SHAUN BROWN (AKA DOG) is out in BAD STANDING from the Rock Machine MC Canada.*
> *Rock Machine Canada National Secretary*

ROCK MACHINE MC NOMADS

On the following day, the Rock Machine Nomads chapter in the US, who had sided with Brown even though they had little knowledge of what was going on in Quebec, were also let go, although they were out in good standing and were bid "a fond farewell." They were quickly replaced by younger and more aggressive American recruits.

Winnipeg contractor and bodybuilder Joseph "Critical J" Strachan took over as national president. A former member of the

LHS who had left the club after the Zeneli murder, Strachan was well known to his former friends in the Hells Angels. Notably, like many of the old Canadian Bandidos, Strachan (though approaching 40) still lived with his parents. Hells Angels supporters found that fact hilarious.

Days later, and with surprisingly little fanfare, a provocative Quebec chapter was formed in Montreal.

A few days after that, on November 30—although media did not catch on to it until well into the new year—Brown, Korne and their friends were accepted as prospective members of yet another large American gang, the Vagos.

Founded in 1965 in the semirural area around Corona, California, the club was originally called the Psychos. Not long after, they changed the name to Vagos—the Spanish word for "vague," but more commonly "gypsy" in Mexican slang—adopted Loki, the Norse god of mischief, as their symbol and chose the color green to represent themselves. Over the years, they became very popular in California, Nevada, Arizona and New Mexico. More important, however, is the fact that they have expanded into Mexico and have 10 chapters in cities there.

While the US Department of Justice accuses the Vagos of producing, transporting and distributing methamphetamine and marijuana, as well as of assault, extortion, insurance fraud, money laundering, murder, vehicle theft, witness intimidation and weapons violations (and has a number of convictions to back up those claims), the Vagos have also been successful at fighting off claims of their outlaw status.

In 1974, four Vagos were released from death row when the FBI informant who had put them behind bars admitted to the murder they were convicted of committing. In 2002, the Vagos turned in a woman who had attempted to pay them to kill her police detective husband. And in 2011, they were cleared after being accused of a plot to bomb the houses of police detectives in Hemet, California, and received an apology from Riverside County officials.

Of course, the mere fact that they were a motorcycle club in California made them enemies of the Hells Angels. That, in turn, put them on positive terms with the Bandidos, Outlaws and Mongols.

Brown found no problem recruiting for the Vagos in Ontario, quickly assembling perhaps two dozen supporters—mostly the remains of the old Ontario Rock Machine. The Canadian Vagos were collected as one prospective chapter with no set clubhouse—a concept known in motorcycle gang circles as Nomads (although the Rock Machine Nomads behave differently). Aware of recent failures by what amounted to this same group of guys, the Vagos hedged their bets a little, allowing the Canadians to wear only support gear (like T-shirts and hoodies) and instructed them to keep their Web and media presence low.

That strategy did not convince everyone they were small time. "They're at war with the Hells Angels in California," OPP Biker Enforcement Unit detective sergeant Len Isnor said, pointing out that the two gangs had recently exchanged gunfire in broad daylight in Chino, California, leaving five injured. "If they spread into Canada, the Ontario Hells Angels will do whatever it takes to support their brothers in California. So, there could be violence."

While the Vagos appeared to be attempting to assume the mantle of Hells Angels opposition in Ontario, no such groundswell happened in Winnipeg. The Rock Machine were strong and popular there, and what other few remaining tough guys were on the street had already been snapped up by the Hells Angels to fill out the Redlined Support Crew. Korne found himself the only Vago in Winnipeg.

Things took a tragic turn for the Rock Machine just before Christmas 2010. Andrew Block, an Edmonton-born hip-hop musician and father of two, was one of the most popular members of the club. The 31-year-old with a shaved head and three teardrop tattoos on his face, also known as Andy Rock and Blakli$tid, had two favourite quotes, according to his Facebook page—TALK SHIT GET HIT and TRUST NO. 1—that he frequently wrote on the Rock Machine's Web site, always in all caps. The Rock Machine's current site has a memorial page that names Block as a full-patch member.

On December 15, in an alley behind a duplex near the corner of 127th Street and 116th Avenue in the Inglewood neighbourhood of Edmonton, police alerted by a 911 call discovered a heavily customized black pickup truck with a flat front tire and smashed windows. Inside they found Block's bullet-riddled body.

The discovery started an alarm of sorts. Media speculated that a Rock Machine–Hells Angels war was starting in Edmonton. Many of Block's friends and family claimed that he was no longer in the gang world, instead concentrating on his music and children. The Rock Machine begged to differ as tributes to their "brother" poured in from all over the world.

My own sources in both Edmonton and Winnipeg have told me that Block's death was the result of a random robbery and was not a targeted assassination, but it did nothing to relieve the tension between the two clubs. And when violence erupted in Winnipeg again, people were quick to call it the start of a war.

Tension rose in January 2011 when it was learned that Jean "le Français" Duquaire was to be released from prison. Notorious not just as a drug dealer but also for his part in the Quebec Biker War, in which he had attempted to assassinate Mom Boucher, Duquaire was one of the Rock Machine leaders who helped the club become Bandidos. Convicted of the assassination attempt in 2003 and sentenced to twelve years, he was released after eight despite being caught with steroids in prison and another incident in which he and some friends nearly beat a Hells Angels affiliate to death for not spitting on or urinating on a photograph of Boucher.

Duquaire was released with the following conditions: He must live in a halfway house; he must provide bank statements to his parole officer; he must abstain from drugs, except for prescribed medication and he must not communicate or meet with convicted criminals. Although that final condition would make it difficult for him to be involved with the new incarnation of the Rock Machine, his release was a metaphorical shot in the arm for them.

In the spring of 2011—while a shooting war had erupted between the Australian Rock Machine and a Hells Angels–affiliated club called the Rebels—a story emerged that put the Hells Angels' reach in Winnipeg into perspective. Back in 2008, an RCMP constable named Todd Glasman fell in love with a woman who had a checkered past. In fact, she was a Hells Angels associate. Aware of this, Glasman would park blocks away when visiting her, so that neighbors would not connect the two. Eventually, the couple married.

In March 2011, Glasman's wife was detained for an interview when trying to cross into the US. As is standard protocol, the US border service alerted the RCMP, who did a routine check of her file on the Canadian Police Information Centre (or CPIC, a high-security database of Canadian arrestees, verdicts and sentences). What they saw surprised them. The woman's CPIC file had been accessed without authorization dozens of times with 186 documents viewed by the same officer—Todd Glasman, according to the CBC.

When confronted, Glasman admitted that he had accessed the files (and others regarding her friends in the Hells Angels) illegally but said he did it for the RCMP's "protection," according to the CBC. A polygraph test indicated that he had shared the information with his wife but nobody else. His wife, however, was known to have many friends associated with the Hells Angels and even frequently visited one convicted full-patch in prison. A disciplinary board concluded "that a reasonable person, having the knowledge of the relevant circumstances, including the realities of policing in general and those of the RCMP in particular, would conclude that conducting numerous unauthorized national crime databank checks for personal reasons without an operational requirement is disgraceful." Glasman was suspended eight days without pay.

That same month, the Rock Machine made headlines in Winnipeg again. On March 22, 2011, Ashley Sandison (who was widely believed to be a Rock Machine full-patch) decided to visit his wife, Kerri-Lynn. It was a bad idea. Not only was his dropping by in violation of a no-contact order that had been placed on him due to a previous incident in which he had assaulted her, but he was also wanted after failing to appear in court for two other unrelated assault arrests.

A neighbor overheard the Sandisons arguing and called police. By the time they arrived, Ashley was in his pickup truck. The police blocked him in and approached with weapons drawn. Ashley then floored it. The pickup reversed into a police car, damaging it, but not moving it enough to allow him to escape. So he slipped it into reverse and did it again. And again. And again, which finally allowed him enough space to exit the driveway and make his escape. An officer fired at the pickup, hitting it but not stopping it.

Two days later, he surrendered himself to police, escorted to the station by his wife. "Well, they didn't have to fire no weapons," Ashley Sandison told media, including Global News, when he arrived. "They stormed my truck with rifles. It's scary! Cops just come running at my truck, and they wanted to shoot me. I didn't know what to do, so I put my truck in reverse, and I tried to get out of there."

His tearful wife offered her support. "I feel awful because we didn't really do anything, and I know we had a fight and I know we got physical, but you know, how many other people fight with their husbands and wives and they get to go to Victim Services and it's forgotten about?" She said in the same piece, "'Cause it happens all the time! We had one fight because of financial stuff and now we're being penalized because maybe he got in trouble before. It's not fair and it's not right."

While the Rock Machine appeared to be gaining traction in Winnipeg, the Hells Angels received a huge boost in manpower in Quebec at the end of May 2011. A Quebec Superior Court ruled that the province did not have enough resources to guarantee fair trials for 31 of the 155 Hells Angels and associates arrested as part of Operation SharQc in April 2009, so they were free to go. Although the Hells Angels were still desperately short of manpower in Quebec, the 31 who were released represented a profound windfall. To make things even more intriguing, two of them were Salvatore Cazzetta and Gilles Lambert, founders of the original Rock Machine who had since become top-level Hells Angels and had been accused of running a trafficking ring in association with men inside Quebec's Kahnawake reserve.

The low-intensity war in Winnipeg was still going on. At 4:00 a.m. on June 29, 2011, authorities received a number of calls about a house on Stranmillis Avenue in Saint Boniface. They were told that neighbours had heard shots fired and that there was smoke billowing from the house. They quickly doused the fire, which caused $70,000 damage to the small, plain, one-story home.

The blaze was considered suspicious and because it happened to be the house Joseph "Critical J" Strachan, president of the Rock Machine, shared with his parents, and since shots were reported, it bore further investigation. Further complicating matters was the fact that the previous night—at about the same time—police had responded to another call about shots fired in the same neighborhood, at a house inhabited by Redlined Support Crew member Justin MacLeod, which also caught on fire.

Investigators determined that the Stranmillis fire was the result of a Molotov cocktail thrown through a basement window from the house's backyard, while the other had begun when a lit road flare was thrown through a window.

Police could not track down any suspects, but they did admit that they too believed that a biker war was imminent or had already started. "The evidence that we do have to date suggests that it looks like it's two opposing motorcycle clubs that have been involved in different incidents in the last week," said Winnipeg police spokeswoman Natalie Aitken at a press conference. "When we have these types of incidents with individuals who are arming themselves, in this case, either with firearms or other weapons of choice, that's something that the police service is taking very seriously and is working as quickly as we can to locate and apprehend any individuals who would be responsible."

Less than two weeks later, it appeared as though the Rock Machine had struck back. At about midnight on July 10, units responded to a raging fire at DC Automotive, the same place where Fat Corey had been beaten up. Hours later, they went to another suspicious fire, this one at a residence on Royal Avenue in West Kildonan. A member of the Redlined Support Crew lived there. "The incidents on St. Mary's Road and on Royal Avenue are connected and are part of the current conflict between rival groups," police said.

When he was reached for a comment, DC Automotive owner Svenn Tergesen denied any involvement with the Hells Angels. He admitted that he knew bikers but said that members from both the Hells Angels and Rock Machine frequented his shop without incident. It was also at about this time that visitors' posts were no longer being published on the Rock Machine's Web site.

Two nights later, a quiet little street behind a community recreation center exploded with gunfire. It was 3:45 in the morning, and the racket woke the whole neighbourhood. As the car containing the gunmen sped away, people on the street collected themselves. A number of houses were riddled with bullet holes. One of the houses, which had nine people, including an infant, inside, had at least 20 bullet holes. One of the bullets made its way into the leg of a 14-year-old boy. The boy was rushed to hospital and survived. None of the other eight people in the house would talk with police or media, but neighbours indicated that at least one man from the house had connections with the Redlined Support Crew.

In the Great Quebec Biker War, public opinion of the bikers had turned to outrage after the death of an 11-year-old boy, killed when shrapnel from a car bomb penetrated his head. Many Montrealers—particularly mothers—rose up and protested against the bikers, making things more difficult for them in every way they could. But there was no similar outcry in Winnipeg after the 14-year-old was shot. Perhaps it's because he survived.

The tepid public response in Winnipeg was not for a lack of effort by police to keep the public apprised of the rising violence. "We are concerned that these incidents are occurring. We have homes that are being targeted. We have shootings where houses are being struck by numerous bullets. . . . When we have firearms being discharged in our community, it's putting a lot of people at risk," police spokesman Jason Michalyshen said at a press conference. "It's about drugs, it's about illegal activity. They are trying to get a foothold on our communities and our city for the sale of those drugs. They are doing everything in their power to intimidate one another."

While there was no public outrage, that doesn't mean people were not aware of the low-level war in their midst. On July 15, the Winnipeg police issued a public advisory "in an effort to inform members of the public regarding the potential for violence surrounding gang members residing in their neighbourhood."

It appeared as though the war had become more violent at 2:00 a.m. on the night of July 17, 2011, when a fire at a rooming house on Austin Street North killed five people and severely injured three more. When it was revealed that the fire had been intentionally set and the exits of the building had been deliberately blocked by furniture and other clutter, both media and people in the neighborhood openly attributed the blaze to bikers.

They were wrong, though. The culprit was Lulonda Flett, who had been in a long and repeatedly violent conflict with her sister-in-law Lynnette Harper, a resident of the house, which was well known as a place people with addictions came to dry out. Harper was one of the survivors. Flett pleaded guilty to five counts of manslaughter and one of arson.

Even so, the violence between the bikers in Winnipeg continued, but with property getting the damage, not people. At about two o'clock on the afternoon of August 11, 2011, the house that had had the road flare thrown through the window in June was attacked again but this time with Molotov cocktails. The house was empty at the time. A neighbor who did not want to be identified told the *Free Press* that MacLeod and another Redlined Support Crew member lived in the house. "You see all the Redlined Crew come by once in a while," he said and mentioned that they had a few big parties.

At about 4:00 a.m. the following night, 187 Ink, a tattoo and body-piercing shop in trendy Osborne Village, was attacked by firebombs. At the time, 187 Ink's flamboyant owner, Wayne Nuytten—who is well known for offering $25 maple leaf tattoos every July 1st—said that the bombing was a case of mistaken identity. "People get the wrong idea, big tattoo, big truck—I'm just a businessman, that's all," he said. "Whether they targeted me, if that is the case, they targeted the wrong person, I guess."

It should be noted that "187" is slang for murder, especially for the murder of police. It comes from the code used by police in much of the US and was popularized by the Snoop Dog song "187."

Still, Nuytten bristled at police characterizations that he was involved with the local gang war, even though he was a known friend of full-patch Hells Angel Anthony "AJ" McLennan, who was arrested in Project Divide and later admitted in court to helping recruit and oversee the Zig Zag Crew. In fact, Nuytten was so nonchalant, he came close to thanking the bombers for the free publicity. "In the end, with all the news and papers, I'm going to get free advertising to the point where I'm just going to gain more clientele off it," he told Global News. "I'm going to make all that money back, plus some." He had a point. Despite the hype and furor, the firebombing managed to cause only $2,000 in damages.

Despite Nuytten's claims of neutrality, nobody was surprised that the men arrested for the feeble firebombing were associates of the Rock Machine. Taylor Morrison and Shaine Stodgell were arrested almost immediately. Stodgell was also charged with the firebombing at DC Automotive. Both pleaded guilty to arson charges.

The arrests did little to convince the police, at least, that there would not be an escalation of the gang war. "I think it'd be naive for us to say that this is over," said Michalyshen to the *Free Press*. "This is ongoing and we're not letting up in any way, shape or form. From our perspective, I think things have escalated already. I think it's sheer luck that we haven't had further injuries or even fatalities as a result of some of these violent acts. We're hoping that due to our efforts and due to the good work of many officers these incidents will stop, but we can't assume that and we can't let up in any way, shape or form. I can assure you that further arrests are pending."

While the police were trying to get the people of Winnipeg to believe that there was a gang war brewing, if not already raging, the city's government was putting forth a completely different opinion. "We don't want to create panic," Winnipeg mayor Sam

Katz told reporters at a press conference. "Keep in mind, the WPS [police] has done its job. They've taken gangs and basically put them out of business. When they're out of business, something new emerges and that's basically what's happening. There's gang violence going on all the time. This isn't new; quite often, it's lower key and you don't hear about it."

But while the mayor seemed to find the level of gang violence not unexpected, the police were still making attempts to quell it. Although they stopped short of identifying gang members and affiliates by name and address, they did send officers into affected neighborhoods and told residents that there were gang members and associates in their areas. "We're going to be identifying with the residents that an individual who has gang affiliations, gang ties, resides in your community, resides in your neighbourhood, and we are informing you of that," said Michalyshen at the same press conference. "It's about notifications and it's about creating that heightened awareness. Members of the public can take that information and absorb it in any way they see fit and certainly bring forward any questions or any additional concerns that they might have." Of course, it was also a way for law enforcement to find out who was visiting whom and when.

One tip they received told them that a specific Hells Angels associate who lived on Antrim Road near Rockspur Street was being targeted for assassination by the Rock Machine. Police set up surveillance of the residence and shortly after midnight on Tuesday, August 9, 2011, they saw a Dodge Avenger slowly circle the otherwise quiet block a couple of times. Just as it was making its third pass, the alleged target opened his front door and stepped onto his porch.

Preempting any potential violence, the police surrounded the Avenger, boxing it in with their own vehicles. Instead of surrendering, the driver attempted to smash his way out, colliding with and severely damaging three police cars, leading to three officers suffering injuries. When the Avenger was finally brought to a halt, police arrested the driver, Guy Stevenson, and passengers Amanda Freeman and Joseph "JJ" Choken.

Police said that both Stevenson and Choken were members of the Vendettas and were also prospective members of the Rock Machine. Freeman, the car's owner and front-seat passenger, was characterized in the media as Stevenson's girlfriend. Inside the car, police found a piece of paper with the alleged target's address written on it, photos of four local Rock Machine members and, most importantly, a loaded .45-caliber handgun concealed in a bag. Choken was already wanted for an outstanding warrant, Stevenson was accused of breaches of his probation related to firearms convictions and Freeman had no previous criminal record.

The three had very different reactions when questioned by police, according to the *Free Press*. Choken remained silent, refusing to cooperate. Freeman maintained her innocence through ignorance. She claimed that she had been on a few dates with Stevenson and let him use her car but had no idea that he was in a gang, that there was a gun in the car or what the purpose of the trip was. Stevenson, on the other hand, seemed proud to be a foot soldier in the war against the Hells Angels. "I don't think there's any contention that he's not a gang member. He admits it clearly in his statement," prosecutor Brent Davidson said to Global News when the case came to trial. "He says the war is ongoing. He says it's a badge of honor. He says he's willing to die for this cause. This is the first we've seen any of the individuals confirm they are involved in this type of conflict." All three pleaded guilty to lesser crimes, Freeman to being an occupant of a vehicle with a firearm. Stevenson plea bargained and was sentenced to time served; charges against Freeman were dropped. Choken was sentenced to five years and six months.

Later in August, a trial that put a face on the Rock Machine for many Winnipeggers came to a close. Back in November 2002, Winnipeg had been shocked by the beating death of a man named Guy Pouliot. It was, like most Winnipeg (for that matter, most Canadian) murders, over a drug dispute. What stood out in Pouliot's murder was the incredible amount of brutality involved. The 46-year-old crack dealer was hog-tied, attacked first with a stereo speaker, then a snow shovel and finally a curtain rod. He had more than 100 individual injuries to his head alone. The pathologist who investigated the case told the media at a press conference that Pouliot's skull had been "cracked open." His body was wrapped in a shower curtain and dumped behind a nearby apartment building. Police followed a trail of blood from the body to Pouliot's house and arrested the two men inside.

One of the assailants, 17-year-old Chevy Ballentyne, was tried as an adult because of the seriousness of the crime. It was determined in the trial that he had sold drugs out of Pouliot's home of behalf of the Manitoba Warriors. The conflict started over how much Ballentyne was to pay Pouliot for the use of his house.

Ballentyne was found guilty and was sentenced to nine and a half years in prison. Despite 33 charges of assaulting fellow inmates and a widespread belief that he was intensely involved in the prison's drug trade, Ballentyne was released on October 10, 2009, after five and a half years. He was under several conditions and broke two of them when he drank alcohol and left the halfway house he was assigned to, effectively making himself a fugitive. Alerts were immediately put out for a six foot three, 203-pound aboriginal man with a shaved head and a tattoo of a skull on his neck.

Ballentyne turned up at a house party on December 23. After having a few drinks, he started assaulting people at random. He pulled out a knife and sliced one person as he flailed about with it. Eventually, he forced some of the partygoers to a second house.

When one person, a 19-year-old woman, attempted to leave, he dragged her by the hair caveman-style into a bedroom. There, Ballentyne hog-tied her, assaulted her with a chair leg and threatened to kill her, then "chop [her] up." After about ten minutes, he fled for reasons unknown and the other partygoers freed the woman.

Ballentyne was quickly arrested and charged; he was denied bail. The CBC reported that he tried to send a letter to the victim from behind bars, offering to "make it worth her while" if she lied in court. He laid out the offer in no uncertain terms. "Just for doing that I'll give you $500 up front . . . and I'll give you $1,000–$2,000 after the actual trial and I'm on the street," he wrote. "Or I can pay a couple of years university for you, any courses, I got you. Do this for me and believe me when I say this, I'll never forget you saved my life." The jail guards who intercepted the letter where surprised that he even went so far as to instruct her to say "Chevy is a sweet guy" and to warn her that the cops might try to "threaten" her into telling the truth. He then appealed to her sympathies. "If I was to get convicted of that . . . I'd get hit with the book."

He did get convicted. On August 17, 2011, Ballentyne was given a five-and-a-half-year sentence, much to the chagrin of Crown attorney Mike Desautels, who claimed to the *Free Press* that "Mr. Ballentyne is beyond rehabilitation." It was at that sentencing that the public learned how he could stay concealed on the streets of Winnipeg for months as a fugitive and how he could finance his attempted bribe. He was selling drugs for the Rock Machine.

While the Rock Machine was threatening to take the streets of Winnipeg from the Hells Angels and their allies, the post–Operation SharQc Hells Angels made a profound strategic decision. Except for British Columbia (and the Hells Angels there have never really been all that close to the others in Canada), the only region where the Hells Angels still had available manpower was Ontario. With the rest of the country in dire need of reinforcements, leadership in Ontario decided to put boots on the ground where they were needed most—Montreal. Ontario bikers were sent in to form clubs to serve the Hells Angels' needs in La Belle Province—the Thunder Bikers in Saguenay, the Iron Beast in the Lower St. Lawrence, the Black Mask on the South Shore and the Dark Souls in Montreal itself. Another puppet club, the Soul Takers, emerged in Ottawa, and the Brotherhood, an American club with good relations with the Hells Angels, opened chapters in Montreal and Ontario. Clearly the Hells Angels found it preferable, or at least more feasible, to protect their interests in Montreal than in Winnipeg.

The conflict in Winnipeg began to heat up again as the weather got colder. On December 3, 2011, a massive blaze at Logan Radiator sent a cloud of black smoke into the sky and knocked out power in the neighborhood. Police revealed that it was the third fire at that same location in one year—the others were on June 14 and July 6—and indicated that all three were related to the Rock Machine–Hells Angels war. Speaking to the CBC, an employee of Logan Radiators referred to the June blaze as "the firebombing."

While both the Rock Machine and the Hells Angels were waiting for the other side to make the next move, it was the police who altered the balance of power in Winnipeg.

Evidence gathered from a paid informant and phone taps in an operation called Project Deplete led to the arrest of 13 people for drug and weapons offenses on February 2, 2012. Also seized, according to the police department's official release, were 6,912 grams of cocaine, 465 grams of crack, 272 grams of methamphetamine, 9,811 tablets of Ecstasy, 1,063 grams of MDMA, 501 tablets of oxycodone and 891 grams of marijuana.

Two of the initial arrests were particularly interesting. Former Hells Angels Billy Bowden and Joshua Lyons, who had since joined the Rock Machine, both faced multiple trafficking and proceeds-of crime-charges. The trial is still pending and the pair have entered not-guilty pleas.

A few days later, evidence from Project Deplete was used to issue a warrant for Jamie Korne. He was finally tracked down in the rural Manitoba community of Newdale on February 22, 2012, and charged with trafficking based on intercepted text messages on his BlackBerry. Korne pleaded guilty to trafficking and received a three-and-a-half-year sentence.

When his arrest became public, the Vagos—he claimed to be their Canadian president—distanced themselves from him. A representative of the gang approached Winnipeg media and told them that, although they had some contact with Korne, he was not a member, let alone president of a chapter. They had never even met him in person. "I don't want my motorcycle club associated with that crap," the man said.

The gang had, however, acknowledged on their Web site that there were Vagos in Canada but did not specify who or where, or whether they had formed a chapter yet.

It didn't take long for the police to strike the other side even harder. On March 16, 2012, more than 150 Winnipeg police officers raided eight locations in Winnipeg, including the luxurious home of Hells Angels Winnipeg chapter president Dale Jason Sweeney. In all, 11 suspects were arrested, including Dale Sweeney; his older brother, Roderick Patrick "Rod" Sweeney, a full-patch Hells Angel; Carmine Puteri, another full-patch; Kurtis Donald Scott, an associate; Christopher Allan Gerula, another associate; Brendin Kyle Wall, a full-patch Redlined Support Crew member: Donovan Michael Lafrance, a Redlined Support Crew prospect; and two Redlined Support Crew associates, Thomas Clinton Barnecki and Jonathon Stewart. All were found guilty or pleaded to lesser charges. Dale Sweeney received an 11-year sentence for trafficking.

The raid was called Operation Flatlined—a tongue-in-cheek

reference to the Redlined Support Crew's motto, "Get Redlined or get flatlined," itself a reference to an EKG with no pulse reading—and it was a significant operation because it left the Winnipeg Hells Angels with just four full-patch members, three short of the minimum seven needed to maintain a charter.

After the 10-month investigation—the first major bust of a biker gang in Canadian history that did not rely on an informant—police revealed that the Winnipeg Hells Angels–Rock Machine war had been much more violent than the public realized. "There have been almost as many unreported incidents of violence between them," police said in their application for search warrants. "The war has been quiet the past few months, but the rivalry is still existent. More violence is predicted between these two groups."

In fact, the bikers had been so quiet about the violence that police found out that Rod Sweeney's house had been firebombed only when they overheard him telling his brother, Dale, about it over a tapped phone. "I guess somebody tried blowing up my house last night," Rod Sweeney said on tape, pointing out that he wasn't home at the time, but his children and "old lady" heard something going on. He then told his brother that the video cameras he had installed on his house clearly showed masked culprits throwing a Molotov cocktail that, luckily for his family, burned out instead of exploding. After telling his brother about the firebombing, Sweeney then made a series of phone calls in which he allegedly ordered six low-ranking associates to exact some revenge. That vengeance came in the form of a smashed windshield on a pickup truck owned by a Rock Machine member. "This is an example of how the Hells Angels take care of their own business, as they like to say," Winnipeg police commented to the *Free Press*.

Other conversations caught on tape, police allege, explained their methods. They used the code words "Knock, knock, ginger man" to mean a home invasion and "convoys" to mean a group of Hells Angels and associates who wore their colors and frequented Rock Machine hangouts to conduct surveillance or intimidate their rivals.

More important to the case, however, were conversations about how the proceeds of drug sales were allegedly divided between Hells Angels and Redlined Support Crew members and instructions on money laundering. There was one almost comical set of conversations as the Hells Angels frantically tried to compensate for a kilo of cocaine that had been seized by police but had already been promised to eager clients.

With just four members on the streets, the Zig Zag Crew essentially relegated to history and the Redlined Support Crew facing serious manpower problems, the future for the Hells Angels in Winnipeg looked grim. "They'll have to shut down until they can recruit some other people," Winnipeg organized crime inspector Rick Guyader said to CBC News. "It's a very big deal."

To add further insult to injury, police showed up at the World of Wheels motorcycle show on March 19 and seized a Harley-Davidson belonging to Dale Sweeney. Some friends had brought the jailed president's bike—with the notorious winged skull of the Hells Angels painted on both sides of the gas tank—to the show and protested when the cops came to get it. There was some shouting and shoving, but no arrests were made.

On the same day, Puteri was released from custody and all charges were dropped in exchange for his exit from the Hells Angels. He was freed pending 14 conditions including a midnight curfew, a ban on his owning gang paraphernalia and an agreement not to communicate with a list of Hells Angels members and associates that ran three pages long. The Crown said it offered the same deal to Rod Sweeney, but he decided against it.

Instead of bail, the arrested Hells Angels and associates

who were freed to await trial were offered peace bonds with complicated restrictions that included not associating with one another. In effect, many of the Hells Angels, Zig Zag Crew, Redlined Support Crew and associates were on the streets but unable to act. Legal challenges were mounted against the peace bonds but to little avail.

The Rock Machine, on the other hand, was growing. Chapters in Alberta and Ontario were gaining members and even Montreal was seeing their presence once again. In January 2012, police in Montreal said they saw two men wearing Rock Machine jackets exit an east-end bar—something that would have been unthinkable just a few months earlier. Before that, visiting Rock Machine members from the rest of Canada, Germany and Australia had been spotted in Montreal in April and July of 2011. On March 24, 2012, no fewer than twenty guys wearing Rock Machine colors were spotted in Cabaret Les Amazones, a downtown strip joint.

Things remained quiet in Winnipeg until October 14, 2012. Jean Paul "JP" Beaumont had a long history of minor arrests dating back to his teens. Aged 22 in 1995, he received a 13-year sentence for firing shots in a holdup of a Little Caesars pizza joint in St. Vital.

He made news again after an incident in March 2005 at the Dirty Laundry Bar in Winnipeg's Little Italy. On March 11, some Hells Angels, Zig Zag Crew members (including Beaumont) and their associates were relaxing in the bar. A man wearing body armor—now widely believed to be a member of Sandham's Bandidos—walked in and shot Billy Bowden, at the time a full-patch Hells Angel, in the chest.

Beaumont returned fire, slightly injuring the intruder.

Bowden survived, as the bullet missed any major organs or blood vessels.

Neither shooting victim, both of whom were arrested, cooperated with police. Others in attendance placed Beaumont at the scene, and on March 24, 2005, he was arrested. At the time, police described him as a "full-patch member of the Zig Zag Crew."

Although they were unable to make any shooting charges stick, just being where he was, with whom he was when the shooting took place while he was on parole for the St. Vital stickup was enough to end his freedom.

After Beaumont left prison again, police, acting on a tip, searched his house on June 3, 2009, and found a Norinco CQ (a Chinese-made copy of the Colt AR-15 assault rifle). This time, the police described him as a "full-patch member of the Rock Machine." In fact, many sources claim that he was the gang's sergeant at arms or chief enforcer.

At the trial, Beaumont claimed that he had no knowledge of the gun's presence in his house and he claimed that his DNA was on the weapon because he had sneezed on it shortly after the cops found it. It worked, he beat the rap.

But his bad-boy lifestyle caught up with him. On parole after going to prison for committing a crime while he was on parole for committing another crime, Beaumont had acquired enough less-serious charges—dangerous driving, flight from police and missing court dates—for a warrant to be issued for his arrest. He was found in Toronto and returned to Winnipeg after making a stop in Thunder Bay, where there was another warrant for him.

Beaumont was sent to Brandon Correctional Centre, and at 10:00 a.m. on October 14, 2012, a guard found him motionless in his cell in Unit C. Police and emergency services were called. He was pronounced dead on the scene.

It was widely rumored in the prison (and reported in the media) that Beaumont had been stabbed. To avoid violence, the already contentious Brandon Correctional Centre was put on lockdown. An autopsy was performed, but its results were not made public "due to privacy issues." What Brandon police did say to the CBC was that Beaumont's death, although he was just 39 years old, was due to "non-criminal" causes. They also said that they would not discuss the case any further.

While nobody would be charged in connection with Beaumont's death, a Manitoba Hells Angel and a Hells Angels associate in the same prison were charged with a different murder just a month later. Full-patch Manitoba Hells Angel Jeffrey David Peck and associate Robert Simpson—who had a couple of murder and manslaughter convictions from Montreal, including that of an 80-year-old woman—were both serving life sentences for a gang-related murder. In November 2012, they were charged with first-degree murder for the 1982 death of 19-year-old drug dealer Robert Frank Conroy while all three were in Kingston, Ontario's Collins Bay Institution. Simpson later admitted to the murder and was convicted of it while already serving a life sentence. He said that he and Peck were ordered to kill their old friend Conroy by the now-deceased Claude "Co Co" Bard—who, as Simpson said, "ran" their cell block—because of an unsubstantiated rumor that Conroy was a child molester. Bard, he said, threatened to kill Simpson if he did not carry out the plan because he had brought Conroy into their midst. He also told him to kill Peck as well if he "had time." Peck's charge is still pending, and he has pleaded not guilty.

Although the Rock Machine outnumbered the Hells Angels on the streets of Winnipeg—though just barely—and had plenty of fuel to be outraged, they did not strike. Instead, it was law enforcement that landed a decisive blow.

On January 30, 2013, an RCMP-led multi-force raid called Project Dilemma descended on several addresses in the Winnipeg area. A six-month investigation led to 11 warrants. Arrested for trafficking and firearms offenses were Rock Machine president Strachan (at his parents' house), Rock Machine full-patches

Todd Murray, John Curwin and Cameron Hemminger and Rock Machine prospect Shannon Campbell, along with associates Christopher Camara, Donny Syraxa, Danny Tran, Patrick La, Teagveer Singh Gill and Richard Lund. It's not coincidental that while all of the Rock Machine members and the prospect were white, the dealers they allegedly worked with were from diverse ethnicities.

The police seized the usual: cash, 16 pounds of cocaine, 1,800 tablets of BZP (imitation Ecstasy), 8 pounds of marijuana, a 2009 Audi S5 and plenty of Rock Machine–related clothing and paraphernalia. More importantly, they uncovered six firearms, ammunition, two pipe bombs and nine other explosive devices. It certainly looked to many as though law enforcement had preempted an attack on what was left of the Hells Angels in Winnipeg.

It was considered a major coup because the Winnipeg chapter of the Rock Machine had proven to be their strongest—certainly the only one that would challenge the Hells Angels face to face. "The chapter that they had there was by far having the most success," OPP biker expert Len Isnor told *Vice* magazine. "They formed a very strong chapter, with some strong personalities and they were able to be successful in an area where other groups were down. Over the last few years the police in Manitoba and Winnipeg delivered a lot of blows to the Hells Angels . . . so it was perfect timing for another group to come in."

After the arrests, the cops started beating their chests. "Here in Winnipeg and in Manitoba there are currently no full-patch wearing members and prospects on the streets," said RCMP sergeant Travis Charlton, who had led the raids, at a press conference. "There's a few associates on the streets for the Rock Machine that are still friends with the members. They weren't targets of our investigation; we just targeted the club members themselves. The Rock Machine is very fluid here as far as their recruitment and members, as members have gone in and out from the club."

But there were plenty of Rock Machine associates (or at least Hells Angels enemies) still left on the streets in Winnipeg. In fact, many of the people who had originally aligned with the Rock Machine in Winnipeg had either left the club or operated with them at arm's length due to a widespread disgust for Strachan and his methods.

"Nobody trusted him," a Manitoba Rock Machine associate who preferred not give his name told me. "He was only after one thing—money. And he'd do anything to get it." In fact, it has been widely circulated that Strachan offered full-patch status to anyone who agreed to move product and pay him $500 up front.

Many members of the Rock Machine outside Strachan's inner circle in Winnipeg were happy to see the 11 men arrested in Project Dilemma gone. Few of them shed tears when Strachan was sentenced on June 25, 2013, to nine years after plea bargaining and admitting to trafficking and gangsterism. Curwin pleaded guilty to trafficking and was sentenced to 9½ years. Murray received 11 years after pleading guilty to trafficking and weapons charges. Hemminger also pleaded guilty to trafficking, as did Syraxa, La, Lund, Tran and Gill. Charges were dropped against Campbell and Camara.

With the power vacuum in Winnipeg, Canadian and international leadership was assumed by the Toronto chapter. Shortly after the news of the Project Dilemma arrests, Rock Machine representatives from all over Canada mobilized a recruiting drive in Winnipeg.

By late spring of 2013, there were at least three full-patch members of the Rock Machine in Winnipeg. That wasn't enough for a chapter, but at least there were boots on the ground, making new friends and keeping old friends calm.

While the Rock Machine, in any incarnation, have never been associated with great strategic leadership, even they knew that Winnipeg was too vital a city to lose. There was no way they'd just hand it over to the Hells Angels.

CHAPTER 16

WHY EASY MONEY MEANT LOTS OF CRIME IN THE LOWER MAINLAND

While the people of Winnipeg may have been wondering what to expect of organized crime and the drug trade once the Rock Machine had been officially demolished and the Hells Angels were experiencing manpower issues, their answer could be seen a couple of time zones to the west.

The Hells Angels had been present in and around Vancouver since 1983, but the chapters there had always operated differently than their "brothers" to the east. In Quebec and Ontario, bikers had traditionally been shaped, supported and supplied by the Italian Mafia. But there was never a large, certainly not a dominant, Mafia group in Vancouver. Instead, the West Coast bikers were supplied by a variety of sources.

Marijuana originally came from California, but the explosive growth of local weed—known internationally as BC Bud—turned British Columbia from a net importer of marijuana to one of the world's biggest exporters by the time the Hells Angels started throwing their weight around.

Cocaine came from Mexico and Colombia through a number of go-betweens in California or Washington. From time to time, Canadians would try to establish their own connections in Latin America, usually with disastrous results.

Heroin came from East Asia—grown and manufactured in Southeast Asia and trafficked through middlemen usually from Hong Kong, Taiwan or Korea. Many of the organizations that brought drugs from East Asia were very powerful in their own right, but they never established the kind of united front and solid infrastructure that the Mafia enjoyed east of the Rockies.

That doesn't mean there weren't drugs in Vancouver. Quite the opposite: It has long been as drug-soaked as any North American city. If anything, there were more drugs there than the Hells Angels had the manpower to move.

And, unlike in the rest of the country, the West Coast Hells Angels had very little competition in the way of other bikers. There were never any Rock Machine or Bandidos or Outlaws there. That's not just because the Hells Angels did such an efficient job of keeping them out. It was also a question of demographics.

Because of their history and image (and because most of them have a whites-only rule), outlaw motorcycle gangs did not have an unlimited group of men there from which to recruit.

The call of the open road meant little to the residents of a city hemmed in by mountains and salt water, one that did not have a single expressway in or out of town. The warrior mentality didn't exactly resonate with the largely blasé residents. But more important than anything else, there weren't the large numbers of disillusioned, angry and uneducated whites that the rest of the country had so many of. The Vancouver area never suffered from mass factory closings and layoffs, so it never had a large class of the uneducated, unskilled whites that outlaw motorcycle clubs in other places found so easy to recruit from.

That doesn't mean there weren't lots of people who wanted to make money selling drugs. It's just that there weren't that many who were attracted to the militaristic, loud-pipes and leather-biker ethos with its skulls-and-dragons imagery.

While organized crime had existed in the Vancouver area for about as long as it had been settled, it didn't have its first star gangster until the early 1990s.

Just like Rocco Perri and Mom Boucher and Vic Cotroni and Johnny Pops and all the other big-time Canadian gangsters, Bhupinder "Bindy" Johal showed signs of his vocation early. Kicked out of two high schools for assaults (including one in which he sent a vice-principal to a hospital), he soon turned to crime.

At the time, organized crime in the region was mostly segregated by race. Chinese dealt with Chinese, whites with whites and so on. Johal hooked up with other men from the Indian, predominantly Sikh, community and eventually they formed into a semi-cohesive group. Called the Indo-Canadian Mafia or the Punjabi Mafia, like most other gangs, they started with small-time crime like stickups and fencing before moving up to cocaine trafficking.

Their boss was Jimsher "Jimmy" Dosanjh. After he went away for the March 14, 1991, murder of Colombian importer Teodoro Salcedo, Johal muscled in and took over control of the group. When Jimmy Dosanjh was released on parole early in 1994, there was something of a power struggle. He expected to retake control of the gang, but Johal had no intention of letting it go.

On February 25, 1994, some of Johal's men lured Dosanjh, who must have believed they were his own men, into an alley with the promise of some stolen electronics. Once he was out of plain sight, they shot and killed him.

Jimmy's brother, Ranjit "Ron," was enraged at the young upstart and swore revenge. He was shot in the face on April 19, 1994, ending the threat from the old guard and any real opposition to Johal within the gang. Even so, a man named Glen Olson was shot and killed a few days after Ron Dosanjh was murdered because somebody thought he was Johal.

Johal did, however, have to deal with law enforcement. On the day of Ron Dosanjh's cremation, Johal was arrested along with Preet "Peter" Sarbjit Gill, Rajinder "Big Raj" Benji, Sun News Lal, Michael Kim Budai and Ho-Sik "Phil" Kim for the Dosanjh murders. Kim was said to be an assassin hired by the conspirators.

While in jail, Johal shared a cell with a minor-league member of his gang named Bal Buttar. The two became good friends, and Johal set up Buttar as the leader of the Indo-Canadian Mafia's enforcement branch (similar to the Rockers in Montreal), later known as The Elite.

In one of the most expensive and strangest trials in Canadian history—disrupted and made famous after Gill was caught having an affair with juror Gillian Guess—Johal was acquitted. He was clearly the boss, and now he had The Elite to back him up.

After that, he started to exhibit many of the eccentricities that the newly powerful often do. He ordered assassinations not only of enemies but also of his own gang mates if he suspected them of wrongdoing or if they did not show him enough respect.

Eventually, it all caught up with him. The Crown had announced that he and Peter Gill would be retried after their first trial was so poorly handled. Out on bail, Johal went to go party at his favorite nighclub, the Palladium, on December 20, 1998. He was shot in the back of the head and died on the dance floor. Police had plenty of suspects, but since not a single one of the 350 people at the club that night would talk to them, no arrests were made. Years later, as reported by CBC, Buttar later admitted he had masterminded the whole thing because Johal was getting out of hand. He spoke up in 2004 from a nursing home he lived in after a 2001 shooting left him paralyzed. The Crown decided that his physical condition made it impractical to pursue any legal action against him.

Johal was important not just for what he did as a trafficker and gang leader but for what he stood for in the community. He played up the part of the gangster in the media, admitting he sold drugs and even once threatening the life of another gangster in front of CBC TV news cameras.

He was larger than life, driving around town in expensive cars and showing off his wealth. To many young men in the area, he was something of an outlaw hero. A decade later, many of the key players in the drug trade were men who admitted they were either directly taught or at least profoundly inspired by Johal.

As one anonymously told Indo-Canadian expert Arthur J. Pais, "To many young people in the immigrant community who feel that Canadian society does not give them enough chance to succeed, joining gangsters is an exercise in building their self-esteem. Why do you think Bindy Johal was a hero to many young Indo-Canadians? His legend had spread wide in the past few years among Indians not only here but also in Toronto and Montreal, New York and San Francisco. He stood up to his school principals, he beat up those who called him racial names—and he was making a lot of money even though he was in his midtwenties. He drove fancy cars, he had girls falling all over him."

With Johal gone, the Indo-Canadian Mafia lost its dominance. It would survive in many forms, re-emerging years later as the Dhak-Duhre organization.

With their decline, a familiar group swept in to take advantage of the power vacuum on the streets. The Hells Angels in British Columbia had been around since 1983 but never had a great deal of manpower. Instead, they relied heavily on other organizations and individuals to do their work for them (which had the extra advantage of further protecting them from law enforcement).

Many of these groups—by necessity—would be made up of other ethnicities or be multiethnic, their ancestry preventing them from ever being full-patch Hells Angels. While many were more than happy to get rich as associates—a model demonstrated by Mom Boucher's loyal black friend, Picasso Wooley—the overall effect was to make many of the organizations something more than traditional puppet clubs. With no hope of, and often no interest in, becoming Hells Angels, these gangs worked more independently and would even challenge and oppose the Hells Angels when they could. It was a strange situation but one not too different than that which gave rise to the Alliance and later the Rock Machine in Montreal. Without any natural opposition, the Hells Angels—through their greed, arrogance and violence—created one.

The emergence of three major groups set the stage for the gang war that started in British Columbia. The first began with a bar fight—actually, two bar fights—in Abbotsford that established not just the existence of an opposition to the Hells Angels but also the fact that they were prepared to defend themselves.

For years, the young men who wanted to be Hells Angels in British Columbia were given the same rigorous auditioning as they were everywhere else. Manpower shortages led to many of them being given fairly major responsibilities even before they attained hangaround status. These intern Hells Angels were known in the area as "supporters" or "81." Both terms derive from the fact that since nonmembers may not wear the Hells Angels logo in any form, the club opened a new revenue stream by selling what they called "support gear" to their admirers and recruits. It consisted of clothes—mainly, but hardly limited to, hoodies, T-shirts and caps—that were usually red and white and always had the slogan

SUPPORT 81 on them. Of course, "81" is slang for "Hells Angels," derived from the fact that *H* is the eighth letter of the alphabet and *A* is the first.

They were the Hells Angels' foot soldiers, working as entry-level dealers and tough guys. Not surprisingly, their work took them mainly to bars and nightclubs, where their customers congregated.

But the Hells Angels and their support crew had anything but a monopoly on drugs in the Vancouver area. The kids in the nightclubs had plenty of different sources for drugs—keep in mind that the border to the US was hardly more than a hedge in most places around there—and that many largely Asian gangs had access to drugs from across the Pacific.

As has always been the case, competition in illegal markets led to violence. At first it was small time, just big white kids in SUPPORT 81 T-shirts beating up on other kids—often smaller and usually Asian—when they caught them selling drugs or even buying from someone other than themselves.

That status quo held fast for years. In May 1997, a group of drug sellers and their friends decided to do something about it. Under the auspices of a failed restaurateur named Clay Roueche, they formed a new club. United by little more than their hatred for the Hells Angels and their strong-arm tactics, the growing group had no interest in Harley-Davidsons or leather. Instead, they wore distinctive hoodies and identifying tattoos and were expected to master the basics of mixed martial arts fighting. Proud of their multiethnic membership, they called themselves the United Nations.

They operated under the Hells Angels' radar for the first period of their existence, avoiding confrontation with the tough guys who they believed outnumbered them. That changed in 2000.

One Friday night—the date is not exactly clear—according to the CBC, a number of the United Nations were hanging out at a bar in Abbotsford called Animals when a few Support 81 guys showed up. Such incursions were not uncommon, as the Hells Angels would often show strength in an attempt to intimidate rival drug dealers.

Unlike what had always happened up until then, this time the United Nations actually fought back. Banding together, they forcibly ejected the Support crew from the bar and went back to partying. Shocked, the Support 81 guys threatened to come back the following week with reinforcements.

They did. In fact, there were about 15 of them. But they were facing at least 70 members of the UN. The Support 81 guys regrouped in the parking lot and called for backup. About 30 showed up. Certain that their reputation would make up for their lack of manpower, the red-and-white side was wrong. They were thoroughly beaten. When it was all over, the UN had made a statement—they were established in the Lower Mainland, and they weren't going anywhere.

The second important group also emerged from an internecine set of brawls. In Coquitlam, there was a group of young toughs of Korean descent who had a habit of beating up smaller, non-Korean teenagers, especially those from the Southeast Asian community. In 2000, they happened upon two such guys, 14-year-olds Quang Vinh "Michael" Le and Eddie Narong, and assaulted and humiliated them.

Le and Narong had no intention of letting it go at that. Instead, they gathered about 20 of their friends and showed up at the Hi-Max, an all-ages strip-mall karaoke joint the Koreans frequented. When one of them, 16-year-old Richard Jung, got up to go to the men's room, the other group jumped him. According to the case before the British Columbia Supreme Court in the trial of Kai Chao, Nan Feng, Thanh-Son Huynh and Jasben Lai (who were there), the place erupted in a melee and when it was done, Jung was dead.

Hardly sophisticated criminals, both Le and Narong were caught, found guilty and sentenced. Because of their youth, they were sentenced to serve time at the Willingdon Youth Detention Centre in Burnaby. It was a notorious place, full of gangs and with a code of silence. Le and Narong quickly aligned with other put-upon kids and formed a mutual protection society called the Red Scorpions.

It didn't start out as much, but after Le and Narong were released, the Red Scorpions morphed into the same kind of gang as the UN. Multiethnic and identified by tattoos, mainly of Eastern imagery, the Red Scorpions quickly gathered steam. As with the old gangsters in places like Montreal and Hamilton before them, the connections made and lessons learned behind bars prepared its members for careers in drug trafficking.

The third group who would play a major part in the road to gang war in the Vancouver area were the Independent Soldiers. Originally a coalition of Indo-Canadian gangs operating in local parks and high schools, the Independent Soldiers were just one of many groups brought up by the rising tide of the drug trade in the Lower Mainland.

BC Bud was so plentiful—although exports to the US and other countries took away a huge share—and popular that the market was immense. The standard means of distribution at bars and nightclubs expanded to include dial-a-dope services in which a discreet phone call to numbers handed out all over town guaranteed prompt delivery of weed. The delivery guys, often recent immigrants or young teens, were deliberately kept in the dark so that if caught, they couldn't give up any incriminating details to save themselves.

The Independent Soldiers grew rapidly and, like all of the other major drug-dealing organizations, became increasingly multiethnic as they sought manpower to run their operation. As they evolved, the Independent Soldiers found themselves growing increasingly close to the Hells Angels, both as suppliers and as a source of recruits. Many of the old Support 81 crew—and other wannabes drawn from other parts of British Columbia less afflu- ent than the Vancouver area—turned to the Independent Soldiers for employment.

The close relationship the Independent Soldiers had with the Hells Angels was demonstrated by the fact that the two groups shared a hangout. Back in the 1990s, many of the Hells Angels were acquiring legitimate businesses, often through intimidation. One of them, Donald Roming, was—according to an area source who'd rather not be named—well known for having savagely assaulted tiny 67-year-old Vancouver impresario Jack Card for standing in his way. Roming owned a Gastown nightclub, Loft Six.

Roming himself was murdered outside another club, Bar None, on the night of March 9, 2001. In retaliation, an independent drug dealer named John Rodgers was killed and his associate badly injured after they were lured to a gas station on April 27, 2001.

Even after Roming's death, both Hells Angels and Independent Soldiers (and other gang members) hung out peaceably at Loft Six.

Normally, a guy like John "JJ" Johnson would be welcome there. But he made a mistake. As a bouncer at Brandi's, a Hells Angels–associated strip joint, he made the executive decision to beat up an obnoxious customer. It just so happened that the cus- tomer in question was also a big-time drug dealer connected to the Independent Soldiers, so when Johnson showed up at Loft Six on August 16, 2003, fireworks erupted.

After the shooting stopped, Johnson was dead and so were bar patrons John Popovich, who didn't have any obvious gang con- nections, and, some 20 blocks away after he tried to drive to a hos- pital, Mahmoud Al-Khalil, a member of the Independent Soldiers and little brother of Khalil Al-Khalil, who was murdered in Surrey in 2001. Among the injured was Gerpal Singh "Paul" Dosanjh—a cousin of two of the original Indo-Canadian Mafia members, Jimmy and Ron Dosanjh—who was shot in the head but survived.

According to police, a person called in to report a handgun in the street. Moments later, another caller told them that a bicyclist had picked it up and ridden off.

After the Loft Six incident, the membership and leadership of the Independent Soldiers changed. In effect, they became less independent as they recruited and promoted more and more Hells Angels–friendly members. Already the most likely gang in the area to work with the Hells Angels, they essentially became a puppet club after that.

Among the polyglot of drug-dealing gangs in the area at the time, there were the decidedly anti–Hells Angels UN, the pro–Hells Angels Independent Soldiers and the not-especially-fond-of-either-side Red Scorpions.

Outside of the densely populated and diverse Lower Mainland, where the demographics and culture more closely fit the traditional biker environment, the Hells Angels set up puppet clubs in much the same way they had other places. In drug-hungry Prince George, for example, the dirty work was generally done by the Renegades, a 1%er club, who handed off duties to a street gang known simply as the Crew. A number of unnecessary assault arrests led to the incarceration of the Crew's president, Scott Payne, and his second-in-command, Joshua Hendrick, so the gang was disbanded. Its members were merged with some other tough guys—some imported from other parts of the province—to become the Prince George chapter of the Independent Soldiers.

Their cooperation was working well until the Independent Soldiers chapter president, Billy Moore, started cooperating with police. His bullet-riddled body was found on March 25, 2005, in the front seat of his car. The club carried on with a new leader,

Romano Brienza (according to the RCMP), imported from the Lower Mainland.

While there was plenty of money to be made selling crack in places like Prince George, the real money was in getting BC Bud over the border. The primary method was to hide the weed in legitimate commodities going over the border in tractor-trailers, but the loss rate was high and truckers were demanding more and more money to play along.

So, according to dozens of published reports, enterprising smugglers tried everything from backpacks to kayaks to tunneling under the border. But the most efficient way to get drugs over the border was to fly them over. A small airplane or helicopter could easily wander into US airspace—even for just a few seconds—to make a low-level drop of a few hundred pounds of weed at a pre-determined location.

CHAPTER 17

A DIFFERENT KIND OF WAR IN MONTREAL

While the cold war was heating up in places like Winnipeg, the ancestral home of organized crime in Canada, Montreal, saw the two superpowers, that dominant Mafia family and the Hells Angels, face off against each other again. They'd also be taking on other challengers. To understand what happened, you have to go back to the US.

If there was ever a perfect undercover agent, it was Joe Pistone. He was of Sicilian heritage and spoke the Sicilian dialect of Italian fluently. He knew how the Mafia worked from his experiences with them growing up in Paterson, New Jersey, but neither he nor any of his family or close friends were directly involved, so he'd never be recognized by anyone important. He knew how to drive everything from a bulldozer to an 18-wheel tractor-trailer. Best of all, he had an uncanny talent—no matter how stressful the situation, he would never, ever let anyone see him sweat.

By the early 1970s, he was a young veteran FBI agent eager to get to work undercover. The FBI gave him a chance in 1974. They deleted his government identity file and gave him an entirely new identity—Donnie Brasco. His first operation as Brasco was a huge success. He busted up a truck-hijacking ring on the US East Coast that resulted in 30 arrests. Since his testimony was never needed in court, his cover was not blown.

The FBI put him back to work. After a few gemology classes so he could talk the talk, Brasco was sent to Miami Beach to pose as a successful jewel thief. Hanging out at local nightclubs and bars, flashing cash and fancy jewelry, it didn't take long for the bad guys to come to him. His first connection was with a guy named Giuliano "Jilly" Greca, who ran a Florida truck-hijacking and fencing ring for the Colombo crime family in New York.

After realizing Greca was small time, Brasco started hanging out with Anthony "Tony" Mirra, who was well connected with the Bonanno family. Mirra was well known in Mafia circles—both in Miami and New York City—as being a little bit nuts. He was temperamental, cruel and unpredictably violent, but he was also a top earner, so the Bonannos tolerated him—from a distance.

Mirra seemed to sincerely like Brasco and set him up with his buddy, Benjamin "Lefty Guns" Ruggiero. Ruggiero ran a number of different operations and put Brasco in charge of his illegal casino-style gambling branch. Brasco proved adept at the job and even started his own side businesses. In fact, he was such a good earner that the top Bonannos in New York began to take notice of him, particularly Dominick "Sonny Black" Napolitano. He was a powerful ally to have. A longtime soldier for the Bonannos, he was elevated to caporegime in the Williamsburg neighborhood of Brooklyn after Carmine Galante was assassinated in 1979.

It was a dangerous time. The Bonanno family was still at war with itself as loyalists and rebels were shooting each other in the streets. Always looking for suitable manpower, Napolitano decided to sponsor Brasco for membership—in the parlance of the Mafia,

Brasco was going to become a "made man," the equivalent of what bikers call a full-patch. While the FBI wanted to pull Brasco from the case because it was getting too dangerous, Brasco—who had come to hate the Mafia—wanted to keep going, to prove that no crime organization was completely safe from infiltration.

There were two problems with that. The first was that everybody wanted a piece of him, and nothing could happen until it was determined who he'd report to, since Mirra (who discovered him), Ruggiero (who employed him) and Napolitano (their captain) all claimed him as their own.

The second problem was that in order to be made, he was required to assassinate Anthony "Bruno" Indelicato, a rogue Bonanno captain who had basically signed his own death certificate when he attempted to kill Gambino family boss John Gotti in broad daylight on a major expressway.

Aware of that, the FBI pulled the plug. On July 26, 1981, FBI agents met with Napolitano and told him that Brasco was one of theirs, working undercover. He didn't believe them, he even laughed in their faces, but, as a matter of protocol, he carried the message to his superiors. They did believe it. Within days, Napolitano and Mirra were killed for allowing a cop into their inner circle. Ruggiero was spared when he, along with about 200 other mafiosi, including Bonanno boss Philip "Rusty" Rastelli, was arrested.

Although Brasco never actually met Vito Rizzuto, his undercover work made it possible for US authorities to implicate the alleged Montreal kingpin, in a massive sweep, for his part in the murders of three rival gangsters on May 5, 1981. On January 20, 2004, Canadian authorities arrested him. Though he fought extradition, the Americans eventually got him in August 2006 and sentenced him to 10 years in the notorious ADX maximum security (supermax) facility in Florence, Colorado, where he was held alongside Richard Reid, the notorious "shoe bomber" and Ted "the Unabomber" Kaczynski.

While Rizzuto was fighting extradition, the results of Project Colisée—a three-year long operation in which police bugged the Consenza Social Club, Rizzuto's headquarters, later renamed Associazione Cattolica Eraclea—did even more to cripple the family.

Project Colisée revealed that sacks of money would be brought into the café and be divided among the bosses, who would leave through the back door with the cash stuffed in their pockets or socks. The *Montreal Gazette* reported that one crew boss, Rocco Sollecito, was recorded telling a soldier named Beniamino Zappia: "When they do something—and it doesn't matter when they do it—they always bring something here so that it can be divided up among us five: me, Vito, Nicolo, Paolo." Vito, of course, was Vito Rizzuto, Nicolo was his 82-year-old dad, and Paolo was Paolo Renda, Vito's brother-in-law. Although he didn't mention it to Zappia, the fifth share went to crew boss Francesco "Compare Franco" Arcadi. After Vito was arrested, it was the hesitant Arcadi who took the reins of the family business.

The recordings even gave an insight into how the Mafia worked its racketeering operations in town. In one taped conversation, two men were recounting how they got a local restaurateur to pay up. They told of how three men went into a café, ordered three coffees and then demanded to see the manager. They told him that his coffee tasted terrible, and that they could supply him with much better coffee. The manager said that decision was up to the owner. The three guys then told the manager to call the owner to set up a meeting that night. The manager called, but the owner refused to come down. The three men then trashed the place and beat up the manager. When the owner finally arrived at his busted-up café, he found out that the men involved were representatives of the Rizzutos. He started serving the coffee they so aggressively suggested.

Far more important in a historical context, the tapes revealed how organized crime was changing in Montreal (and also in the rest of Canada). At the time, there was no significant Rock Machine–Bandidos presence at all on the streets of Montreal, and the Hells Angels had been reduced to little more than skeleton crews.

For the most part, the bikers' place in the food chain had been largely taken over by mostly black, primarily Haitian, gangs—much like Master B, the one Rockers president Picasso Wooley came from years earlier. Although there were some differences between them and the Mafia and the bikers, there were also stunning similarities as far as ranks, discipline, prospective membership and initiations, their use of aligned and puppet clubs and, of course, their involvement in drug trafficking.

Like the Mafia and the bikers, they fell into two competing groups with no love lost between them. While the Italians divided themselves based on where their families came from, the black gangs in Montreal were more like the bikers in that they divided themselves according to whether they were for or against the dominant power. Also like the bikers, they showed their affiliation by wearing—or, in their cant, "flying"—their colors. And like the Canadian bikers, they took their names and colors from more established gangs in the US.

Among black street gangs in Montreal, as in much of Canada, the primary color was blue. As everyone involved in the drug trade knows, blue represents the Crips. Formed not far away from where the original Hells Angels were established, the Crips evolved from a number of small organizations of young black men, many of whom had law-abiding beginnings.

In the late 1960s, however, many of the same forces that drew poor whites to motorcycle gangs were exponentially visited upon black youth in southern California. The lack of jobs was more acute, the white and mainly East Coast–dominated government was engaged in a very unpopular war in Southeast Asia (which many believed intentionally put black men into the line of fire in disproportionate numbers) and they also faced the daily grind-down of deeply embedded racism, especially from the LAPD, which had a hard-earned reputation as one of the most violent and racist forces in the developed world. In fact, black youth couldn't even become Boy Scouts in some parts of southern California until 1974.

Some young black men in that era joined black nationalist organizations and other activist groups like the Black Panthers, but far more joined smaller, local groups that offered a chance to make money, often by selling drugs or committing other crimes.

One of the most noteworthy of these men was Stanley "Tookie" Williams. He was born in Shreveport, Louisiana, in 1953 and had a youth that was some parts Bindy Johal, some parts Mom Boucher and some parts Vic Cotroni. His father abandoned his family almost immediately after Tookie was born. His mother took him and his little brother to South Central Los Angeles on a Greyhound bus when he was six in hopes of a better future. At first, Tookie later said, he hated the gangs he saw around him, but as he became a teenager, he got increasingly involved with them, earning a reputation as a vicious street fighter. By 15, he was one of the most powerful gangsters on the west side of South Central, which included his home community of Inglewood. Arrested while stealing a car in 1969, he went to prison and became a devoted weightlifter. Upon his release, according to his autobiography, he was asked what he wanted to do with his life. He replied that his plan was to be "the leader of the biggest gang in the world."

Once out of prison, he was introduced by a mutual friend to Raymond Lee Washington, who ran a gang (the Baby Avenues) on the east side of South Central, centered in Watts. The two, both thick with muscle and with reputations as enforcers, had much in common. But what really stunned Tookie Williams about Washington was that they dressed exactly alike. Both wore black leather jackets and starched Levi's jeans held up by suspenders, and both had diamonds in their left earlobes and walked with canes despite not having any mobility issues. They decided to join forces—uniting their two gangs to span both the west and east sides of South Central—for the extra manpower to fight off more established rival gangs like the Brims, the Drill Company and the Bishops.

The idea took off, and soon more and more young men began to join, eventually outnumbering their rivals in South Central by a significant margin. At first, the organization did not have an official name, but its members were often called cribs, because "cribbing," at the time, was slang for small-time crimes like stick-ups and burglaries. That all changed, according to the *Los Angeles Times*, when an elderly woman who would not give up her purse to some gang members who all carried canes told the media she had been attacked by "a bunch of cripples." The name stuck, and the Crips were established.

Neither Williams nor Washington had any better-than-ordinary organizational skills, and the Crips never became a unified group with a central command like the Hells Angels. Instead, they were a very loose federation of groups (known as sets) that had varying degrees of allegiance to the concept and to their fellow Crips.

One of those sets, from Compton's Piru Street and often referred to simply as the Pirus, was disgruntled when neighboring Crips sets regularly invaded their turf and sold drugs in their territory. Despite several attempts to negotiate, the Piru Street Boys were left unsatisfied. Eventually, they recruited several other sets who were also unhappy with how they were being treated and formed their own loose federation called the Bloods. In order to hold their own while vastly outnumbered, the Bloods, who wore red as an identifier, were extremely violent. That started an arms race that saw fists turn to bats turn to knives turn to handguns turn to AK-47s and MAC-10s.

As conditions worsened in South Central—the region of fewer than 500,000 residents saw 70,000 workers laid off between 1978 and 1982—gangs flourished. The resulting poverty and the appearance of crack (a much cheaper form of cocaine that proved incredibly lucrative) in 1984 caused gang membership to skyrocket. According to an LAPD report, there were 18 black gangs in South Central in 1972, 60 in 1978, 155 in 1982 and an astonishing 274 in 1996.

Similar to the effect media depictions had on the Hells Angels in the 1960s, media portrayals of these gangs—in movies like *Boyz n the Hood* and in the popular gangster-oriented lyrics of rap and hip-hop music—imparted to the Bloods and Crips legendary status, and they expanded throughout North America. Of course, no movie or song ever made a gangster, but the media of the era did point those who would be gangsters in the right direction, just as *The Wild One* had so many years earlier.

Unlike the Hells Angels, though, neither group had a copyrighted logo nor did they have a central command. Anyone who wanted to wear red and call himself a Blood or wear blue and call himself a Crip could, if he could defend himself. As a Kansas City gang cop told me, "Never call anyone a 'wannabe' gangster; those are the dangerous ones, the ones who have to prove something."

Thousands took up their flags. Although the original Bloods and Crips were exclusively African-American (although they quickly added Samoan-American and Tongan-American sets), outside of Los Angeles, Crips and Bloods sets could be of any mixture of ethnicities (even all white in some places) but generally had black leadership.

No matter who their membership was, Crips and Bloods traditionally did not get along, and violence between them was at ridiculous levels in Los Angeles and other cities affected by crack until a truce was signed in 1992. According to *Time* magazine, in 1980, the homicide rate in all of LA was 34.2 people per 100,000. In 2011, it was 7.8. The lion's share of those murders occurred in South Central, despite its meager population.

The animosity got so bad at one point that, hilariously, an LAPD officer I know told me that the Crips banned their members from saying the sound of the letter *B*, while the Bloods banned the sound of the letter *C*. Depending on where you were, you might hear the word *because* pronounced "bebause" or "cecause."

There are still occasional flare-ups between the two (as well as violence between Crips and other Crips and Bloods and other Bloods, as there's not much of an alliance within the groups themselves aside from hating the other side), but it's nothing like it was between 1980 and 1992.

The concept of Crips and Bloods came to Canada eventually, mostly through pop culture, and implanted itself into the consciousness of many of the same communities that had bred Mafia and bikers before them. Hamilton police, for example, identified 22 different gangs operating in the city in 2010, including the Oriole Crescent Crips, the Downtown Crips, the Driftwood Crips, the Dawes Road Crips, the Front Line Bloods and the Cutthroat Bloods.

In Montreal, the Crips and Bloods concept resonated with the city's black, mainly Haitian, community. As the Mafia and bikers saw manpower reduced through arrest, assassination and retirement, both found recruiting among their traditional communities become more difficult. By the time Vito Rizzuto was arrested, most of the lower-level jobs that had been done by bikers at the Mafia's direction were being performed by largely black gangs, often at the bikers' behest, depending on which side—the bikers' or the Mafia's—they were on.

The Consenza Social Club tapes indicated that the mafiosi had mixed feelings about the black gangs. Some were impressed by their ability to import and move drugs, while others despised them for not showing due respect to the Italians, invading their territories and even stealing from them. Not surprisingly, there was a healthy dose of racism, as the mafiosi were recorded comparing the black gangsters to animals and saying that they were impossible to reason with.

At the top of the street gang food chain in Montreal were some new organizations. Picasso Wooley's old Montreal-North gang, Master B, fell apart after he left to form the Rockers. Some of its former members regrouped under the leadership of a Haitian immigrant, Beauvoir Jean, and took the name "Bo-Gars" (local slang for "handsome boys"). As many had before them, they made their money with a combination of strippers, prostitutes and drug trafficking.

Wooley was something of a legend in the gangster community. Not only had he become extremely wealthy, but he had broken the biker color line (given his patch personally by Mom Boucher, no less) and had beaten three separate murder raps. When the cops arrested Stadnick, Boucher and all the other important Hells Angels and Rockers after Operation Printemps in 2001, they had no problem finding Wooley because he was already in prison for trying to take a loaded .44 Magnum onto an airplane.

After the Rockers collapsed due to those arrests, Wooley started a new gang composed mainly of Caribbean immigrants and known as the Syndicate. I'm told that it was Wooley and the Syndicate who provided the muscle that helped the Hells Angels retake the drug trade in many of the towns hit hard by mass arrests, including Trois-Rivières.

As Wooley and the Syndicate began to muscle in on Montreal North, the Bo-Gars went on an ingenious propaganda campaign to maintain their dominance in the area. They convinced many in their community that the Syndicate were simply doing the bidding of predatory white gangsters, flooding their community with drugs and vacuuming out money. They pointed to Wooley's past—noting that he had left his black gang behind to wither away while he was getting rich with the clearly racist Hells Angels—as evidence.

While their claims were true, they were also ridiculous. The Syndicate did get their drugs from the Hells Angels, but the Bo-Gars got theirs from the Rizzutos, and also frequently worked for them as hired muscle. If either of the groups was more under the thumb of a largely racist white organization, it was the Bo-Gars.

Stalemated, the two sides acted predictably. Like everybody before them in the cold war that characterized Canadian organized crime, they organized their allies, acquired small gangs and found flags to fly to foment a more solid identity.

What happened next would be funny if there hadn't been so much violence involved. Both sides claimed to have made the decision first, but whichever did, the Bo-Gars became Bloods and the Syndicate became Crips (each using both names interchangeably), and the Syndicate aligned with gangs like the upstart and surprisingly successful Crack Down Posse. Ironically, Wooley, who had spent his entire adult life defending the red and white of the Hells Angels was now suddenly bedecked in blue and forbidden to wear red.

The transformation of the two gangs didn't really have that much meaning. It's not as if the Syndicate were the Rock Machine, having to woo the Bandidos in Europe and Texas for the right to wear their patch. The LA Crips and Bloods were not asked or consulted. In all likelihood, they had no idea that there were Crips and Bloods in Montreal, if they even knew where Montreal was. To be a Crip or a Blood, all you had to do was wear one color and hate the guys wearing the other color.

Wooley was too smart and had worked too long and too hard to get involved in alleyway beatings and other small-time crimes.

The Syndicate moved into a godfather role. Just as the Mafia had the Hells Angels to do their bidding and the Hells Angels had the Rockers, so the Syndicate had a number of gangs—all wearing blue, including the Crack Down Posse and the 67s—take care of business for them.

The cold war was back on, but the superpowers were now the Rizzuttos on one side, pitted against their old allies, the Hells Angels (who still dealt with the severely weakened Calabrians)on the other; the actual combatants were primarily the sons of Caribbean immigrants who were certain that it was the other side that was too compliantly serving its white bosses. Although it may have seemed like nothing had changed in the cold war, one important detail had: These young gangsters, raised on gangster behavior in movies and TV, were not impressed by the existing hierarchy based on power and privilege. A few years earlier, a biker, knowing his place, would never flex on a made guy—unless it was a psycho like Apache Trudeau who had been hired by some even more powerful made guy—but these new guys had no respect for that. To them a gangster was a gangster. And a bullet could end anyone's life no matter who pulled the trigger.

That became apparent just after the clock ticked over from March 8 to March 9 in 2005. About 250 people packed Laval's hottest club, the Moomba Supperclub, for its weekly Latin night. It attracted a wide and diverse crowd, including two guys who really did not like each other. Thierry Beaubrun, boss of the 67s and out on parole facing armed robbery charges, was on the floor dancing when he spotted Michael "Big Mike" Lapolla, an enforcer for the Rizzutos. Leaving his partner bereft, Beaubrun elbowed his way through the dance floor until he was face to face with the huge, burly Italian. Without a word, he pulled a gun and shot the big man in the heart. Perhaps suddenly realizing the grave danger he had put himself into, Beaubrun ran for the exit. He made it but didn't get much farther. Friends of Lapolla's, once they had gathered their wits after the initial shooting, killed Beaubrun with a spray of bullets as he tried frantically to unlock his Jaguar.

Lorenzo Giordano, who co-owned a transport company with Lapolla and had been at Moomba when it all went down, went to Consenza to inform the higher-ups that Big Mike was dead. The tapes recorded an organization divided. Arcadi, the boss, warned the others that it might be foolhardy to act; the best plan of action, he said, was to wait and see what happened. That opinion was met with outrage by many, who desperately wanted to teach the upstart 67s a lesson.

While they were waiting to do so, more challenges arose, ones that might not have emerged if Vito had still been around. Mafia expert André Cédilot reported that a group called the D'Amicos, a Calabrian family who allegedly ran things in Granby, came to the Consenza. According to them, the Montreal Sicilians had run up a $900,000 debt to their friends, the Sherbrooke Hells Angels, and they demanded something be done about it. Arcadi pompously refused to pay. The ensuing argument was not recorded, but much later Arcadi mentioned that the D'Amicos had threatened to behead him.

What the Rizzutos decided to do was to rattle their saber. They rented a helicopter to fly low over the D'Amicos' houses and shine bright lights into their windows late at night. Also under the cover of darkness, the Rizzutos set fire to one of the D'Amicos' cars.

Police wiretaps made public included conversations in which the Rizzutos alleged that the D'Amicos met that pathetic show of non-force by kidnapping Nicolo Varacalli, one of Arcadi's best friends. They revealed that, on Halloween night 2005, four costumed men knocked on his door. When he answered, they picked him up, carried him away and threw him into the back of a van. The wiretaps recorded discussions in which the men claimed that members of the

D'Amicos then allegedly sent Arcadi a videotape of Varacalli in captivity, according to Cédilot. He spoke directly to the camera, saying, "Don't think you're untouchable. There are lots of them, and they can get you." No charges were ever laid in connection.

Arcadi didn't budge. The wiretaps recorded conversations in which his men said that the D'Amicos allegedly went to ancient Nicolo Rizzuto, hoping the old man had a better grip on things than the interim boss did. He convinced the D'Amicos to release Varacalli as a gesture of good faith. They did, but Arcadi didn't pay them. A few days later, Cédilot claims in his book, men associated with the allegedly enraged D'Amicos and an associate marched into the Consenza with weapons. No shots were fired, but Arcadi ordered all of his men to travel with armed bodyguards and imported four contract killers from his contacts in Venezuela.

That wasn't all the tapes revealed. Much to the outrage of ordinary, hard-working Quebecers, the *Montreal Gazette* reported that the mafiosi were overheard musing about whether to buy Ferraris or Porsches, boasting about spending $1,000 a day on vacation and sitting in the second row for World Cup games. They compared diamond-studded Rolexes, $60,000 bracelets, $75,000 pinkie rings and even how much they had paid for hair transplants (and how much they had hurt).

When it all came to pass, Project Colisée led to the arrest of 91 people, including Arcadi, Renda and the old man, Nicolo, himself.

At about the same time, changes were also happening among the Calabrians. Frank Cotroni was still head of the family but had been withdrawing from its operations after getting out of prison in 2002. He even published a cookbook. In 2004, he was diagnosed with brain cancer. On August 16, 2004, heavily sedated as he had been for months, he died in his daughter's home.

Pundits all over Canada paid tribute to Frank, referring to him as the last of the old-time gangsters, mainly because he was the last of the four Cotroni brothers to die. It wasn't strictly true. Unlike the other brothers, Frank had never even visited Italy, let alone been born there. And while the other Cotronis preferred to do business in Italian, Frank always used French, and the men he chose to deal with were far more likely to be French-Canadian than from the old country. He wasn't the last of the old guard; instead he marked a transition between them and the next generation. He was more the first of the new than he was the last of the old.

Not long after Frank died, his old "nephew" Réal Simard turned up. After ratting out the family in 1986, he served some time and was paroled under a new identity in 1994. But it was an uneasy relationship between him and his keepers. They often berated him for taking high-profile jobs, including one as a personal driver for notorious Quebec politician Richard Holden, which could comprise his identity. Simard complained that even low-level officers frequently and freely bandied about his real name and those of others under protection. He published a book about it called *Trahisons* (Betrayals). When the police caught him in a welfare fraud scam in 1999 and stripped him of official protection, he fled to South America.

While that may have led many to close the book on him, Simard actually secretly returned to Montreal just 18 months after he had left. He was somehow able to stay underground until 2004, when someone at Collège Jean-de-Brébeuf—Canada's most prestigious French-language high school and junior college, which had educated both Pierre and Justin Trudeau—noticed that a security guard looked familiar. Simard had acquired the job, after two security checks, by using the identity of Charles Bouchard, who had died as an infant in 1957. After he was arrested, he immediately started petitioning for parole. It was denied.

This was also a time of transition for the bikers in Montreal. When the first set of Canadian Hells Angels went down—by arrest, turning rat or murder—there were others to replace them. In fact, the students of Boss Buteau had transformed the Hells Angels from a small band of drunken thugs into a sophisticated nation-wide crime organization that dictated the rules of the drug trade and enforced them with zealous brutality. When the second generation went down, however, their replacements proved far less capable. There were no Walter Stadnicks or Mom Bouchers in this new group.

Instead, there were guys like Salvatore Brunetti. A former Devil's Disciple who admitted to manslaughter during the gang's war with the Popeyes, Brunetti later became one of the founding members of the Dark Circle and the Rock Machine. But with the war nearly over, he was one of the original eight Rock Machine–Bandidos members—the others were Nelson Fernandes, Stéphane Trudel, Daniel Leclerc, Éric Leclerc, Jimmy Larivée, Gaétan Coe and Stéphane Veilleux (Sasquatch Porter would join later)—to join the Hells Angels. In fact, the easily swayed Brunetti was actually scheduled to become a Nomad, but when the group was "frozen" (Hells Angels–speak for being temporarily suspended) due to a lack of manpower, he went to the notorious Sherbrooke chapter, which had seen many of its members and prospects arrested for violence and trafficking.

On March 15, 2006, police unleashed Project Piranha, in which they determined that Brunetti was a ringleader of a group that was flying cocaine and Viagra into the Laurentians from British Columbia. Several Hells Angels associates were also arrested, including Vancouver-based pilot, Michael Russell; Alain-Louis Dauphin and Louis Pasquin, the lawyer who represented Brunetti at several trials, including the one that arose from Operation Printemps. Pasquin was convicted of drug trafficking, possession, conspiracy and gangsterism, for which he was disbarred. All the others pleaded guilty: Dauphin to trafficking, Brunetti to gangsterism and Russell to lesser offenses.

CHAPTER 18

WAR SPREADS TO ONTARIO

Fears of a biker war in Ontario flared at about the same time. In late 2006, Bandidos hit man Sylvain Baudry was released after serving his sentence for the Christmas Eve 2000 murder of Toronto Viet Ching gangster Quan "Ah Cham" Cham Lu. That led many in the media to speculate that the Bandidos might be regrouping, but they weren't. The Bandidos were officially done with Canada. They wanted nothing to do with the country that they frankly considered insane. There were some minor flirtations between other big American gangs—like the Vagos and the Mongols—and unaffiliated Canadian bikers, but nothing all that solid ever materialized.

There were always bikers who resisted the Hells Angels' hegemony, and in Ontario this resistance was centered around a homegrown, often overlooked gang called the Loners. Over the years, the Loners had been characterized by internal strife—they once fought a war, essentially with themselves, across a suburban street—and poor decision making.

When Walter Stadnick did his great Ontario recruitment drive in 1999 and 2000, some Loners were welcome to join the Hells Angels but others, including their leadership, were not. One of them was their mercurial founder Frank "Cisco" Lenti, who Stadnick neither liked nor trusted and would not allow into his club, although the Loners often say it was the other way around. At any rate, in the post-Printemps, post–Shedden Massacre days, the Loners were players in Ontario.

• • •

Just as the Mafia and bikers in Montreal were depending on Bloods and Crips to move product, so were the Ontario bikers. The Toronto Hells Angels found something they did not expect: a white Crip. David "White Dread" Buchanan's family came to Toronto from Nova Scotia's economically disadvantaged Cape Breton Island, and he lived in the almost all-black Mount Olive housing complex, eventually becoming a member of the Mount Olive Crips. Known to police as a drug and weapons trafficker, Buchanan was soon a full-patch member of the West Toronto chapter of the Hells Angels and was quickly promoted to sergeant at arms. His connections with, and respect from, the Crips would prove invaluable for the Hells Angels.

When Buchanan and three other Hells Angels walked into Club Pro, the Woodbridge strip joint Lenti frequented, on December 1, 2006, trouble was almost guaranteed. It was more than just a rivalry. When an informant named Stephen Gault told police that the Hells Angels had planned to murder Lenti and hang him in his colors from a busy overpass, Mexican-cartel style, they passed that information onto him. After that, Lenti—who had been with the Loners, Rebels, Diablos, Satan's Choice, Outlaws, the Rock Machine and the Bandidos at various points in his career—carried a handgun with him everywhere he went and was understandably jumpy.

The Hells Angels recognized Lenti and began to argue with him. Lenti pulled his gun, killed Buchanan and seriously injured Dana "Boomer" Carnegie and prospect Carlo Verrilli. The other Hells Angel, Scott Desroche, was unharmed—he managed to hide in a closet until police arrived. Lenti was later convicted of manslaughter.

The Hells Angels were so protective of the lucrative Toronto area that when a former Hells Angels prospect named Jason Pellicore started shooting off his mouth about starting a Bandidos chapter in the area (which clearer-thinking minds would have realized would never happen), he was shot and killed just outside his health club.

They were hardly as powerful outside the city, however, where other bikers ran unmolested—except when they were in the sights of law enforcement operations. One such operation, Project Touch Up, targeted a cocaine ring that was operating from the Lend A Hand auto shop in Kingston, Ontario. According to law enforcement, a guy named Samy Tamauro would bring half-kilo bags of cocaine from Montreal to the shop in Kingston, where Roger McIlroy would distribute it to his dealers, primarily for sale at Queens University and the area's prisons. Among his dealers were former Rock Machine and Bandidos full-patch Carl Bursey. Tamauro, McIlroy and Bursey were arrested. Also arrested was Shirley A. McMahon, a Kingston police dispatcher who was charged for giving information to the accused. None of the accused would say where the coke came from, nor would they admit to any biker gang affiliations, but it was clear that the Hells Angels were not involved. All were convicted or pleaded guilty to lesser charges. McIlroy's shop, the Lend A Hand, closed.

In Montreal, law enforcement continued to put pressure on what was left of the Hells Angels there. After several raids made news of them almost routine, one—on October 17, 2008—raised many eyebrows because instead of the usual haul of drugs and cash, the cops recovered 41 cases of explosives, more than a ton. To a city that still had memories of regular firebombings, it was chilling.

Montrealers' fears were realized, at least partially, three days later. In a scenario that reminded some of the 9/11 attacks on New York and Washington, a stolen tanker truck burst through the front gate of the Hells Angels' Sorel clubhouse and crashed into the fortified bunker's edifice, setting the building ablaze. Witnesses saw two or three men then jump from the tanker into a blue pickup truck and take off at top speed.

With tongues of flame stretching more than 60 feet into the night sky, the ensuing blaze obliterated the building and the tanker and prompted the evacuation of the residents of 50 nearby buildings.

The following day, the media went crazy. An unsigned editorial in the *Montreal Gazette* blamed unnamed "Haitian gangs" and said that the theory some police were bandying about—that the Hells Angels had done it themselves—was ridiculous, that "the idea a Hells Angel would torch it is unthinkable, as if the pope burned St. Peter's." They went on to predict an all-out war between the Haitians and the Hells Angels. Even the official police mouthpiece turned up the stress level. "It's sure that we're going to consider whether the biker wars have started again," Sûreté du Québec spokesman Ronald McInnis told CBC News. "Perhaps there are other gangs that have issues with the Hells Angels."

Of course, it didn't happen. In fact, sentimentality aside, it made perfect sense that the Hells Angels would destroy the old Sorel headquarters and any evidence inside it, although no party was ever found responsible. I have even been told that the fire actually set back or even cancelled at least one major police operation. Either way, no war erupted.

If a war was going to have happened, it certainly would have after April 2009, when Project Axe dismantled the Syndicate. Wooley was already in prison (again), but several of his closest allies, including former Olympic weightlifter Jean Lavertue, and 46 others were arrested in raids in Montreal, Laval, Longueuil, Ottawa and Kingston. The cops issued a press release claiming that they had seized 2,300 crack rocks, 49 kilograms of cocaine, 225 kilograms of marijuana, 11 kilograms of hashish, small amounts of methamphetamine, Viagra and Ecstasy, 25 guns and ammunition, several bulletproof vests and about $60,000 in cash. That haul of people, equipment and merchandise gave the anti–Hells Angels gangs operating in the north a very strong advantage. Lavertue was sentenced to eight years for trafficking.

If the Hells Angels had hoped that the fire would slow the police down, they would be disappointed. Back in 2006, the police, as they so often do, approached several prominent Hells Angels and offered them deals to become informants. One of them, according to the CBC, was Sherbrooke full-patch and former sergeant at arms Sylvain Boulanger, who said he could be swayed for $10 million. When the cops countered with $2.9 million ($300,000 on signing; $600,000 if any arrests were made; four annual payments of $400,000 afterward and $400,000 after any trials were finished) and immunity, he took them up on it.

As is custom, when an informant turns, he or she must report everything he or she has done to break the law. Boulanger had an enormous list, including the murder of an unnamed member of the Rock Machine. "The door was open, I come up on the side and I shoot," the CBC reported he told police. "I hear 'Ow! Ow! Ow!' I see him there and, in my head, he's dead. So I get out of there running."

His cooperation led directly to Operation SharQc, which dug up evidence on the Hells Angels and their associates not only for drug and weapons trafficking but also their war with the Rock Machine. On April 15, 2009, no fewer than 1,200 police officers in Quebec, New Brunswick, France and the Dominican Republic arrested 156 Hells Angels and their associates. In fact, they claimed that every single one of Quebec's full-patch members, all 111 of them, had been taken down.

Still, there was enough of a Hells Angels presence on the streets of Montreal that 55 more associates could be taken down on June 3, 2009. An operation called Project Machine dedicated to stopping a cigarette and weapons trafficking ring on the Kahnawake Mohawk reserve just south of Montreal led to trafficking charges against two Hells Angels and three members of the Rice family, Peter and his sons Francis and Burton. Burton was the publisher of *Naked Eye* magazine, which shared an office with Cintron, an energy drink company owned by the Rices and, of all people, Salvatore Cazzetta. The trafficking charges were later dropped against the Rices and replaced by tax evasion charges, which are still pending.

While it looked like the Hells Angels had been eliminated from Montreal's crime scene (at least temporarily), and their pals in the Syndicate were also crippled, still no war broke out.

At least not among the bikers and the street gangs.

With Vito Rizzuto still in supermax in Colorado and most of his inner circle following the bumbling Arcadi into prison in Quebec, the Mafia had been particularly quiet in Montreal. At least on the outside.

The Calabrians had been gathering some steam. They were widely rumored to be linked to the Violi and Luppino families in Hamilton. When the Rock Machine, such as it was, came from Winnipeg in full colors looking for permission to operate in Montreal, they went to Chez Paree, the strip joint that had been a Cotroni stronghold since the 1950s. But no other evidence of an alliance emerged.

• • •

The Cotronis didn't show up in the mainstream media until September 18, 2008, when the *Montreal Gazette* reported that Frank Sr.'s grandsons—Francesco Bruno Cotroni and Nicolo "Nicky" Bruno Cotroni—had been arrested for their part in a marijuana grow-op that featured 1,100 plants hidden away in Casey, a logging town 300 miles north of Montreal. Both served brief sentences in prison. Afterward, Francesco Bruno Cotroni went back to work as a professional boxer.

The Mafia came back to the front pages at the end of December 2009. About a month after police raided FTM Inc., a Notre-Dame-de-Grâce construction company, looking for signs it had connections to organized crime, its offices received a visitor. Nick Rizzuto Jr., Vito's son and Nicolo's grandson, had just stepped out of his black Mercedes-Benz SLK roadster at the corner of Wilson and Upper Lachine when a man approached him. Just as Nick Jr. noticed him, the man pulled out a gun and fired at Nick four times. After assessing the damage, the gunman shot Nick's prone figure again twice more before running away.

The brazen daytime killing of such a well-known and well-connected figure was obviously a message to Vito Rizzuto that with him away, his family was no longer in charge. "This is an unprecedented challenge to the Rizzuto crime family," Canadian Mafia expert Antonio Nicaso told the CBC. "Since the '70s they were in charge of criminal activity in Montreal—without any challenge to their authority. There will be, for sure, a retaliation. The son—the eldest son—of Vito Rizzuto was killed. This is not just an ordinary member of the family."

The US Federal Bureau of Prisons refused Vito Rizzuto's request to attend his son's funeral.

Against whom that retaliation would be was not as easy to figure out. The police blamed the Haitian gangs, who they said were now in charge of much of the city's crime. It would turn out to be more complicated than that.

On January 23, 2010, police rushed to a McDonald's at the corner of St. Jacques and Ste. Anne de Bellevue in Notre-Dame-de-Grâce, not all that far from where Nick Jr. had been killed. Witnesses directed them to the bullet-riddled corpse of Kirk Murray in the parking lot. Not far from him, another man, Anthony Onesi, was dying of gunshot wounds he received while sitting in the driver's seat of his car nearby.

Murray was a career criminal with several violent offenses on his record. Onesi had given Murray a lift that day but was reputedly unaware of his friend's criminal lifestyle.

The next gangland-style murders in Montreal did not involve the Rizzutos but, actually, one of their competitors. Mark Stewart was a Longueuil resident who, in January 2010, visited Truro, Nova Scotia. On his way back, he went missing. His body was later recovered in a wooded area in Saint-Honoré. Stewart was black but not Haitian and was not known to be connected to criminal activities.

Before long, informants helped the police to arrest Nomads full-patch Jeffrey Lynds for ordering the Murray and Stewart murders and two other men, Nova Scotians Robert and Timothy Simpson, for carrying them out. When the Simpsons cooperated with the investigation in exchange for lighter sentences, Lynds went to prison. Lynds was one of the founding members of the ill-fated Halifax chapter of the Hells Angels and had already served time for the 1999 murder of Hells Angels associate Randy Mersereau in Truro.

After Lynds died in what authorities called a jailhouse suicide in January 2012, many refused to believe them. One of those skeptics was Lynds's own lawyer, Al Bégin. "You know, if we hear he's cremated then I think there'll be conspiracy theorists going on forever," he told the *Montreal Gazette*. "By all accounts, Jeff Lynds is not the type of person who would kill himself."

If Murray or Stewart had been involved in Nick Jr.'s murder, it would have been odd for a veteran Hells Angel to do anything about it, considering the two sides were facing off via proxy in the Montreal cocaine trade at the time. More likely, Murray, Onesi and Stewart died for other reasons.

There was a hit that struck against one of the Rizzutos' enemies, but it went shy of eliminating the man it was intended to kill. On the afternoon of March 18, 2010, a 911 call was made that directed emergency personnel to an upscale clothing store called Flawnego in Old Montreal. The caller reported, according to the *Montreal Gazette*, calmly and in French, "Two people entered. They were masked. They shot people inside the store."

Police arrived, and the *Gazette* reported that one officer recognized the store's owner, Ducarme "Kenny" Joseph, outside, speaking on his cell phone. Inside, he saw two victims dead on the floor. He recognized one of them as Peter Christopoulos, Joseph's bodyguard, and, although he didn't realize it, the other man was Jean Gaston, the store's manager and Joseph's uncle. Another man, Frédéric Louis, had also been shot in the head but, before police arrived, was able to drive himself to a nearby hospital in a Cadillac Escalade he said Joseph had loaned him. The man the cop made as Joseph left before he could be questioned.

The reason the cop recognized Joseph and Christopoulos is because he had been on the gang squad and Joseph was reputed to be one of the most powerful Haitian gangsters in town—the leader of the 67s—and Christopoulos had been his bodyguard and constant companion.

The CBC reported that police said they saw Joseph 90 minutes after the incident, talking with a well-known triggerman they refused to name other than by his nickname, "Gunman."

Later that night Joseph spoke with police about the incident and was, by several accounts, visibly shaken.

Joseph was arrested the following day at the same construction company Nick Jr. had been killed in front of. He was taken in because he was consorting with two known criminals, which was against his bail restrictions. In fact, the men in question, Stanley Stevenson Fleurant and Dutroy Charlotin, were also taken in for consorting with him and each other. When Joseph was arrested, he had a slip of paper in his pocket with the sketch of a face and the words "Are there photos of the guys to be eliminated" written on it. No charges were ever laid against the men.

There weren't any more eliminations. The police arrested Carey Isaac Regis, Terrell Lloyd Smith and Kyle Gabriel—members of a rival Haitian gang—for the killings. Regis and Smith were arrested in Montreal. Gabriel was taken into custody later in Richmond Hill, Ontario. Their trial is pending.

In fact, while everyone in Montreal was waiting for the Rizzutos to exact their revenge, their impotence looked more like utter powerlessness when on the afternoon of May 20, 2010, Paolo Renda went for a drive and never came back. After he did not return to his Cartierville home at an appointed hour, his family called police. Aware that Renda had been out of prison a little more than a month, had been Nicolo Rizzuto's right-hand man, was Vito Rizzuto's brother-in-law and that it was open season on Rizzuto allies in Montreal, the police mounted a search immediately. Before long, they found his late-model Infiniti—windows down and key in the ignition—two blocks away. The media decided he was "alive and well" because it's easier to shoot a man than to kidnap him (even a 70-year-old like Renda), but everybody else knew better. Renda was never spotted again. For years after he went missing, whenever the body of an older man was found—as one was, encased in cement in Toronto Harbor in May 2010—the media speculated it was Renda's. He has yet to be found.

While the media didn't seem to know what was going on,

the police certainly did. With candidates for the leadership of the Rizzuto family rapidly becoming an endangered species, the cops warned the obvious next-in-line, 66-year-old Agostino Cuntrera, that his life was, in all likelihood, in grave danger. His reaction was better than that of most bikers—like the ill-fated Scott Steinert and Donald Magnussen, who ignored similar warnings—but not much more effective. Instead of getting out of town, Cuntrera invested in an armored car and made one of his crew, Liborio Sciascia, carry a gun and travel with him everywhere he went.

It would have been better for him if he'd left town. Just after four in the afternoon on a sunny June 29, 2010, the two men were exiting Distribution John & Dino, a squat blue-and-tan warehouse with barred windows and more than a few italianate features. Witnesses told the CBC that two men in a large black car, perhaps a Chevrolet Impala, pulled up and it occupants filled both Cuntrera and Sciascia full of lead.

Cuntrera's funeral was attended by more than 600 mourners, but all eyes were on Leonardo Rizzuto, Nicolo's oldest remaining grandson, and Calogero "Charlie" Renda, Paolo's son. The two of them must have been as nervous as they were mournful.

Also in attendance was Ennio Bruni. Said to be a money-runner and bodyguard for more important men, Bruni had survived an attempt on his life on November 24, 2009, in which he took four bullets but kept on walking. He refused to cooperate with police while being treated for his wounds. On September 29, 2010, though, he was not so lucky. Enjoying a drink at the Cafe Bellerose in Laval at 3:15 in the morning, he was approached by a pair of men who, after getting his attention, shot him in the head several times.

At every one of those funerals was 86-year-old Nicolo Rizzuto. He wasn't considered much of a threat by some anymore. Scooped up in Project Colisée, Nicolo in 2008 pleaded guilty to possessing goods obtained through criminal gains and possession of proceeds of crime for the benefit of a criminal organization. Because of his age and ill health, he was given three years' probation. He was in trouble again, according to CTV News, in 2009 after the Canada Revenue Agency accused him of not paying taxes on $5 million he had deposited in three separate Swiss bank accounts in the mid-1990s. Rather than fight, he had his accountant write a check for $209,000 to cover the taxes, interest and penalties, and left the courtroom smiling. Ironically, it would come to light in 2013 that the CRA had sent him a $381,737.46 rebate check in 2007, even though his tax return indicated he owed them $1.55 million. Nine CRA employees were fired over the scandal, six of them charged with criminal offenses, according to the CBC. The trial is pending.

In fact, that very 2007 tax bill had been used by the government to put a lien on his house on Avenue Antoine Berthelet in luxurious Ahuntsic-Cartierville. It was next door to Renda's, which was next door to Vito's.

Because of Nicolo's age, of course, nobody saw what an inviting, even obvious, target the old man was. Whoever was killing the Rizzutos was making it personal and had no regard for the Mafia's code of ethics.

It was at 5:40 on the afternoon of November 10, 2010, when Nicolo, his wife, Libertina, and his daughter were preparing dinner that a shot was fired from a wooded area behind the home's solarium. It pierced the two layers of glass of the solarium's sliding doors and embedded itself in Nicolo's chest. He was taken to Sacré-Coeur hospital, but could not be revived. The old man was dead.

Since Nicolo had been killed by a single shot from an extremely powerful sniper rifle, speculation was rampant that it was the Mafia, whom the media considered better equipped than the bikers or street gangs and more likely to take on the Rizzutos, especially in their severely weakened state. "It can't be bikers; it can't be street gangs," former Hells Angels and Mafia enforcer Normand Brisebois told reporter *Toronto Star* reporter Peter Edwards, pointing out that neither would gain as much as they would lose by killing Nicolo.

Suspicion fell squarely on the Calabrians. In fact, Giuseppe and Dominic Violi—the two sons of Paolo Violi who had been living in Hamilton since their dad was assassinated in 1978—were seen in Montreal's Little Italy just days before the hit. Their mere presence made media and amateur Mafia watchers start making their own calculations and predictions. No charges of any kind were laid against them.

Not everybody believed that Nicolo was too old to wield much power at the time of his death, especially with so many of the generation after his behind bars or dead. "I think he was still the guy," Brisebois said. Mob expert Antonio Nicaso agreed, telling the CBC, "Whoever killed Nicolo Rizzuto wants to control the narcotics traffic, the construction industry, the extortion business. Recently, he looked more like a great-grandfather than an underworld lord; probably, however, he was the only one capable of organizing the family."

While the Rizzutos were down, the forces against them would not stop kicking. But just as Nicolo's assassination was distinguished by its professionalism, the next strike against them was as amateur as any crime Montreal had ever seen..

Not unlike the Magaddinos in Buffalo, the Rizzutos owned a funeral home, the Complexe Funéraire Loreto. It was owned by Vito Rizzuto's wife, Giovanna Cammalleri, and his sister, Maria, and its president was Charlie Renda. It was, according to some media, the family's sole remaining legitimate business.

On the night of January 5, 2011, a security guard inside the building heard a window break. He ran toward the sound and saw that an area of carpet beneath a broken window was on fire. He called 911. At about the same time, a passerby also heard the crash and walked over to investigate. He saw two young men dash away from the window and into an already running car and speed off. He too called 911 and gave the dispatcher an accurate description of the two men and the car, including its license plate.

The police stopped the car a few blocks away. Nervous and smelling of gasoline, Alexandre Toualy, Julien Bourassa-Richer and Sounthone Chareunsouk were arrested. Chareunsouk was also found to be in possession of cocaine. The men were so soaked in gasoline, in fact, that the police had to open the windows of the cars transporting them because the scent was so strong. All three men were convicted.

Quick thinking and action limited the bomb's damage to about $1,400 worth, said CTV News. The Loreto opened for business the next day without any delay.

The identity of at least one group targeting the Rizzutos also became clear after the arrests. Chareunsouk was already facing charges of trafficking cocaine (for which he was also convicted) and was known to be a member of the Montreal-North street gang d'Allégeance bleue (Blue Alliance). Of course, the blue in question shows that the allegiance was with the Crips. The fact that Chareunsouk was Laotian and his alleged accomplices were French-Canadian indicated the increasingly multiethnic nature of Montreal's new set of street gangs. The gang first emerged in the public eye after their allies in the area, Wooley and the Syndicate, were taken down by 2009's Project Axe.

If d'Allégeance bleue were behind the bombing, it put the picture of the anti-Rizzuto forces into better focus, and it put the Hells Angels and their friends well into the frame. It would appear that types like Chareunsouk were at the bottom of the army, mere foot soldiers, and that other forces—the Calabrian Mafia, the Hells Angels—were in command and calling the shots.

The killings continued. Lorenzo "Larry" Lopresti always denied involvement with the Rizzutos, but his dad, Giuseppe "Big Joe" Lopresti, worked for them until his body was found wrapped in a sheet in a Montreal alleyway in 1991, and his mom was one of their cousins. The last time the younger Lopresti was in the public eye was at Nicolo's funeral, for which he provided an ostentatious wreath.

At just after ten on the evening of October 24, 2011, people near the corner of Côte-Vertu and Hocquart in the Saint-Laurent neighborhood heard gunshots. At least one of them hit Lopresti while he was standing on his balcony. He had just stepped outside for a smoke when he was killed.

The Rizzutos certainly were reeling, but there was still a lot of money to be made from what remained of their empire. The men who were left tried to put together a consensus of who would be in charge of the empire. Joe Di Maulo was a candidate, but his age and his lack of any leadership experience worked against him. Far more capable was his brother-in-law, 59-year-old Raynald Desjardins, but his obvious failings, in Mafia eyes, were that he was French-Canadian and had close ties with the Hells Angels. He also suffered from multiple sclerosis.

There was also a new contender, Salvatore "the Ironworker" Montagna, from New York. Montagna was born in Montreal, moving to the Bronx when he was 15. As an adult, he lived in Elmont, Long Island, and ran a metal fabricating shop in the Bushwick section of Brooklyn. He was largely immune to prosecution but was listed in a 2003 FBI report as a capo after a conviction for illegal gambling. Two years later, when Bonanno acting boss Vincent "Vinny Gorgeous" Basciano was arrested, Montagna became acting boss. His reign came to an abrupt end when US customs agents noticed he had never finished his application for a green card. He was deported to Canada in 2008.

The initial part of his stay in Canada was quiet. He was a soldier in the Rizzuto family with no claims on its leadership. But when he saw the family falling apart, he had a sit-down with Nicolo, advising him to step down and promote some of his younger men.

After Nicolo was killed, it seemed obvious to many that the next natural godfather of the Rizzuto family would be a Canadian who had actually been the acting boss of the mighty Bonannos.

Not everyone agreed, though. I have been told by sources who would rather not be named that Desjardins felt that it was his job. He had, arguably, been the family's second-in-command while Vito was still running things, and he had an army and a knowledge of the city Montagna could not match. If there was any chance he was going to play the good soldier and watch some guy from the Bronx take over his city, it dissipated on September 16, 2011, when a car stopped at a stoplight next to his own, lowered its windows and the men inside opened fire. Desjardins was not hurt nor was his driver, but he was, law enforcement told the CBC, on the warpath.

According to police, a gang kidnapped Montagna on November 24, 2011, and intended to take him to the home of one of the alleged conspirators, Jack Simpson, on Île Vaudry, just east of Montreal. Before they got there, witnesses saw a man leap from a white van on Île aux Tresors, just upriver from Île Vaudry. Other men inside the van opened fire on him, hitting him once. Wounded and leaving a red trail in the snowy, wooded area, the man kept running, losing his shoes in the process, until he reached Rivière l'Assomption. Without stopping, he leaped into the rushing, freezing water. He made it to the other side (ironically, it was Île Vaudry, where the killers were headed anyway) and was shot again. This time the bullet stopped him in his tracks. Montagna, the man they called the "Bambino Boss" when he was at the height of his power, lay dead in the snow.

About a month later, Desjardins, Simpson (who was already in prison after being caught with 300 kilos of cocaine), Vittorio Mirarchi and Felice Racaniello were arrested for murder and conspiracy. Two other men, Calogero Milioto and Pietro Magistrale, were arrested in connection to the case and face weapons charges. They are still awaiting trial and have pleaded not guilty.

It's important to note that although the Rizzutos were still fighting with the Hells Angels and their allies in Montreal North over the cocaine trade there, both Desjardins and Simpson had a history of cooperating with the Hells Angels and their allies in the past.

It didn't matter for very long that both Montagna and Desjardins were out of the picture. The Rizzutos got their undisputed leader back in October 2012. After a hasty deportation process following completion of his sentence at Florence, Colorado, he was seated in the back of an airplane with four federal agents, taking off at 6:22 p.m. mountain time and touching down at Toronto's Pearson Airport at 10:41 p.m. eastern time (the flight took about two and a half hours), on October 5. The last person off the plane, he was escorted through the airport by heavily armed (and armored) Peel Region police officers who took him to an armored limo that ferried him back to his home in Montreal.

Everybody in Montreal knew heads would roll, and the first one came quickly. On the morning of November 4, 2012, a 911 call was made from inside a luxurious Blainville residence. When emergency crews arrived, they found the house's owner facedown in his driveway. There were two holes in his head. The man was Joe Di Maulo.

While it's not clear why Di Maulo was targeted—it may have been because he had done nothing while the family was being annihilated before his eyes—the local media hinted broadly at which side had done it. No charges were laid. While every other

Rizzuto ally who had been killed, regardless of why or by whom, had a lavish funeral studded with well-known mafiosi at the Rizzutos' funeral home, Di Maulo's service was small, quiet and at a different mortuary. Not a single well-known mafioso attended, but there was a big floral display from his brother-in-law, Raynald Desjardins, who was in jail at the time.

The next victims were also Desjardins associates.

The first to go down was Domenico Facchini. He was shot and killed inside the Café Domenica-In, where he had hung out for years. Before it had become a café, the building had housed a motorcycle repair shop that had been owned and operated by Facchini's former boss, a Desjardins friend and Hells Angels associate named Giuseppe "Ponytail" De Vito. He was charged in Operation Colisée—he had been recorded negotiating a shipment of 218 kilos of cocaine into Canada and even complaining that his traffickers were cheating him—but managed to escape arrest. After four years in hiding, De Vito was arrested as he exited a Laval gym on October 4, 2010.

Not long after he was sentenced to 15 years in prison, he was called upon to testify at the trial of his estranged wife, Adele Sorella, who was accused of murdering their daughters—Sabrina, eight, and Amanda, nine—while De Vito was avoiding law enforcement. Sorella was found guilty and sentenced to life with no chance at parole for 25 years.

At about 11:30 on the evening of July 7, 2013—two weeks after Sorella was found guilty—De Vito was recorded on video walking in a common area in Montreal's notorious Donnacona prison before he waved at a security camera and retreated into his cell. Shortly after midnight, a guard found De Vito unresponsive. He died about 90 minutes later at a nearby hospital.

Authorities have not disclosed a cause of death but reported no signs of violence. While Donnacona—which was full of Rizzuto allies and enemies—was full of suspects, another explanation has gained more popular support. Several personal sources have told me that there is a widely circulated rumor saying that De Vito isn't dead and that the RCMP faked his death after he agreed to help them find evidence against Vito Rizzuto.

Gaétan Gosselin was shot and killed as he exited his Saint-Léonard home on January 22, 2013. He had once been related to Desjardins by marriage and still lived in a building owned by the Desjardins family. Four men were rounded up and charged with murder—Edrick Antoine, Olivier Guay, Standley Minuty and Kevin Tate. All of them had lengthy records, but it was especially interesting that Antoine was reputedly a member of the Bo-Gars and had been arrested for trafficking with Bo-Gars boss Chenier Dupuy 17 years earlier. Their trial is still pending; if convictions follow, it will look as though neither side was above using the mainly Haitian street gangs to do their dirty work because the suspects were all involved with such groups. But it would appear that the anti–Hells Angels side preferred Bloods to Crips.

Two more men, both with ties to Desjardins, were shot and killed a week later. On January 31, 2013, Vincenzo Scuderi was hit outside his home in Montreal's north end, while Tony Callochia got his on the morning of February 1 just outside a Laval restaurant.

It appeared that the tide had definitely turned in the war that pitted the Rizzutos and their street gangs who flew the Bloods' red flag against Desjardins loyalists, the Hells Angels and the gangs that identified themselves as Crips. However, there was also a third side—law enforcement.

CHAPTER 19

THE CHARBONNEAU COMMISSION
SHOCKS, VITO RETURNS

Just as the Bourassa organized crime inquiry did its best to disrupt organized crime in the 1970s, a new inquiry was launched by Premier Jean Charest in 2012. Under the auspices of Justice France Charbonneau, best known to the public as the prosecutor who finally put Mom Boucher away in 2002, a new inquiry was launched on May 22, 2012, to investigate organized crime's effect on the City of Montreal's construction projects. Its mandate, according to the commission's official Web site, was "to examine the awarding of public construction contracts by a wide variety of public and para-public entities in Quebec over the last 15 years, to identify the specific techniques used by organized crime groups to infiltrate the province's construction industry and to find routes toward solutions."

Almost as soon as the Charbonneau Commission started and was televised on CBC, witnesses gave shocking testimony about just how corrupt things were in Quebec, mainly Montreal. The first big bombs came on June 15, 2012, from former Montreal police chief and anticorruption specialist Jacques Duchesneau, who reported that the anticorruption unit at Transport Québec suffered from severe staffing and resource shortages and that when its final report was handed to Transport Minister Sam Hamad, he greeted it with "complete disinterest." Duchesneau, who has since been elected to the provincial legislature for the Coalition Avenir Québec party, also testified that about 70 percent of all political contributions in the province were made illegally.

After a summer break, the commission heard from Mafia experts, including Italian academic Valentina Tenti, who explained how the Mafia works and warned the commissioners not to think of the organizations as local, but as international.

She was followed by York Regional Police detective Mike Amato, who had investigated many Ontario mafiosi and who told the commission that the Mafia works in plain sight and has its tentacles everywhere, often infiltrating the legitimate business market, and using restaurants, transportation companies, construction firms and other businesses as fronts for trafficking and other activities.

He was followed by Joe Pistone (Donnie Brasco himself!), who explained that the Mafia can exist only with the help of corrupt officials. "Organized crime cannot operate without corruption," he testified live on CBC. "So, in these types of situations, who do they need to corrupt? They need to corrupt public officials. They need to corrupt building inspectors."

Those experts were followed by details from Operation Colisée, including lists of visitors to the Consenza Social Club, transcripts and videos. The room fell silent as spectators watched a video showing a construction boss hand Nicolo Rizzuto cash.

Then on September 27, 2012, came the shocking testimony of disgraced construction boss Lino Zambito, who had already been charged with trying to illegally influence an election. He explained how his company, Infrabec, would include certain kickbacks into any bid on municipal jobs. According to his testimony, 2.5 percent would go to the Rizzutos, 3 percent to the Union Montreal party of Mayor Gérald Tremblay and 1 percent to Gilles Surprenant, who had been the city's chief engineer. To make up for those losses, Zambito would simply bill the city for nonexistent extras, like charging for union labor, while actually employing much cheaper nonunionized, sometimes illegal, immigrant workers.

Tremblay—who up until then had had a very clean, even boring, reputation among Montreal mayors—answered the allegations by denying involvement and saying "my conscience is clear."

Zambito was far from done. On October 1, he testified in front of CBC cameras that Infrabec had bid on a $25-million contract to take part in the construction of the l'Acadie interchange, but that he had received a phone call from Simard-Beaudry Construction owner Tony Accurso, a rival, telling him to retract his bid. Instead, he had done what many Italian Montrealers did when they had a beef—he went to Vito Rizzuto and presented his case. Rizzuto, he said, sided with Accurso and told Zambito to back off. Accurso's lawyers immediately denied any of that ever took place.

Zambito also named city employees Yves Themens, Michel Paquette and François Thériault as in on the action (all three were suspended immediately and Themens and Thériault were fired in 2013, while Paquette was reinstated). Zambito said that former city manager Robert Abdallah and executive committee chairman Frank Zampino also had their hands dirty. Both denied the allegations on TV.

Shocked by the scope of the allegations, the city suspended $75 million in infrastructure contracts until stronger anticorruption legislation could be enacted.

Two days later, Vito Rizzuto landed at Pearson.

Finally, and perhaps most damning, Zambito told the commission on October 15 that he had donated to all three major political parties and that each of them benefited from engineering contract kickbacks.

But the bombshells were not limited to testimony. The day after Zambito testified that he illegally funded campaigns, anti-corruption cops raided the offices of Asphalte Desjardins, another construction company that bid on city projects, and—as a by-product of their raid—found that commission chief prosecutor Sylvain Lussier had represented them against one of Accurso's companies in a suit. Lussier resigned later that day. "As you know, some doubts have been raised about me regarding possible appearances of conflicts of interest due to old files unrelated to the commission's mandate," his resignation read. "After careful consideration, even if these doubts are unfounded, factual or legal, it seems that the public interest will be better served if I resign as chief prosecutor." He has since become a partner at Osler, Hoskin & Harcourt LLP, one of Canada's most prestigious law firms. Lussier was replaced by veteran criminal lawyer Sonia LeBel.

While a lawyer for the city tried to discredit Zambito's testimony as tangential, another bomb fell. Surprenant, the retired city engineer Zambito had named, admitted that he had received in excess of $700,000 in bribes from bidding firms. He pointed out that, by spending at least a third of it at Casino de Montréal, he had actually helped the city's economy. Further clearing his conscience, Surprenant surprised the CBC cameras when he brought in $122,800, mostly in hundreds, that he hadn't spent yet and gave it to the commission as evidence.

He didn't stop there. He explained how contractors jacked up prices by 20 percent (on some jobs, as much as 50 percent) between 2000 and 2001 with phony work, like hiring a crew to dig a hole that already existed. Surprenant said that nobody ever questioned the contracts, even though their prices had increased remarkably over a short time. In fact, he referred to the corruption as an "open secret" and said that nobody tried to stop it because there wasn't anyone who felt as though it was their job. He closed by saying that he regretted his part in the wrongdoing and attributed it to an "error in judgment."

While much of what the commission had heard so far was shocking, it was just beginning and would later become mind-blowing. Next up was Martin Dumont, who had worked for Tremblay's Union Montreal party. He testified that his boss, Union Montreal finance chief Bernard Trépanier, once called him into his office to help him close a safe that was overstuffed with cash. Allegedly, with much huffing and puffing, the two large men managed to do it. When those words were broadcast over the CBC, the audience was aghast. As with many other forthcoming allegations, Trépanier denied that it happened. After much criticism from the media and other politicians, Tremblay, who had campaigned on an anticorruption platform, decided to take a few days off.

After Surprenant's testimony, it began to appear that being city engineer could be a lucrative gig if you were crooked. Luc Leclerc told the commission on October 31, 2012, that he had received about $500,000 in cash between 1995 and 2009 from bidders and had received almost as much as that in gifts. He had even had an offer to have a free house built for him. And, just like his pal Surprenant, he played it off for the TV cameras as not a huge moral or ethical deal. He said that receiving gifts was just part of the city government culture and that he did it to fit in. He actually told the commission, "When in Rome, do as the Romans." No charges were laid against him.

With the city, province and country in a state of shock regarding what had been going on during his term, Tremblay stepped down on November 5, 2012. While the city engineers who admitted their wrongdoing sounded only slightly contrite, Tremblay denied to the *Montreal Gazette* that he'd done anything unethical and said that he was actually unaware of the whole bribery scheme. He got downright pompous in his resignation speech. "I cannot help anymore, given the circumstances," he said solemnly. "My father always told me not to go into politics because it was dirty and people would destroy me. I dedicated myself fully to the success of Montreal—with Judeo-Christian values of charity, solidarity, integrity, respect, openness." No charges were laid against Tremblay.

He was hardly the only one affected. Laval mayor Gilles Vaillancourt, who had been mentioned in the testimony as receiving kickbacks and attempting to bribe provincial politicians, took a leave of absence for unspecified medical reasons. After Tremblay's resignation, Vaillancourt's office sent out a cryptic statement that read, in part, "The mayor is continuing his period of rest and reflection. Once his decision is taken, it will be shared with you." After several raids of his home and office, he resigned on November 9, and his party was disbanded. Vaillancourt was charged with two counts of gangsterism and has pleaded not guilty.

On the same day, the city suspended Suprenant's old boss, Gilles Vézina, for what happened under his watch. When it was his turn to testify, he said he had never accepted cash but had been the recipient of gifts like wine, dinner, hockey tickets and even the services of prostitutes. In an effort to explain why, he said that was just how things were done in the office, and had been since he was hired back in 1962.

Tremblay was replaced as mayor of Montreal by Michael Applebaum, a longtime councillor and borough mayor of Côte-des-Neiges–Notre-Dame-de-Grâce. He was the first anglophone to hold the office since 1912 and the first Jewish mayor in Montreal history. A former realtor, he appeared to be a safe choice.

While the testimony thus far had been ridiculous, bordering on hilarious, on November 15, 2012, it turned chilling. The speaker was Martin Carrier, owner of a Quebec City company called Les Céramiques Lindo. After he had done some work for the City of Montreal in 2004, he said he was driving his daughter to a music class when his phone rang. She answered and handed her dad the phone. Luckily, he recorded what happened. The following exchange was played for the commission live on CBC.

> Caller: Mr. Carrier, Martin Carrier?
> Carrier: Yes.
> Caller: You did some ceramic work in Montreal?
> Carrier: Yes.
> Caller: We'd like you to stop coming here to do work.
> Carrier: Who are you?
> Caller: It doesn't matter who I am, okay? Because the next time, you won't be walking away from here. You've been warned.

Later, Carrier bid $400,000 on a job at the Université de Montréal. He testified he received a call from a rival who identified himself as Francesco Bruno of BT Céramique. He said that Bruno told him that it was his company's turn to get the job, and that Carrier would be best served to wait his turn. Carrier told him, "We don't work like that." Worried, Carrier went to the cops. He then received a call from Bruno, who told him, "You didn't listen. We warned you. It's over."

The police identified "Bruno" as Rizzuto ally Francesco Del Balso. Later, after Carrier appeared on a TV show describing his plight, CTV News reported that Del Balso threatened to sue him for defamation. He did not follow through.

Afterward, a pink card arrived at Carrier's office. On the front, it said, "This is a message of sympathy expressed with compassion," and inside, it read: "Dear friend. Don't bid any more in Montreal. You run the risk of having your family receive a card just like this. Final warning."

Charbonneau herself thanked him for his testimony and praised his "exceptional courage" on live television.

The witness after Carrier was a contractor in a similar situation. Michel Leclerc, who owned a company called Terramex, held out as long as he could, but when he realized he wasn't going to get any contracts, he started, reluctantly, to play ball. His partner, he said, reported the problem to the city's auditor general but did not get a reply.

André Durocher, owner of Excavations Panthère, testified that he tried to avoid the corruption but couldn't get any work. He tried to collect other disgruntled contractors and set up an alternative group to bid as a unit, but the effort quickly collapsed.

After him, Michel Cadotte, president of Ipex, testified live on camera that the city was delighted by his latest product, Terra-Brute pipes, and bought plenty of them. After he refused to pay a $150,000 bribe to the usual suspects, his sales suddenly stopped.

After a months-long break, the commission resumed in January 2013. Although the CBC described it as a "bombshell," Michel Lalonde's testimony was actually just more of the same, admittedly astonishing, stuff. Lalonde, president of Génius Conseil, testified that his firm routinely charged 25 to 30 percent more than was appropriate and turned over part of the overbilled revenue to political campaigns.

Lalonde, however, had backed the wrong horse. In 2001, he contributed to Tremblay's opponent, incumbent Pierre Bourque. When he was soundly defeated by Tremblay, Génius Conseil did not receive a contract, despite constant bidding, for two years. Lalonde then received a call from Bernard Trépanier. In it, Lalonde testified on CBC, the Tremblay fundraiser told him, "Listen, everything seems to be going well; we have to position ourselves for the next election. . . . We have to start talking about financing. Listen, Michel . . . you're one of the firms that's well-positioned to get contracts." Then, Lalonde said, Trépanier asked him for $100,000.

Lalonde paid, even though he knew that campaign contributions of more than $1,000 were illegal. "If they want to invest more than what they're allowed in order to win an election, you understand, they want to win, they'll take whatever means necessary to win," he testified. "The only way to do it is with cash."

His reward, he said, was to sit down with Trépanier to select which firms received which contracts, choosing only those who would contribute to Union Montreal. Trépanier denied all such claims.

Prosecutor Denis Gallant asked him under cross-examination, "Would you say the financing of political parties was directly linked to the obtaining of contracts? Without hesitation, Lalonde replied, live on camera, "I'd say yes."

When asked to name politicians who had specifically asked for kickbacks or illegal donations, Lalonde had no problem reciting a list that included Joe Magri, former mayor of Rivière-des-Prairies–Pointe-aux-Trembles; Cosmo Maciocia, former mayor of Rivière-des-Prairies–Pointe-aux-Trembles; Michel Bissonnet, mayor of Saint-Léonard; Gilles Deguire, mayor of Montreal North; Robert Coutu, mayor of Montreal East, and Jean-François St-Onge, borough councillor in Ahuntsic-Cartierville. If those place names sound familiar, it's probably because those were the places where the Rizzutos and their allies operated and lived. Lalonde added that any company that did not pay would not be considered for contracts. None of the politicians responded to the claims.

Lalonde then said that the bribery did not stop at city and borough governments. He testified that Transport Québec contract-selection committee member Claude Millaire told him in November

2007 that bids would be assessed for a project to renovate Autoroute 13 in Lachine. Lalonde said he handed Millaire $25,000 in cash and several other gifts including a cell phone that Millaire used for years with Lalonde picking up the tab. He won the contract. Millaire denied the claims.

The next witness, however, was a bit of a surprise. While Surprenant was holding back tears during his testimony, Giuseppe Borsellino, boss of Garnier Construction, said he was lying. He testified that Surprenant wasn't an innocent carried away in a tsunami of corruption but one of the primary perpetrators, the person who had come up with many of the ideas. "The guy had everything in front of him to promote collusion, promote corruption, losing money if the city didn't pay. They had so much power," he testified. "There's people at the city who are very powerful, and they could tell a contractor, 'You're not going to make any money unless you listen to me.'"

He also went on to testify that he grudgingly paid in excess of $50,000 for an Italian vacation for the former head of Montreal's public works department, Robert Marcil, and the ex-CEO of FTQ-Construction, Jocelyn Dupuis, and their wives. Marcil and Dupuis denied the claims.

As forthcoming as Borsellino was when it came to financial wrongdoing, he clammed up when things got physical. When asked about a 2009 incident in which three large men burst into his office and gave him a brutal beating, he demurred. "I don't know why, and it could have been for a number of reasons," he testified, "It could be linked to construction; I've tried to forget the incident."

Charbonneau, not one to be played with, pushed him. "If you were beaten to the point that you were disfigured and had to be hospitalized for a reconstruction of your face, you must have some idea why you were beaten like that," she pointed out.

"I have some ideas," he replied, sheepishly. "Maybe I didn't pay my debts. Maybe I didn't do a job well. It's maybe two or three reasons. I did not make a complaint, and I went on to my business and went back to work."

He then admitted that he knew the Rizzutos because his family was from the same hometown back in Sicily but that he had had no business dealings with them.

Then the commission was shown a police video from Operation Colisée. In it, a man identified as contractor Nicolo Milioto walks into the backroom of the Consenza Social Club with a paper bag and greets Nicolo Rizzuto. The two then take a huge sum of cash out of the bag and separate it into seven equal piles. Rizzuto then hands Milioto some other cash, which the contractor puts in his pocket.

Prosecutor LeBel claimed that Milioto's job was to collect kickbacks from construction companies and deliver them to the Rizzutos. The job earned him the nickname "Mr. Sidewalk."

Milioto, visibly and audibly nervous while giving his testimony, claimed he knew Rizzuto only because he too was from the same hometown in Sicily. As for the cash, he stammered, "Mr. Rizzuto could have asked me to do him a favor and gave me $100 or $200. . . . It's possible he gave it to me to do an errand—buy something for him."

As the video continued, Rizzuto was seen handing Milioto even more cash, which the contractor then hid in his socks. At first Milioto said he did not recall why he was getting any money and then later happened to remember that Rizzuto had lent him money for his house. Then he changed it to his daughter's wedding.

After being confronted several times by an angry LeBel about the outlandishness of his stories, Milioto went old-school. "I have no idea what the Mafia is," he testified. "Is it someone who kills? Someone who steals? Someone who traffics drugs? I don't know."

On the following day, February 18, 2013, CTV News reported that 120 Sûreté du Québec officers barged into Montreal City Hall and told all elected officials except for Applebaum to leave and take only their coats. A little more than five hours later, Applebaum emerged from the building and told reporters: "My objective is to work with the police, to respond to all their questions and to open city hall so they can find all the information they're looking for concerning the files they're investigating. I am not under investigation—that's clear. I want to reassure Montreal citizens that we are here to cooperate with the police. From the time of my election, I've made it clear I want to shed light on corruption and collusion."

The allegations continued. Charles Meunier, owner of BPR, told of how his firm could not get contracts with the city until he started handing envelopes full of cash to Trépanier. As with everything else, Trépanier denied the claim.

He was followed by Yves Cadotte, general vice president of SNC-Lavalin, Canada's largest construction firm. He testified live on CBC that the Quebec Liberal Party and the Parti Québécois (PQ) asked for money from the company on an annual basis, and that his company paid them in excess of $1 million. "There are still parties in power, and it's the market that is important to us," he testified. "We want to make sure we can take part in our activities and [so we] agree to the demands that are made."

In the midst of all the revelations, the city still had to be run. When city council pulled a $5 million contract to fill potholes from the table because all seven bidders had links to people accused by the Charbonneau Commission, Applebaum felt he needed to step in. On March 21, 2013, he told Montrealers they had two choices: Either give contracts to companies with tainted reputations or live with potholes. Many interpreted his statements as the mayor telling the voters that living with organized crime was an unavoidable part of living in a big city—or, at least, in Montreal.

Then it was up to the man almost every other witness had already accused, the man they started calling Mr. Three Percent, Union Montreal finance chief Bernard Trépanier. Although he had worked on federal campaigns—including Kim Campbell's bid for leader of the Progressive Conservatives, which later made her briefly prime minister—the commission limited its inquiry to provincial and municipal government. The Canadian Press would later calculate that at least $2 million in illegal contributions to the federal government were spoken of in the inquiry.

Trépanier, 74, was visibly nervous and gave very little juicy information but did say that he thought nobody had ever followed election rules in Quebec. He added that he had worked as a lobbyist despite not having registered, as is required under law.

Trépanier admitted on camera to asking companies for up to $200,000 for Tremblay's election fund and to lobbying on their behalf. He denied the repeated allegations that he had demanded a 3 percent kickback. He said the other people who had testified were liars and that he was the victim of a complicated smear campaign. Later, after he and his associates were arrested, his lawyer, Daniel Rock, claimed there was little chance of him getting a fair trial in the province.

Vallaincourt, the former mayor of Laval, was arrested on May 8, 2013, on several different charges, including one of gangsterism that could net him 20 years in prison. "I will devote all the time I have to prove my innocence," he told the media. "And I think I have strong points."

Not everybody agreed. "We executed 70 search warrants," said anticorruption commissioner Robert Lafrenière when asked about Vallaincourt. "We captured approximately 30,000 wiretapped conversations. We have recovered $438,000."

A few days later, federal NDP leader Thomas Mulcair told the media that back in 1994 when he was first elected to provincial government representing the Laval riding of Chomedy, Vallaincourt handed him a "suspicious-looking envelope." Mulcair refused what he took to be a bribe but did not report it until 2011, when investigations into Vallaincourt began to get serious. He also refused to give further comment because the case was before the courts.

Vallaincourt wasn't alone. On the morning of June 17, 2013, Applebaum was arrested and charged with making shady real estate deals, unrelated to the inquiry, before he was mayor. As Gawker.com reported about his arrest: "A major Canadian city woke up to find out that its mayor had been arrested at his home early this morning. And it wasn't even the guy who smoked crack on video!" Two other politicians—Saulie Zajdel, an ethnic outreach officer for the federal Conservatives, and Jean-Yves Bisson, former director of building permits for Applebaum's west-end Côte-des-Neiges–Notre-Dame-de-Grâce borough—were also arrested in relation to the case against Applebaum, but charges were dropped.

In the midst of the furor over construction corruption, on that same day Quebec's 175,000 unionized construction workers went on strike. Their representatives claimed that they were being asked to work 14-hour days and six-day weeks without overtime. The head of the association of builders denied that claim. The unions would later run a TV ad that featured an older man wearing a suit taking money from his pockets and, notably, his socks and stuffing it into an already full safe. Because the commercial had Italian music in the background, some Italian-Canadian groups claimed the ad was discriminatory.

Later that week, Montreal city council selected Laurent Blanchard as mayor. He didn't try to raise hopes—his slogan was "the city continues to function"—but he also promised no more surprises would come from the office.

Up to that point, the commission's only mention of organized crime focused on the Italian Mafia, particularly the Rizzutos and their allies. But they were not the only ones with their hands in the construction business. Although there were no official Hells Angels chapters operating in Quebec anymore, their presence was still felt as they acted as individuals and groups without an actual clubhouse.

Many of those arrested in Operation SharQc made bargains and some were set free simply because the province could not afford fair trials for all of them. After 27 Hells Angels and associates pleaded guilty to charges involving murder and/or manslaughter, Judge James Brunton issued a stay on all other charges, primarily trafficking. He explained that the number of accused and the huge volume of charges would put an unreasonable strain on the province's resources.

In the meantime, even more opportunists had come to the lucrative streets of Montreal to make deals with whomever they could.

One of them was Larry Amero, who had been shot in a gangland assassination in Kelowna, BC. He first came to media attention in Montreal when he was found guilty of driving under the influence and a hit-and-run in July 2012 after he drove his SUV into a woman's car and fled on foot before being tackled by police.

He wasn't just another tourist who had had one too many, though. On October 31, 2012, Amero and his old pals from BC Rabih "Robby" Alkhalil and Shane "Wheels" Maloney were arrested (along with 100 others) by the Sûreté du Québec in Operation Loquace, which was aimed at shutting down what they called a huge cocaine smuggling and trafficking ring. The charges are still pending.

With the bikers still a threat, Sûreté du Québec sergeant Alain Belleau was brought in to educate the Charbonneau Commission about them. He described the gear bikers wear and pointed out that it was intended to intimidate. He said that while the bikers had traditionally made their money like old-fashioned organized crime groups, with drug and weapons trafficking, money laundering and loan-sharking, the scrutiny brought on by Operations Printemps and SharQc had led them to infiltrate legitimate businesses. While many of them chose businesses with plenty of cash transactions (strip joints were popular) or that brought them close to people they already knew (sports drinks and mixed martial arts fighting), others became involved in construction.

That knowledge would help the commission after hearing the testimony of Paul Sauvé, owner of LM Sauvé, a construction firm that had a contract to renovate the Parliament Buildings in Ottawa until it went into bankruptcy with the project nowhere near finished.

Sauvé spoke of how his business and others had been infiltrated by Trois-Rivières Hells Angel Normand "Casper" Ouimet. Just five foot five but weighing in excess of 250 pounds, Ouimet, he said, used intimidation as a bargaining tool. After he went into business with Sauvé, Ouimet warned his new partner to keep quiet, saying, "By the way, if you talk about what happened, we have this motto: Without a body, there won't be a trial."

The cops had tried to arrest Ouimet in April 2009 as part of Operation SharQc in connection with 22 murders during the Quebec Biker War but could not catch him until November 2010 when a Montreal cop saw him go by in the back of a taxi. He was convicted and received a 27-year sentence for conspiracy to commit murder, gangsterism and money laundering.

Sauvé then alleged that former PQ leader André Boisclair authorized a $2.5 million subsidy for his company in 2003. That prompted Jacques Duchesneau, of the rival Coalition party, to say to the *Montreal Gazette*, "In 2005, Mr. Boisclair himself admitted that he used cocaine while he was a cabinet minister. So the question is, with Mr. Sauvé being associated with the Hells Angels, and a subsidy of $2.5 million being granted, did that influence Boisclair's decision?"

Boisclair, a former police chief, first threatened to sue Duchesneau, then stepped down from his post as the province's official representative to New York City. He didn't sue.

Another big player was heard from. The Fédération des travailleurs et travailleuses du Québec (FTQ) is the biggest union in Quebec, representing half of all unionized workers in the province. With witnesses on tap to speak about the union, the FTQ asked that wiretap evidence of any of its conversations not be presented because it had not led to any charges. The request was denied.

The FTQ was already implicated. A former FTQ employee, Ken Pereira, testified in front of CBC cameras that he had taken expense reports and other incriminating documents from the union's offices. When this was found out, the union bosses, he said, offered him $300,000 for his silence. A few days after he refused, a minivan blocked him in and two large men approached him. Fearing for his life, he was relieved to find out they were Sûreté du Québec officers.

He testified that the 2008 election for FTQ leadership was fixed and that a candidate, Dominique Bérubé, dropped out of the race because one of the bikers, Jacques "Israël" Émond, who was hanging out at the polling station told him to.

Pereira also exposed his boss, Jocelyn Dupuis, head of the FTQ's construction arm, for billing at least $50,000 in fraudulent expenses.

Dupuis denied those allegations and any involvement with organized crime figures. He did, however, say that he had a policy of trying to give people who had had problems with the law second chances. "The past is the past, the future is the future," Dupuis said. "When you've paid your debt, your past is put aside and you try to reintegrate these people into society." One of those people was Raynald Desjardins, the Rizzuto lieutenant and Hells Angels ally who was in prison at the time of the commission (although it could be argued that it was Desjardins's ninth or tenth chance, not his second). Dupuis acknowledged that when a company co-owned by Desjardins bid on a government contract, he took Desjardins's name out of all the documentation.

Soon after Pereira's testimony, FTQ president Michel Arsenault resigned.

As revealing as the Charbonneau Commission was, I'm not sure it actually accomplished all that much. A few guys were arrested, some more lost their jobs, but, by and large, the fingers were pointed away, to bikers and Mafia. Besides, it was limited to government construction contracts, a small slice of the organized crime pie.

The mood of the region could be gauged by the November 3, 2013, municipal elections. Instead of an energized populace fueled by disgust and rage filling the polling stations, turnout was very low (43.32 percent), reflecting the cynicism that had engulfed the area. Montreal elected Denis Coderre, a former Liberal member of Parliament and career politician. Laval went with Marc Demers, a former cop.

But all the while the commission was dominating headlines, it was business as usual on the streets of Montreal.

• • •

While the Mafia killings drew more attention, a crime that was perhaps more illustrative of how organized crime now works in Montreal was committed in November of 2012.

Chenier Dupuy had been the boss of the Bo-Gars for 20 years and had been arrested, according to the *Gazette*, in 2008 with 900 crack rocks, 361 grams of cocaine and 2 kilos each of marijuana and hashish. He was a tough guy, someone to be feared, and his authority extended beyond the Bo-Gars to all of the street gangs who flew the red flag of the Bloods.

Several sources say he was invited to a summit meeting with Picasso Wooley, who, it could be said, held a similar position with the Crips. They say that Wooley offered peace under the condition that all of the gangs align and get their product from his sources. Defiant, Dupuy slapped Wooley in the face.

Two weeks later, Dupuy and his right-hand man, Lamartine Paul Sévère, were both shot to death in broad daylight.

Business is, after all, business.

CHAPTER 20

THE VICIOUS CYCLE

While organized crime exists in every Canadian city of a certain size, it always seems to come back to its roots in Montreal and Hamilton.

It was a warm, sunny autumn day when I found myself in Hamilton, a couple of blocks away from Roxborough Park, the first school I ever attended, so I thought I'd drop by. Built in 1964, like most architecture of that era, it hasn't held up well. It's low and squat, nearly windowless and an almost universally drab brown. A week later I learned that city council had just heard a recommendation to close the school to curb costs.

The yard looked about the same, except there was an old shopping cart in it, and most of the moms waiting around for their kids to get out were wearing guntiino dresses and head scarves, leading me to believe they were recent Somali immigrants.

The neighborhood—which a Hamilton historian once told me "doesn't matter"—had certainly changed. Located on and around the site of Hamilton's first airport, it was converted into housing in the 1950s as the airport moved to the suburbs and the steel factories kept hiring more and more workers. Originally, Roxborough Park was populated almost entirely by people from Britain and Ireland who had left behind the rapidly diversifying central city and the rising prices of the west end. It was then enhanced by immigrants from places like Hungary, after that country's 1956 uprising against Communist rule, and then other Eastern European nations. They were followed by Caribbean immigrants, Southeast Asians, Latin Americans and then Africans.

It's always been a blue-collar, even poor, area. In the 1960s, it was one of the first places in Ontario to experiment with subsidized housing for the underprivileged. Hamilton has become increasingly impoverished as jobs have left the city—the steel industry now employs about one-twentieth as many people as it did in its heyday. In fact, Tim Hortons recently featured Roxborough Park in an ad campaign called "50 Hours to Discover," in which they sent kids from the neighbourhood to camp so they could escape "an area where gangs and gang violence do dominate," at least for a little while.

When I was a kid there, everyone in school knew that the area was biker territory. Satan's Choice was in charge, but we also heard talk of the Red Devils, who were maybe a mile or two to the north on the Beach Strip. I even knew one kid—Pat, his name was—a little older than me, who idolized the bikers. He'd somehow managed to get someone to weld two new sets of front forks to his bike and attach a tiny front wheel to them to make it into a chopper. He also ripped the sleeves off his fake leather jacket and wrote SATAN'S CHOICE on the back in ballpoint pen. I think he was nine.

Times have changed. The area now belongs to the Oriole Crescent Crips. You can see the kids emulating them. I don't have to describe the style.

In the central city, where I went to high school, we knew about the Mafia. We frequented pizzerias and bakeries our parents told us were connected, and whenever one caught fire, and they did with frightening frequency, our parents would all claim they knew who did it. Friends of mine went to an all-boys Catholic school in the shadow of John Papalia's Gold Key Club hangout. I knew who Fat Pat Musitano was, but he didn't know me. When a friend of mine had his jaw broken and the cash box stolen from an event he was holding, everybody blamed it on the Musitanos. But no one did anything about it.

Now, police and others in the know tell me, if you want crack in that neighborhood, you've got to go to a member of the Downtown Crips or one of their associates.

That doesn't mean there aren't still plenty of bikers in Hamilton. After Project Retire put most of Ontario's Outlaws out of business in 2002—most important of them, of course, was national president Mario Parente, who (as well as Hamilton's most notorious murderer, Evelyn Dick) lived on the same block as me—the Hells Angels set up their first chapter in Walter Stadnick's hometown in the old Satan's Choice clubhouse in the north end. It didn't last. In 2009, the clubhouse was seized after Project Manchester, in which several prominent members of the club, including its president, were arrested.

It was part of a huge crackdown in which the police reversed much of Stadnick's efforts, shutting down chapters in Niagara, Oshawa, Thunder Bay and London.

In the summer of 2011, however, they were back again. The Hells Angels had occupied a once-popular north-end tavern and put a huge sign out front, letting everyone in the city know who they were. "We're introducing ourselves; we're letting people know we're here," James "Bubba" Sherwood, spokesman for the club, told local television station CHCH. "We tried the other approach, by hiding in an industrial area and minding our own business, but the cops didn't seem to like that. They took that place away from us." Sherwood, who stood in front of the clubhouse on Hamilton's

Gage Avenue with another full-patch named Joel Rollin, presented quite the photo op for local media. Both men were huge, not just beefy, but close to obese. Both had goatees, black baseball caps and lots of jewelry, and Rollin, who was the fatter of the two, wore a black T-shirt that read HELLS ANGELS HAMILTON and had a giant skull pendant on his droopy chest. Sherwood, who was wearing a leather vest, sported a full patch on the back but no patches on the front signifying any accomplishments for the club. These were not the same Hells Angels who had conquered organized crime in Canada.

Sherwood wanted to make it clear that the club was not a collection of criminals. "We're not doing anything illegal," he told reporters. "This is strictly a social place for us and our friends to meet, have a few beers and talk about bikes." When asked about the security measures, like video cameras and barbed wire, he responded, "That's just the type of neighbourhood you're in." To be fair, it was.

But it was in a somewhat nicer neighborhood that some doubt was cast on Sherwood's words, in a case that was made public by the Ontario government. At the corner of Greenhill and Mount Albion, there's a small strip-mall bar and live music venue called Our Dog House. In the autumn of 2010, its owners—a married couple who, by court order, can be identified only as RB and MB—offered to sell it to some friends, Linda Muraca and Dennis Dreher, for $70,000 because they planned to move to the US. A deal was made in which Muraca and Dreher would pay some outstanding taxes and apply for a liquor license.

The liquor license, however, was held up because of the lack of a bill of sale. In June 2011, after RB and MB moved back to Canada (they were staying at Dreher's house until they could find lodging of their own), RB agreed to make one. He insisted on not using a lawyer, and Muraca found the document RB made unsatisfactory and riddled with errors. She refused to sign. RB assured her he'd make a new, more accurate version.

As he dragged his feet, he exhibited some bizarre behavior including removing the temporary liquor license Muraca and Dreher had acquired from the bar, which put them in violation of the law. Whenever he entered the bar, he maintained that he was still the owner. Nerves frayed. Dreher booted the couple from his house in July.

On Saturday, August 6, 2011, Muraca returned to the bar to find that RB had dropped off a bill of sale and a confirmation of purchase. Both had been signed by RB and MB. Muraca then called RB to let him know she had received the documents and that she'd look them over when she had a chance. RB then asked her to consider dropping Dreher as a partner and cutting him in instead. That offer took Muraca by surprise because Dreher had told her that RB had made a similar offer to him. Muraca politely declined. Angered, RB gave her until Sunday night as a deadline to sign the documents. After the discussion, she learned RB had entered the bar and removed the interim liquor license again.

While the new bill of sale was better than the first, it still bothered Muraca. One clause in particular—one that made it seem as though RB could reverse the sale whenever he felt like it—made her reluctant to sign. She called RB on Monday morning and left a message saying that she felt like she had to consult a lawyer before signing. Later that day she received an angry phone call from a man known by the court as RY, who shared a house with RB and MB. He told her that RB was also seeing a lawyer. Muraca told him she thought that was a great idea and offered to come along. RY refused. That evening, she went over to RB's house but was met at the door by RY. Shouting at her, he would not allow her in the house and angrily told her to leave.

Muraca's lawyer couldn't help her with the bill of sale because he was in the process of moving his practice, but he did provide a letter stating that she had visited him about it and that he had advised her to seek help from one of his colleagues. That was good enough for the Ontario Registrar of Alcohol and Gaming, and she was granted a liquor license.

Sensing something foul, however, the registrar called the Ontario Provincial Police's Biker Enforcement Unit. They assigned the case to Hamilton police detective Steve Stone. Checking the files, the first thing he noticed was that on the night of Monday, August 8, there had been a report of a dispute at the house RB and MB shared with RY. A neighbor had seen one of RB and MB's children run from the house, clearly in distress, and called the cops. When police arrived, the house was empty.

They found RB nearby and questioned him. He said that some Our Dog House regulars had dropped by his house, which was about two blocks from the bar, and there'd been an argument. No big deal. Then the cops went down to Our Dog House and checked that story with Muraca and Dreher; both denied any knowledge of the incident.

On the following Monday, RB, MB and RY arrived at the Hamilton police's mountain station and made statements that were recorded on DVD. They claimed that the incident didn't go down the way they first claimed it did. They said that at about 6:00 p.m. on Sunday, two men walked into RB's house through an unlocked front door. RB recognized them immediately as Hells Angels, because he had been involved with the Lobos—a Windsor, Ontario, motorcycle club who were patched over to the Hells Angels in Stadnick's massive takeover—and then the Montreal Hells Angels. That allowed him to party at the Gage Avenue clubhouse, where he had run into both men before.

RB said that they first asked him where the liquor license was. Then they hit him—once, in the neck—hit RY as well and produced two documents that RB recognized as the bill of sale and the confirmation of sale, demanding he sign them both without reading them. RB and MB complied.

Then one of the two intruders accused RB of using the club's name for his own gain, which is expressly forbidden by the Hells Angels. Although he denied it, the bikers said that the penalty— they used the term "tax"—was $5,000 and that they would be back to collect it the following week. If he didn't have it, they would take his truck instead.

After the intruders left, their frightened child returned to the house and told RB that a neighbor had called the police. Sure that if the Hells Angels thought he himself had called the police things would be far worse for him, he told everyone to evacuate the house. Shortly thereafter, RB ran into the cops, who were looking for him, and told them his story about the minor disagreement at the house. Sure the coast was clear, RB returned home to make some calls, while the case transcript says that RY went to various bars "trying to find out what possibly was going on and how much damage had been created, you know, against the club and how, how much, you know, what we were facing, like were we just facing a beating or were we facing, you know, more than a beating."

The first call RB made was to the Windsor Hells Angels, where he still had friends. After he explained, they told him there was nothing they could do. The situation was in Hamilton, so the Hamilton Hells Angels were in charge. It was their decision.

Then he called the owner of the building that housed the Hells Angels clubhouse in Hamilton, who happened to be one of his friends, to see if he knew anything. From his friend's tone, RB surmised that he was in very, very deep trouble.

The following day, he, MB and RY again went to the Hamilton police and told them their story, which was recorded on DVD. On the strength of their statements and his own investigation into the incident, Stone arrested Hells Angels Bubba Sherwood and Joel Rollin as well as Muraca and Dreher. The Hells Angels both pleaded guilty to extortion and assault. Sherwood received a three-year sentence, Rollin got six months. Muraca and Dreher were both acquitted because the prosecutor could not prove that the Hells Angels were working on their behalf.

It was hardly the crime of the century, but it was illustrative of a few important trends in the history of organized crime in Canada. First, it shows that Hamilton, one of the birthplaces of Canadian organized crime, and still a lucrative drug market despite falling on hard times, had changed.

It had, since the 1930s, been dominated by the 'Ndrangheta until they were overshadowed by the Cosa Nostra when Johnny Pops brought his heroin money to town in the 1960s. After he and his band were taken down through attrition and assassination in the 1990s, the 'Ndrangheta took over again. They were quickly taken down by law enforcement and their own hubris. That left the city open for the Outlaws—the former Satan's Choice—but without their own strong leader, Parente, they were easily supplanted by Stadnick and the Hells Angels. After Stadnick went down, the Hells Angels became less and less vital and less and less important. By the time guys like Sherwood and Rollin were on the scene, they had been reduced to pulling small-time strong-arm acts, like what happened in the Our Dog House incident.

Indeed, the Hells Angels were down in Hamilton, losing manpower and respect on the streets. For years, one of their enforcers was an ex-fighter named James "Louie" Malone. He'd officially retired from the club after Project Manchester but was still, according to police, active in the city's underworld. On the night of November 8/9, 2013, he was hanging out at Main Billiards—an old-school pool hall with a public ashtray and a payphone out front, located at what locals call the "Delta," the intersection of King and Main Streets and the unofficial border between central Hamilton and the east end.

A little after midnight, a fight broke out between Malone and, allegedly, a pair of brothers he grew up with in the neighborhood. In fact, Malone and the accused, John and Mato Josipovic, had known each other since kindergarten at Holy Family School on Britannia between Robins and Kenilworth. They were even described as friends.

The fight resulted in no arrests or major injuries. But it appears as though feelings, at least, were hurt. Later that morning, Malone was walking his dogs on Robins just north of Cannon when he started arguing with another man. The dispute, according to witnesses, heated up and the other man pulled a shotgun. Malone began to flee and the gunman shot. He hit Malone and also blew out the front door of the house they were in front of.

Badly hurt, Malone started running eastbound down Cannon Street, one of Hamilton's busiest. Witnesses said he was pursued by the gunman and another man in a gray pickup. He turned north on Kenilworth, and the gunman caught up with him one block later at Britannia, shooting him again. Leaving a trail of blood behind him, Malone ran the last block of his life. He collapsed in front of the New Image rent-to-own electronics store. The gunman, witnesses said, tracked him down and gave him a couple more blasts from the shotgun, blowing out New Image's windows, before jumping into the gray pickup and taking off.

On November 18, 2013, police arrested John Josipovic at home in Grimsby. His brother lived next door but had already left for work in Milton. While police were reluctant to make any gang connections between the Josipovics—calling the matter "personal"—in their first court appearance, both men were read a long list of people with whom they were forbidden contact during the trial. Aside from the names of the brothers themselves, all the listed names were put under a court-ordered publication ban. John found it perfectly appropriate to wear a Harley-Davidson T-shirt while facing the judge. They pleaded not guilty and the trial is still pending.

Whether the Malone killing was gang related or not, it definitely showed that the Hells Angels had become pretty small time in the Hammer. Although Malone was officially out of the club, he was still a beloved character in the neighborhood. The fact that after he was killed, the alleged culprits were rounded up by the cops nine days later with the cooperation of many in the community revealed the difference in how the public and police viewed the Hells Angels in 2013 as opposed to in their heyday. There was little to no public fear of reprisals. A few years earlier, for ordinary people to see a recently retired Hells Angels enforcer brutally murdered on city streets would have led to abject silence in the community, as the culprits would likely be the Hells Angels cleaning house or the Outlaws staking a claim. By 2013, nobody cared. The bikers were just not as scary as they used to be.

It wasn't them selling crack on the streets, although they may have been the source of it; it was the street gangs. In fact, the days of the bikers as the dominant force in the drug trade in Hamilton were over. There were a couple of reasons for that.

The first is that they became the primary target of law enforcement throughout the country. Operations like Printemps, SharQc, Amigo and Dismantle ended in mass arrests that put hundreds of bikers—whole organizations—behind bars. Sure, many of them got out right away, but not the important ones, not the leaders. And those who did get out often had so many court-ordered restrictions that they couldn't re-form as effective groups.

To be a biker in Canada during the era after the mega-arrests was to live a paranoid, stressful existence, not knowing when you were being recorded or watched, or which one of your friends or associates was secretly working for law enforcement.

The other reason the bikers were fading was that they just weren't cool anymore. The allure of loud pipes, leather jackets and the rebel lifestyle had largely waned. It's not a coincidence that Harley-Davidson stopped publishing its rapidly rising average age of purchasers when it climbed to 48 years old in 2009. Young men who wanted a flashy vehicle were more likely to start with a tricked-out Honda Civic, and, if all went right, eventually move on to a Mercedes-Benz SLK or a Cadillac Escalade.

The men the bikers had to choose from—keep in mind that they had to be white in most places—shrank significantly. Most of those who were eligible weren't interested. That's why the Hells Angels were now represented by people like Bubba Sherwood rather than Walter Stadnick.

Of course, there are still some places in Canada where outlaw motorcycle gangs can find new recruits. In December 2011, the Loners, who by default had become the Hells Angels' primary biker opposition in Ontario, opened a chapter in Peterborough. Law enforcement members who are familiar with the area have told me that they're at the top of the heap as far as trafficking in the area is concerned.

That set up a conversation between me and several members of law enforcement who pointed out something I already knew but had not yet articulated to myself. The bikers do have recruiting grounds in Canada, but they are diminishing. To put a face on it, take a look at the kids in your community. If they listen to classic rock or country, if they think hunting is a pretty reasonable hobby, if they are wearing black leather jackets and if Satan or skulls are a primary part of their cultural imagery, then the bikers are probably running the drug trade in your area.

Conversely, if the kids are listening to something closer to hip-hop or rap, if they prefer to wear bright colors instead of black and if they have an interest in mixed martial arts, then the bikers have probably already been replaced by street gangs.

For the most part in Canada, street gangs are multiethnic in varying degrees, but their leadership often reflects whichever ethnic group is the most marginalized in the area. For most urban centers in Canada, that usually means that the leaders are aboriginal, Jamaican, Haitian or Somali.

Of course, nobody's ethnicity ever made them a gangster. But when the catalyst elements of poverty, a disconnect with government and mainstream society and a history of violence come together, the elements of any group who are inclined toward crime tend to organize. Like the original Mafia, all of those groups that now run street gangs suffered through poverty, indifferent government and discrimination, but most of the current generation of immigrants has had experiences far worse than those of the immigrants from Sicily and Calabria in the last century.

Even more than many immigrant groups, Canadian aboriginal people are, on average, at or near the bottom of the Canadian economic spectrum and have lived through centuries of discrimination that has included war, slavery, forced resettlement and other concepts we used to promote but now recognize as atrocities.

Jamaica is a drug-distribution hub rivaling any in the world, has a generations-long history of corrupt government and now has one of the highest murder rates in the world—about ten times that of the US and nearly double that of Mexico. It is a country many consider to be in a state of civil war between its government and drug cartels. Haiti has been the poorest country in the Western Hemisphere for as long as such records have been kept and even required a US military intervention in 1994 to restore its legally elected (but reputedly quite corrupt) government. Somalia, though, actually has dibs on being the worst country in the world. Basically governmentless for a generation, it has been Balkanized into tribal clans run by local warlords who often employ child soldiers. It fell off the bottom of the UN's Human Development

Index in 2013 because of insufficient data, but it had occupied the bottom spot for many years until then.

The trajectory of these recent immigrants upon arrival in Canada is not so different than that of the hard-done-by Sicilians and Calabrians from so many years before. The membership of these new multiethnic gangs has been swollen by uneducated whites (and others) who were frustrated with their own lots in life and were either not cut out for, or not interested in, the biker lifestyle.

While street gangs existed almost everywhere in Canada, they were mostly shadowy organizations, and public knowledge of them was limited for a very long time. For the most part, they lived—as it seemed both sides preferred—in a separate reality than the mainstream. Unlike the Hells Angels, whose name guaranteed the front page, reports of their activities were few and far between. Even when there were killings, coverage would generally be perfunctory at best. Mentions of gangs or the "gang lifestyle" would be made, but the gangs would be unnamed, and the overall tone would reek of judgment, as though the victim should have known what was coming to him by being involved with such people.

For example, at 3:57 in the afternoon on November 9, 2005, Toronto police received calls about a shooting at a parking lot on Marlee Avenue just north of Eglinton. When the police arrived, they found two young men, one very badly injured. Despite desperate efforts by emergency personnel, he died at a nearby hospital.

The victim was 17-year-old Jamal Hemmings, and he was with his best friend, 18-year-old Amon Beckles, when he was shot. On the day of Hemmings's funeral, Beckles was waiting just outside the church's rear entrance when he was approached by three masked men who shot him several times and killed him.

Media coverage focused on topics that included Hemmings's two-month-old son, how brazen it was that Beckles would be shot at a funeral and the fact that both boys grew up without fathers at home.

An advocacy group for inner-city children in which both Hemmings and Beckles participated named a college scholarship after them.

What never came into the public consciousness was what gang they were affiliated with, who their enemies were or what they were doing. It was as though street gangs were an amorphous, impossible-to-understand mass.

In fact, Hemmings and Beckles were both members of the Five Point Generalz (5PG), police told me, a street gang known to be among Toronto's most violent. In August 2005, one of its members, Gregory Sappleton, was charged after a drive-by shooting injured four people, including four-year-old Shaquan Cadougan. It made news, particularly because of its young victim, but the case never saw trial due to a lack of witness involvement.

Later, Sappleton and another gang member named Akiel Eubank (who usually had the 5PG logo shaved into his hair) were allegedly involved in a shootout with another north Toronto gang called the Baghdad Crew. Sappleton and Eubank were charged with the murder of 11-year-old Ephraim Brown, who fled through an alleyway when he heard gunshots but was hit and killed. But there was a lack of people willing to testify, and they were acquitted. "All those guys out there that are doing the wrong," Ephraim's mother, Lorna Brown, told the *Toronto Star*, "I don't think they have an education. . . . They shoot and kill and I don't know what they get out of it."

What they got out of it was money. Because of how big and how readily available that money was, they had terrorized their communities into not cooperating with police.

While many of their rivals in the area—mostly aligned with the Crips—had ties to the Hells Angels, a May 2010 raid called Project Corral revealed that the 5PG were receiving their drugs and weapons directly from Jamaica's notorious Shower Posse. That gang, long a shadow government in the poorest parts of Jamaica as well as a crime organization in the style of the Mafia and Latin American cartels, made international news when an intervention by the Jamaican military, backed by US intelligence aircraft, to arrest its leader, Christopher "Dudus" Coke, caused the death of at least 74 people and led to more than 700 arrests.

The reaction to the local violence among Toronto's media and citizens was very much like Montrealers' original reaction to the biker war there. It was generally considered tolerable as long as the gangsters killed only their own people. Unfortunately, in Toronto, black children like Ephraim Brown counted as their own people.

Then Toronto had its own Daniel Desrochers moment. Just as the Hells Angels were widely believed to have killed 11-year-old Desrochers, an innocent fell to street gangs, and her death riled the community.

Boxing Day, the day after Christmas, is traditionally the busiest shopping day in Canada. Retailers slash prices on all of the merchandise they couldn't move before Christmas. The busiest shopping spot in Canada is the Eaton Centre, a giant mall that spans most of the area between Yonge and Bay Streets and Queen and Dundas Streets in the heart of downtown Toronto. In fact, it was built in 1976 at that spot in part as an attempt to reduce the rampant street crime in the area.

On December 26, 2005, one of the bargain hunters in the throngs was a pretty, blond 15-year-old high school student named Jane Creba. She and her sister had just stepped out of Sam the Record Man, about two blocks north of the Eaton Centre, when Jane told her sister she had to drop by a Pizza Pizza to use the washroom. She didn't make it. A gunfight broke out, and a slug went through Creba's chest, perforating her aorta. She died soon thereafter at St. Michael's Hospital.

About 40 minutes after the shooting, police arrested two men—Andre Thompson and Jorrell Simpson-Rowe—at Castle

Frank subway station, several blocks away from the incident. Simpson-Rowe was carrying a Ruger nine-millimeter semiautomatic handgun. After his arrest, sure that his youth would prevent him from being prosecuted, he told police that he had been at the shooting, and that he was handed the gun by Louis "The Big Guy" Woodcock, who'd asked him to get rid of it. Since Simpson-Rowe was just 17 and the bullet that had killed Creba was a .357, he was released. But the evidence he gave police allowed them to tap the phones of several of his associates.

Over the following months, the cops learned that the shooting started because members of two rival gangs—the Silent Soldiers and the Point Blank Soldiers, who were fighting over who had the right to sell drugs in Toronto's notorious Regent Park housing projects (one side wore red, the other blue)—happened to run into each other on Yonge Street just as Creba was passing by. They started shooting, and eight people were hit; Creba, who was the only fatality, was shot accidentally.

Her death threw the city into outrage. If an innocent girl couldn't be safe on the busiest block in town, people wondered, who was safe anywhere? They had a point. While the Mafia and the bikers had strict rules about how such conflict resolutions were performed—when Hells Angel Scott Steinert was suspected of being responsible for Desroschers' death he was beaten to death with hammers for it, among other reasons—wiretaps revealed that when the subject of Creba's death came up among the street gangs, they had no more complex a plan than to tell each other to "respect the G Code," in other words, keep their mouths shut.

One young man who grew up in Regent Park, Canada's first and largest housing project and the area being fought over by Creba's killers—was Christopher Husbands. Originally from Guyana, Husbands had a hard time fitting in once he moved to Canada and was eventually well known in the neighborhood for fighting and running with gangs.

On March 1, 2010, at 1:45 in the morning, Husbands was stopped by a cop in Hamilton because of an expired license-plate sticker on his Nissan Maxima. After he gave her a fake name, he was arrested for breaking curfew and bail conditions for a previous conviction in Toronto that police, even now, do not want to disclose any details about.

He was released, but on March 29, at 2:58 in the morning, another Hamilton cop spotted a Maxima in a parking lot with its lights on. When he looked inside, there was a man sleeping in the front seat. The cop, Keith Malone, woke him up and asked him his name. Husbands gave him the same fake name he had given the other cop earlier. Malone recognized it and searched the car, finding a Heckler & Koch .40-caliber handgun and a small amount of marijuana hidden in the front vents. He arrested Husbands.

Again, Husbands was let go as charges were dropped. In November 2010, Husbands, 21 and the father of a young child, was arrested and charged with sexual assault for having unconsensual intercourse. He was placed under house arrest.

He didn't pay much attention to it. In February 2012, two months before Husbands was to face a judge in Hamilton over the weapons and drug charges, a man named Todd Irvine and his fiancée were returning home from a trip to Home Depot through Regent Park when they saw a man lying in the street. His wrists were bound by duct tape and he was bleeding from several wounds to his face and chest. Irvine stopped the car and went to the man's aid while his fiancée called 911.

The man, barely clinging to life, was Husbands. According to several reports, Husbands had had a dispute with two of his rivals in the Sic Thugs gang all three men belonged to. Ahmed Hassan and Nixon Nirmalendran had bound Husbands, thrown him into a bathtub in an empty Regent Park apartment, stabbed him more than 200 times and left him for dead.

Hassan, whose family came to Canada from Somalia when he was young, was facing charges of cocaine trafficking, obstructing a police officer and possession of stolen goods after an arrest in Fort McMurray, Alberta, at the time. He was also a prime suspect in the 2012 Fort McMurray murder of a drug dealer named Abdinasir Dirie.

Nirmalendran, whose family came from Sri Lanka, had a similarly spotty past. Arrested at 18 for robbing teenagers in Riverdale Park with a pellet gun, he was later jailed for breaching bail from that charge after being arrested for cocaine trafficking. While staying at the city's Don Jail, he was implicated in a murder.

Shortly after his release from segregated confinement after being caught smuggling marijuana in his rectum, Kevon "K-Dog" Phillip was beaten to death in the facility's showers. A career criminal specializing in auto theft, Phillip was rumored to have provided police with the names of several dealers. Ironically, when police interviewed the 38 men on the cell block where Phillip was killed for allegedly snitching, 37 of them provided evidence. Five inmates were named. Four of them—Abdifatah Mohamed, Christopher Fearon, Hussein Nur and Nathaniel Grant—were found guilty of the killing, but charges against Nirmalendran were dropped and he was soon released.

Because Husbands survived the stabbing, the Sic Thugs fell into two rival factions: one backing Husbands and the other, Hassan. Bullets flew. Although there were no reported injuries, police counted no fewer than 90 shots fired on one March weekend.

On April 23, 2012, a recovering Husbands showed up in Hamilton court. The weapons charges were dropped in exchange for guilty pleas for the weed and the breach of probation. He was allowed to leave.

On June 2, though still officially under house arrest, Husbands was sitting down for a bite to eat at the Urban Eatery, the Eaton Centre's gigantic and often crowded downstairs food court, when he happened to see Hassan and Nirmalendran. He stood and opened fire.

Hassan was killed; Nirmalendran was critically injured and died weeks later. Also hit were five innocent bystanders, including a 13-year-old boy visiting from Port Hope, Ontario, who was shot in the head but survived.

While the Boxing Day and Eaton Centre shootings and their white victims caused outrage and arrests in Toronto, they had little effect on drug trafficking or street gang membership. They did, however, reveal that these gangs were multiethnic, trafficked drugs from big-time international connections and were incredibly violent, often putting innocent people into danger as they carried out their business dealings.

Of course, the news coverage of both shootings paled compared to the worldwide scrutiny of Toronto mayor Rob Ford's tribulations in 2013. After reporters from Gawker.com and the *Toronto Star* reported the existence of a video of Ford smoking crack with reputed gang members, a long and sordid series of bombshell events linked the mayor with several people in the drug trade. On November 5, 2013, he admitted to an astonished public that he had smoked crack. Of course, there's no way to obtain crack legally.

Toronto police eventually found the videos featuring Ford on a computer owned by a suspected drug dealer named Muhammad "Ali K" Khattak, who had been photographed with the mayor alongside Anthony "Buck" Smith and Monir Kasim. Months earlier, while the Ford allegations were still in their infancy, Smith and Khattak had both been shot while leaving a Toronto nightclub called the Loki Lounge on March 28, 2013. Smith died.

While the *Star* initially referred to the gangsters as "Somali," the paper later backed off that claim, saying they "overdid" that angle. In fact, the Dixon City Bloods—also known as the Dixon

True Bloods or the Dixon Goonies—are largely, but not entirely, Somali-Canadian. Besides drug trafficking, the gang has been linked to cross-border weapons smuggling, which has led to them having a presence in Windsor, Ontario, and they also have some members stationed in Edmonton, Calgary and Fort McMurray to traffic in those cities.

One big difference between these gangs and the ones that had handled trafficking before became quickly apparent. The Mafia and the bikers recruited their membership from men they knew and trusted. Those men had to undergo rigorous background checks and internships and apprenticeships before they were given a chance to become made men or full-patch members, and then they were sworn to a code of ethics that involved an oath of silence. In street gangs, membership is almost interchangeable. There are initiations and logos and other signs of unity, but being a member of the Doomstown Crips is not like being a Hells Angel. Instead of depending on high-quality recruits and an ability to get others to do their bidding, street gangs rely upon intimidating their entire community and often playing the race card (by portraying police as a tool of white oppression), to ensure the community's silence. That allows them to recruit just about anyone, even very young teens, who can be unpredictably violent.

Another difference between the new gangs and the old ones is that none of the new gangs ever had a capable leader in Canada who could unite and elevate them to a level at which they could call the shots for a large number of soldiers. Contrast that with the Canadian Hells Angels, who, in their heyday, could make their own deals on a national basis and decide on distribution methods, prices and how to deal with competitors. The street gangs can't do that; there's no national organization of Bloods or Crips, just a bunch of gangs who wear red or blue. Instead of making important decisions, they take orders from their suppliers—who include the Hells Angels.

Because, though down, the Hells Angels were far from out. Several chapters still existed, and in places like Alberta and Saskatchewan, they were still going strong. Even in Ontario, where law enforcement had made them priority one, they still kept going.

In April 2007, police managed to seize 32 Hells Angels clubhouses in Ontario, New Brunswick and BC. Most notably, the Downtown Toronto chapter, which had been the Para-Dice Riders before the Stadnick takeover, was shut down when the police broke into the clubhouse by tearing a wall down with a tow truck and proudly paraded the club's possessions, including their prized winged skull sculpture, in front of TV cameras.

At the time, many Hells Angels, even those who weren't arrested, quit. They ceremonially put an exit date on their Hells Angels tattoos and went on with their lives. The remainder regrouped and started meeting in a house in Toronto's rapidly gentrifying Parkdale neighborhood. It was a simple house without any signs or statues or anything that indicated it was where the mighty Hells Angels met other than the fact that they sometimes wore their colors in and out of the building and that there were always plainclothes cops on hand taking pictures and writing down license-plate numbers.

On September 16, 2013, the Toronto Hells Angels opened a bricks-and-mortar store at 98 Carlaw Avenue, just around the corner from the old clubhouse at 498 Eastern Avenue. With a huge red "81" in the window, it hawks items that include T-shirts and other paraphernalia, including, my favorite, a baseball cap stitched with the phrase KNOWN ASSOCIATE. On their Web site, they published a message that indicated their take on their relationship with law enforcement.

Thank you. Downtown Toronto Hells Angels Motor-cycle Club gives a BIG thank you to all our friends and

*supporters! Each and every one of you have helped us
fight the fight.*

The only way the street gangs could evolve to a level even close to where the Hells Angels were would be to find a great leader, a uniter. Previously, organizations had succeeded when they had strong leaders like John Papalia, Walter Stadnick, Mom Boucher, Vic Cotroni and Vito Rizzuto. They got into trouble when they were led by lesser lights like Paolo Violi, Giovanni Muscadere, Raynald Desjardins and Michael Sandham.

Until that happens, the drug trade is controlled by their bosses, which recent arrests have shown may be from Canada, the US, Mexico, Jamaica, China or other countries. Canadian organized crime, which had previously been the domain of large, mostly autonomous Canadian gangs with ties to the US, has been transformed to small, isolated groups working directly for international bosses.

Except for one. In the midst of all these changes, the Sicilian Mafia in Montreal appeared to keep rolling; their enemies were dying. On the other hand, so were some of their friends. And it didn't matter where they were.

One of Vito Rizzuto's most trusted allies, Juan Ramon "Johnny Bravo" Fernandez, was busted trafficking cocaine and was deported. Like so many gangsters deported from Canada, he did not go back to his native country. Born in Spain, Fernandez settled instead in Bagheria, Sicily, and opened a mixed martial arts training center. Italian police said that the dojo was actually a front for drug trafficking. As part of their investigation, police recorded a conversation in which Fernandez claimed to have been "made" by Rizzuto even though he was Spanish, as had Desjardins, even though he was French-Canadian. In May 2013, the bodies of Fernandez and a friend—Fernando Pimentel, a Mississauga-based

Rizzuto associate, who had recently been deported from Canada and had also settled in Sicily—were found on a remote hillside not far from Fernandez's dojo. They had been shot several times and their corpses set ablaze. Whether their deaths were caused by Sicilians who could not tolerate a Spanish made man or by Fernandez's longtime association with Desjardins is debatable. Not long after, Pietro and Salvatore Scaduto—both of whom had allegedly worked for the Rizzutos before they too were deported—were arrested when they were caught trying to sell Fernandez's Rolex.

Their enemies continued to fall. At one in the morning on July 12, 2013, police responded to a call about a shooting at the Terrace Banquet Hall in Vaughan's Woodbridge section. When they arrived, they came upon a BMW X6 SUV with broken windows in the parking lot. Inside were Salvatore "Sam" Calautti, dead from gunshot wounds to his face, and James Tusek, dead from similar wounds to his chest. Both had strong ties to the revitalized Ontario 'Ndrangheta.

Calautti was a short, stocky and brutish man who plied his trade as an assassin. In 1996, a witness said he went to collect a $500 debt from a Toronto man named Giuseppe Congiusta and showed him a handgun to emphasize the seriousness of the situation. The next day, Congiusta's bullet-riddled body was found. There was not enough evidence to convict Calautti.

He was named as an assailant in a case in 2000 in which four men were shot at and later that year was charged with the murder of Gaetano Panepinto. According to prosecutors, Panepinto used his bargain casket store as a front for trafficking cocaine he received from the Rizzuto family. While Calautti was not convicted of either crime, he was clearly in the sights of the Rizzutos.

After years of lying low under the protection of several Calabrian-Canadian chieftains, rumors started flying that Calautti was actually the triggerman who had killed Nicolo Rizzuto. That would explain why he was killed after the Rizzutos appeared to be back on top in Montreal.

On November 10, 2013, exactly three years after Nicolo Rizzuto was shot, yet another enemy of Vito Rizzuto was killed. Moreno Gallo first made a name for himself in Montreal in 1973 at age 28 when he killed a known drug dealer. After he was convicted and given a life sentence, he told the parole board that he killed the man only because he was dealing at his younger sister's school, and they released him in 1983. He quickly rose through the ranks of the Mafia and when Vito Rizzuto went off to prison in the US, he became something of a mediator when it came to Vito's would-be successors. While investigating his son Anthony in 2009, investigators found evidence that Gallo had never become a Canadian citizen. After fighting immigration authorities for two years, he was deported in October 2011.

Gallo did not go back to his native Italy. Instead, he settled in Acapulco, Mexico, one of the most dangerous cities in the world. He became a regular at Forza Italia, an Italian restaurant on Acapulco's La Costera strip, just down the road from the Hard Rock Cafe where Rock Machine member Normand Baker had been killed by the Hells Angels in 1995. One night when Gallo was eating there, a man dressed all in black walked into the pizzeria and put two nine-millimeter slugs into the back of Gallo's head, killing him instantly. Nobody in the bar could provide the police with an accurate description of the perpetrator.

Just as the Mafia war seemed to be peaking, something happened that would change everything. A few days before Christmas 2013, Vito Rizzuto died in a hospital bed of pneumonia, which had been complicated by cancer—a condition he had kept secret. While CBC News opined that it was mostly likely the end of his "dynasty," hundreds showed up for his funeral. If his faction—and, by extension, the war—was finished, it sure didn't look like it that day.

CHAPTER 21

WHAT'S NEXT?

There will always be organized crime in Canada. If there's something illegal that people want, someone will get it for them for a price. If there's something legal but too expensive—as when a rise in cigarette taxes prompts an increase in cross-border smuggling—someone will provide it. Even if we legalized everything from marijuana to crystal meth, there would still be loan-sharking, extortion and a host of other occupations for ambitious gangsters.

While a lot of Canadians seem to want to think that organized crime won't affect them unless they seek it out—you won't have any problems with drug dealers unless you go looking for drugs—it's not true. As we've seen repeatedly, organized crime is not limited to, nor satisfied by, the drug trade. As importing or making and distributing drugs becomes more difficult, risky and expensive due to law enforcement's more sophisticated abilities, crime organizations depend more and more on other sources of income.

We've seen from the Charbonneau Commission that the Mafia and Hells Angels can and will infiltrate legitimate business and even government, and—for the most part—get away with it. Not only does that compromise the integrity of our elected officials, it costs us a great deal as taxpayer money is diverted into mobsters' socks, and it introduces risk as the work we are paying for is not the work we get.

Even while the massive efforts of law enforcement have put hundreds of mafiosi, bikers and other gangsters behind bars for trafficking, the drug trade is still the most effective way to make money illegally. It's so effective, in fact, that there's almost no limit to the people who'd like to get into the game.

For the most part, dominant organizations like the Cosa Nostra and the Hells Angels tend to keep violence down, because it's bad for business. It's when they are weakened, often through mass arrests, that the violence increases as other contenders vie for their lost territory.

As traditional organizations like the Hells Angels, Outlaws and others break down or age without replacements, they are generally replaced by street gangs, who are often nothing more than a collection of high school friends with a few weapons. To survive, they make alliances with other sets, which has the side effect of antagonizing still other sets.

Something of an order has come to it, however, especially after Raynald Desjardins and his allies went down and Vito Rizzuto returned from Colorado. On one side, the Sicilians, based in Montreal, can count on biker gangs and street gangs who are not associated with the Hells Angels. On the other side, the Calabrians, based in Hamilton, have the support of the Hells Angels and the street gangs, many of whom identify as Crips, on their side. The same holds true of the multiethnic gangs of the West Coast and the big cities of Alberta and the aboriginal gangs throughout much of the country. They might not know who Vito Rizzuto is, and they may not get any product from the Mafia, but they fall on one side or the other. That dividing line is often determined by whether they love or loathe the Hells Angels.

With those two armed and antagonistic groups facing off against each other, the effect has been something of a cold war in Canadian crime. For the most part, the two sides respect the other's right to exist and do business, but when one side oversteps its bounds—like with a high-placed assassination or the formation of a new gang in a disputed area—that cold war can suddenly get very hot.

Although we have seen hot wars in which bullets fly in the streets and firebombings destroy whole buildings in cities like Montreal, Vancouver, Winnipeg and Hamilton, violence against uninvolved people in Canada is still, thankfully, rare. These conflicts are caused by imbalances, such as assassinations or mass arrests, that change the level of dominance one group has over another.

It's in the cold periods, when organized crime groups are operating efficiently, that we see the real cost. Their internal and international activities cause us to spend astronomical amounts on law enforcement and border security. Their infiltration of legitimate business puts an unnecessary drag on our economy, and their efforts to manipulate our elected officials and their staffs undermine our very democracy.

It's not enough simply to acknowledge that organized crime is present in Canada or even to recognize how powerful it is. It's more important that Canadians stick up for themselves and work to end the culture of silence and intimidation that allows organized crime to thrive.

A NOTE ON SOURCES

Although you found *Cold War* in the true crime section of your bookstore or library, it's more accurate to say that what you're reading here is a history book. It's about crime, but it's also—actually, even more so—about our shared history. Unlike most other Canadian crime books, which are written about a single case that the author has been following and has a close relationship with, *Cold War* has a broader scope. It is an attempt to explain how organized crime in Canada originated and how it works.

As such, *Cold War* relies on a number of different sources for its material. Much of it comes from personal conversations and interviews I've had with the people involved, but a lot of it—especially, but not limited to, events that occurred before my birth—is from outside sources, including books, newspapers, magazines, court records and other legal documents, law enforcement media releases and the organizations themselves. I have tried to choose the most reliable sources and to credit them appropriately.